THE JIVE TALKER

THE JIVE TALKER

TALKER

Or

How to Get a British Passport

Samson Kambalu

JONATHAN CAPE
LONDON

Published by Jonathan Cape 2008

2 4 6 8 10 9 7 5 3 1

Copyright © Samson Kambalu 2008

Samson Kambalu has asserted his right under the Copyright,
Designs and Patents Act 1988 to be identified as the author of this work

This book is a work of non-fiction based on the life, experiences and recollections of
the author. In some limited cases the names of people, dates and the sequence or
detail of events have been changed. The author has stated to the publishers that,
except in such minor respects not affecting the substantial accuracy of the work,
the contents of this book are true.

First published in Great Britain in 2008 by
Jonathan Cape
Random House, 20 Vauxhall Bridge Road,
London SW1V 2SA

www.rbooks.co.uk

Addresses for companies within The Random House Group Limited can be found at:
www.randomhouse.co.uk/offices.htm

The Random House Group Limited Reg. No. 954009

A CIP catalogue record for this book is available from the British Library

ISBN 9780224081061

The Random House Group Limited supports The Forest Stewardship
Council (FSC), the leading international forest certification organisation. All our
titles that are printed on Greenpeace-approved FSC-certified paper carry the FSC logo.
Our paper procurement policy can be found at www.rbooks.co.uk/environment

Mixed Sources
Product group from well-managed
forests and other controlled sources
www.fsc.org Cert no. TT-COC-2139
© 1996 Forest Stewardship Council

Typeset in Dante MT by Palimpsest Book Production Limited,
Grangemouth, Stirlingshire

Printed and bound in Great Britain by
CPI Mackays, Chatham, Kent ME5 8TD

In memory of Jane and Aaron

CONTENTS

If the natives are not elevated by their contacts with Europeans, they are sure to be deteriorated.

Dr David Livingstone

I am no man, I am dynamite.

Friedrich Nietzsche

FROM HOLY BALL EXERCISES AND EXORCISMS,
CHANCELLOR COLLEGE, ZOMBA:

Whao! Jesus! Just come down on earth and see this!
Work of an artist.
NUKA 02/08/00 1715HRS

Wonders and puzzles always succeed with free wine.
STEVE

Blasphemy.
ANONYMOUS

PROLOGUE

When my Scottish fiancée and I decided to get married, the consul at the High Commission in Malawi asked me: 'Are you marrying Susan to get a British passport?' My reply to that was deliberate. 'Not really,' I said. The consul regarded me for a moment and filled in 'NO'.

'The answer is NO, OK? The answer is NO,' he said.

The Jive Talker

1

My father wore three-piece suits that he had ordered from London in the sixties and seventies when he could still afford them. Back then he looked like Nat King Cole, but when I was growing up, he looked like a scarecrow. This was not because his suits were too old (for a good suit can last for ever) but because my mother was obsessive about hygiene. When my father, who was a clinical officer, returned from his weekly round in the hospital wards, she would undress him in the backyard, before he entered the house, and wash his suit to get rid of the tetanus, whooping cough, measles, mumps, TB and other dangerous diseases that she thought she could trace within the familiar scent of aspirin on him. For some reason she did not trust the local dry-cleaners for that kind of job. Her washing machine was the big boulder in the middle of the yard; she would soak the suit in hot water and Sunlight soap and mash it up to a pulp with her strong hands. Thereafter an eerie silence would descend upon the house because the sight of the suit hanging on the line used to scare away all the birds from the surrounding trees.

But my father did not mind looking like a scarecrow. He said he was a philosopher and walked with his head held high in the sky like a giraffe. His favourite study was the toilet. Apart from the fact that it was the only private space in the house, he believed that it was from the toilet that all great ideas came. It was not a coincidence, he said, that Martin Luther conceived the Reformation in the toilet. Our toilet was therefore usually stuffed with an eclectic mix of books from his huge two-part bookshelf in the living room, which he called the Diptych. Many of the books were by his favourite writer, the nineteenth-century German philosopher, Friedrich Nietzsche. My father said that Nietzsche was the perfect philosopher for the toilet because of his searing aphoristic style and cold truths. He had every book that Nietzsche had ever written among the piles of paperbacks by the side of the toilet: *The Birth of Tragedy*, *Untimely Meditation*, *Human, All Too Human*, *Daybreak*, *The Gay Science*, *Thus Spake Zarathustra*, *Beyond Good and Evil*, *On the Genealogy of Morals*, *The Case of Wagner*, *The Twilight of the Idols*, *The Antichrist*, *Nietzsche vs. Wagner*, *The Will to Power*, *Ecce Homo* and even the one book he is supposed to have written when he went mad towards the end of his life called *My Sister and I*.

My father made quotations and notes from his readings and hung them all over the toilet walls until they spilt over to other places around the house. And, since the time in Blantyre when he had been moved from the leafy suburb of Queens to the rough Nkolokosa township in order to make way for a real doctor from England, we had called him the Jive Talker, not because he lied or talked jive, but because he liked to keep us awake on random nights and inflict his Nietzsche and personal affirmations on us in drunken performances, which he called jive, named after his favourite beer, Carlsberg Brown, which he also called jive.

When my mother asked the Jive Talker not to talk to us about Nietzsche because we were too young to understand the blasphemous ravings of syphilitic philosophers, he protested, saying that we were taught about the equally irreverent Christ even before we could read the Bible and yet we *understood*. And he was right that we understood, or some of us anyway: there I was one morning, in Thyolo District, suffering from diarrhoea and perched on the toilet, a skinny African boy, only eleven years old, and I was hooked on Nietzsche like I had been on the Bible when I was a Born Again. I now wanted to become a philosopher. I was confident that I could do it at that green age because I had read in the Bible that Jesus was already debating the scriptures with the rabbis when he was only twelve years old. My mother also told me the story of Kalikalanje, the wizard boy, who within a year of his birth was conducting profound conversations with grown-ups after he had accidentally fallen into the fireplace and jumped out with the brain of a sage. She thought I was special too: I had been born two months premature, had often fallen from my bed as a baby and had almost drowned in a well when I was three years old. These, she reckoned, were the reasons why the Jive Talker thought I had an eidetic memory, why I always came top at school and why I sounded like I already knew enough jive to invent my own religion in time for my twelfth birthday.

2

I should have washed that piece of fruit first. I had been recovering well from the malaria which I had caught after doing a rain dance in Arthur's nuclear bunker, when, earlier that morning, my little sister, Linda, gave me a piece of mango to make me feel better; instead, I got from it a bad case of diarrhoea that had me glued to the toilet seat for hours. Luckily enough I was home alone and nobody else needed to use the bathroom.

I had made myself a big sugar-and-salt solution and placed it on the bedside table to make sure I would not die of dehydration, but I very soon forgot about it. The trouble was that when I was off school for whatever reason I always enjoyed being in the toilet, nosing through my father's books and notes. I could do it for hours and it was no different that day, especially now that I had decided I would become a philosopher. It was like reading nonsense verse of the 'Jabberwocky' variety, which I loved: meaningless but meaningful. As I thumbed through Nietzsche that morning, I did not understand most of it but that did not deter me because, thanks to the Jive Talker, I did at least understand what each one of his aphorisms meant: the *will to power*, just like my father's personal affirmations.

These were mostly creative visualisations of his professional ambitions and usually began and ended with a mysterious phrase, '*I am a multimillionaire.*' He would habitually type the affirmations on A4 paper and then carefully fold the paper so it could fit in his wallet. Here are a few examples I found in his bedroom when he died from Aids in 1995:

I am a multimillionaire.

This week brings me a chain of successes. Within a few days from now I will be a great success in the eyes of my superiors. I will have performed my work well. Everyone will admire my work. My superiors will be highly impressed by my work. Stacks and stacks of money both in glittering silver and banknotes are on their way to me! I will ride in beautiful cars. Friends will invite me to parties. I shall be in very splendid health.

I am a multimillionaire.

I am a multimillionaire.

My goal at this time is to open tomorrow's course for polio vaccinators with ease and enjoyment so that my audience congratulate me! I will be highly congratulated after opening the course.

I am a multimillionaire.

I am a multimillionaire.

I will manage all government hospitals in Malawi.

My office is at the Ministry of Health Headquarters in the City of Lilongwe.

My office is at the Ministry of Health Headquarters in the City of Lilongwe.

My office is at the Ministry of Health Headquarters in the City of Lilongwe.

My office is at the Ministry of Health Headquarters in the City of Lilongwe.

My office is at the Ministry of Health Headquarters in the City of Lilongwe.

My office is at the Ministry of Health Headquarters in the City of Lilongwe.

My office is at the Ministry of Health Headquarters in the City of Lilongwe.

My office is at the Ministry of Health Headquarters in the City of Lilongwe.

My office is at the Ministry of Health Headquarters in the City of Lilongwe.

My office is at the Ministry of Health Headquarters in the City of Lilongwe.

My office is at the Ministry of Health Headquarters in the City of Lilongwe.

My office is at the Ministry of Health Headquarters in the City of Lilongwe.

My office is at the Ministry of Health Headquarters in the City of Lilongwe.

My office is at the Ministry of Health Headquarters in the City of Lilongwe.

My office is at the Ministry of Health Headquarters in the City of Lilongwe.

My office is at the Ministry of Health Headquarters in the City of Lilongwe.

My office is at the Ministry of Health Headquarters in the City of Lilongwe.

My office is at the Ministry of Health Headquarters in the City of Lilongwe.

My office is at the Ministry of Health Headquarters in the City of Lilongwe.

My office is at the Ministry of Health Headquarters in the City of Lilongwe.

I am a multimillionaire.

NATIVE

1

In around 100 BC a group of Bantu-speaking peoples armed with iron-tipped spears migrated from the Congo Basin onto the East and Southern African plateaux, displacing the Stone Age pygmies from the area down south into the Kalahari Desert. Among these peoples were the Chewa who settled in what is now the central region of Malawi.

When the Dutch Reformed Church came to Dowa District in 1892 the Chewa were a matriarchal society: a man lived with his wife's people and played a marginal role. He did not even own his children or property. He was little more than a sperm donor who sometimes helped with manual work. That was the position my grandfather, oBanda, had in his family before he became a Christian. When his household converted, however, he found himself the head of his family. Not only that: he was given a *name*, Elisa. Before the missionaries, a name was not something you were given, but something you *earned*. Until you earned your name, which for many never happened, you were called by your clan name, which had a slight variation to denote your gender. Thus in the case of my grandfather who belonged to the Banda clan all the males in his household were called oBanda and all the females, naBanda. When the neighbours' child came into their compound to deliver a message and called out 'oBanda!' several men would come out of the mud huts and the child had to point a finger at which oBanda he was looking for. The missionaries, however, had different ideas: they said that every man was special from birth and christened each one of them with relatively unique names. And as if that was not enough, they were also required to pick up a surname to register with the colonial authorities. My grandfather chose the surname *Kambalu*, which means 'splinter'.

Fascinated by the new order of things, Elisa Kambalu sent his son, my father Aaron Elisa Kambalu, to Robert Blake Mission School to get an education. My father's ambition was to go all the way to Edinburgh to study medicine, but his dreams were cut short when one of Blake's Boer teachers called him a 'native' as he worked in the school gardens. He had hated that word ever since he realised its implication. Losing his temper, my father threw his hoe at the teacher, narrowly missing his head. They expelled him from the school and sent him to prison for several months. It was during his incarceration that he read Samuel Smiles's *Self-Help* and embarked on a lifelong project of self-configuration and enhancement through any book he could lay his hands on in that remote part of the world.

Back at home in Misi Village his father sold goats and fowl of all kinds to support him while he completed an O-level correspondence course in English with a college in London. He got an E. The poor result, the Jive Talker reckoned, was not because he did not know his grammar but because he had been too bombastic.

Anyway, at the age of twenty-four, armed with the London certificate, my father left his village for ever. The year was 1964. It was the beginning of a new era. Malawi had just gained independence from the British, with Dr Hastings

Kamuzu Banda, a US- and UK-trained lawyer and physician, as its first president; the young country had never been so optimistic.

2

Aaron Elisa Kambalu moved to the city of Blantyre, named after the birthplace of the Scottish missionary and explorer, Dr David Livingstone. He trained as a medical assistant at Blantyre Medical School. He was then placed at a government clinic in Naperi township: it was there, among half-naked ailing natives, that he found his future wife.

My mother was different. She looked like Twiggy; her hair was parted in the middle, ironed straight down into a bob and decorated with a plastic red rose. And, since this was long before the Decency in Dress Act of 1971, she wore a miniskirt and high-heeled shoes. She carried a handbag. She spoke fluent English. She loved the Rolling Stones too . . .

Upon realising this, my father immediately announced that he had run out of aspirin and sent away the rest of the natives. He then closed the door and turned round to give the young lady a thorough examination.

Her name was Jane Kaphwiyo, she was twenty-two years old, a Ngoni, hence her unusually light complexion and her petite figure. In relative terms, people of her kind were new to this hotter part of Africa: she was more Hottentot than Bantu. The Ngoni were a warrior tribe who had fled British settler excursions from the Eastern Cape, Portuguese slave raiders from Algoa Bay and Shaka Zulu's subsequent *Mfecane* (the Crushing) in South Africa in the mid nineteenth century.

The displaced warriors had fought and looted their way into the interior of Africa until they were slowed down by food poisoning in Malawi: they had come across a stash of *kalongonda* (velvet beans), which they did not know needed days to cook. A good number of the marauding warriors were poisoned to death while the survivors were disarmed by the creation of the British Protectorate of Nyasaland on 14 May 1891. Their exodus thus terminated, some of the Ngoni settled in Ntcheu District in a village they called Chingoni.

When the Montfort Missionaries came to Chingoni Village in 1901 to establish the Roman Catholic Parish of Nzama, my maternal great-grandfather lost his land in a deal that his cousin, the paramount Ngoni chief, Njobvuyalema ('tired elephant'), made with the French missionaries. As compensation, the missionaries offered to teach his children to read and write. When my grandfather, Henry Kaphwiyo, finished school, he left the village to work as a clerk in the copper mines of Zambia, then known as Northern Rhodesia. By then he was already married and had a daughter, my mother, whom he left in the care of the missionaries. The Montfort Missionaries at Nzama Parish were raising my mother to become a nun until some mysterious stranger made her pregnant.

She left the baby on the doorstep of the parish priest and went to Blantyre to study as a primary school teacher at Kapeni Teacher Training College. That's where she met my father one afternoon when she had a headache. Six months later they were married, following an agreement that her bastard child stay back there in the village with the grandparents. They went on to have eight children, who in order of birth are Emily, Lucy, Joyce, Elson, Kondwani, Chikondi, Linda and Bond.

One hungry afternoon I asked my mother why the household was big enough to staff a farm. Was it because she was Catholic? Her reply was ingenuous but brutal: the supply of contraceptives at the hospital was erratic.

3

I was born in Nkalo, Chiradzulu District, on 23 November 1975, the year they killed Sweetman Kumwenda, the police chief from the Northern Region, and exiled the Jehovah's Witnesses to Zambia for refusing to buy Malawi Congress Party membership cards. My mother told me that on that day my father came home late at night, soaked to the bone by the heavy rains. He had been out in the bush administering polio vaccines. We were pretty broke and so the cold supper that awaited him on the table in gleaming china was bad by his normal standards: two lumps of maize meal, pumpkin leaves in a groundnut sauce and a couple of smoked *utaka*, a bitter, finger-sized fish from Lake Malawi. All the same, he sat at the table and said his prayers. When he opened his eyes, the dim light of the oil lamp revealed that there was no cutlery by his plate. He hated that.

'Where is my knife and fork?' he asked the stillness of the house.

There was no answer.

My father, it was well known, loved his cutlery better than his food.

'Where is my knife and fork?' he asked once again. His notorious temper was already steaming but still there was no answer, only the pelting rain on the tin roof and the muffled buzz of a fly keeping vigil at the table.

'Where is my knife and fork!' He bellowed it out this time, banging the table with an angry fist.

His startled pregnant wife suddenly answered from the bedroom: 'You cannot eat that fish with a knife and fork.'

She was still half asleep but she was right: *utaka* is a lean fish when smoked and dangerous if eaten with a knife and fork. In every bit you sawed off there was a bone waiting to lodge into your gums and throat or go down your windpipe and choke you to death. The only way to eat *utaka* is with your hands, feeling your way through it. But my father, a progressive gentleman, valued etiquette above his own life and upon hearing my mother's reply he completely lost his temper.

'You bloody natives! You don't understand!' he roared, and pushed the table away in disgust.

The table was new from the carpenter's workshop – you could still smell the pine – but it was not perfect. Parts of the woodwork had warped and, upon being pushed, the table came off the cardboard stopper under the shorter leg and swayed from side to side. The lantern fell off the table and smashed to the floor with a *boom!*

Suddenly the curtains were on fire, the sofa, the display cabinet, the Diptych . . . the whole house was on fire.

That calmed his temper quickly.

He woke up the whole family, my mum, my sisters, Emily, Lucy and Joyce, my brother Elson and the nanny Ayene, not to lead them out into the safety of the rain outside, but to help him save what was left of the Diptych from the conflagration. The family dragged the incredibly heavy twin bookcases out of the house to the shelter of the banana trees, but it had taken so long that there was no time to save anything else, so the family just stood there, shattered, watching the house burn down.

Then suddenly my pregnant mother's womb began to turn; that's when I crawled out of her like a little mouse, two months before my time, right there beside the Diptych.

There were no incubators at Nkalo Clinic; I survived by the kangaroo method. The midwife told my mother to wrap me warm between her breasts with a *chitenje* and to keep me there until I was strong.

I was born the fifth child, and they named me Kondwani, a Chichewa name, which translates as Meher Baba's expression, 'Don't worry, be happy.'

KASUNGU

1

Dr Hastings Kamuzu Banda constantly shuffled his civil service and so my father was moved up and down the country a lot. As he was a senior civil servant we lived in the big white Victorian houses abandoned by the colonial mandarins. The houses were located in what was called the Bush Line, the cooler areas of the districts, usually up in the hills from where the rivers flowed. But that was after he'd quickly risen up the ranks and become a clinical officer. Around the time I was born, however, he was a medical assistant, and so he was posted to the remotest parts of the districts, where there was no electricity or running water.

My earliest memory is of a roundworm slapping my bottom side to side as it slowly dropped out of my anus into the hole in the ground over which Ayene had me squatted for my toilet. The 'Mama!' shrieks that I unleashed as I quickly ran out of the pit latrine, the nanny chasing after me, put my memory to work: I remember Ayene catching up with me halfway to the house, tucking me under her arm, pulling the rest of the worm out and dangling it in front of my petrified face, scolding me:

'Told you not to eat the soil, *mwana iwe*! This is what happens when you eat the soil!'

Not long after that we were moved from Nkalo to

another remote area called Nkhamenya in Kasungu District.

Moving from place to place every two or three years knitted my siblings and me close together like a nomadic tribe. We rarely played with the local kids, because what was the point when we would be gone again the following day? The house was our main playground and the eight of us kept the place very busy indeed: disorder and ruin reigned everywhere, although you could not easily tell because the nanny tidied up quickly in our wake.

Come in through the bedroom window, the beds had mosquito nets but even the dopey greenfly got through, because there was always a ladder on the side from the last time somebody played fish or fell off the bed in their sleep. Malaria was rife in the house and so there would always be somebody sleeping in there.

We slept in hospital beds that Dad got free from the hospital, that was why they were unusually high. They were of course great for keeping the creepy-crawlies off our bodies, but not so convenient when you fell off the bed in your sleep: the sharp thud of tender bones hitting the concrete floor would wake everybody up confused:

'What's happening?'

'What is it?'

'*Akubaaaaaa!*' (Thief!)

Somebody brave would put on the light and calm things down:

'Oh, it's Lazarus.'

'Again?'

'Again.'

And I would be trying hard not to cry.

Inspect the walls in the corridor, and you soon realised that Dad was not the only one posting his thoughts on the walls. There were pencil and crayon jungles all over the place, inhabited by an array of colourful characters from the Diptych, among them my favourites, the Very Hungry Caterpillar and the wild things from Maurice Sendak's *Where the Wild Things Are*.

Enter the living room: high above the mantelpiece the Swiss cuckoo clock ticked, '*Ever, never; ever, never; ever, never . . .*' but if you looked carefully the hour hand stayed at three and the little bird no longer came out to sing, not since Lucy had reached up on tiptoe and pulled the gold chain right out of her little house. The small silver transistor radio on the windowsill only tuned to a raging storm. The dining table danced up and down, splattering your face with porridge, and the chairs wobbled back and forth like swings. The radiogram had on it the Beach Boys' record 'Good Vibrations' but it never played. My mother said it needed a needle. Sit on the armchair with the pretty doily that my mother had crocheted and you sunk in and got stuck until the nanny came to pull you out. My favourite object in the house, the camera hanging on the wall behind the sofa, zoomed in and out, clicked and shuttered, but took no pictures even though we had opened it with a spoon so many times and tried to fix it . . .

Overlooking the wasteland were the huge twin cedar bookcases, stuffed with books that took you places that you could never imagine: the Diptych. The Diptych was the most sacred object in the house and we all knew we were not to touch the books with dirty hands or defile the pages with our drawings and writings, as that would make Dad very angry indeed.

Above the Diptych hung a crude painting of the defiant St Paul's Cathedral in London during the Blitz. The bold caption at the bottom of the painting simply said, I SHALL SUCSEED. The artist whom Dad had commissioned to paint that picture couldn't spell, but for some reason Dad did not have the caption altered.

2

They nicknamed me Lazarus because I was a frail, malaria-prone child who constantly fell flat on his face from sheer lack of energy. I always had a wound or two from my numerous falls. They would know I had malaria when I was out on the veranda basking in the afternoon sun like a crocodile, trying hard not to shiver. Then they would gather me up, with or without my consent, and take me to the hospital for the nasty quinine jab I was trying to avoid.

But sometimes it was good being ill because my mother gave me her full attention and treated me special: I got to eat custard creams with orange squash while everybody else was eating kidney beans with water.

When I played in the dusty front yard of the house, creating spaghetti roads with my brick bus, big greenflies and a mangy dog called Bobo followed me, licking my wounds and messing up my work as he went. On one of the days when Ayene was not looking, Bobo bit me in the face.

As I lay in my bed, overwhelmed by the huge anti-rabies injections on my navel, Bobo kept coming to our house looking for me. From my perch high up on the hospital bed, I saw him through the window, drooling all over the place. Ayene threw stones at him, but still he kept on coming. 'Woof, woof, woof,' he said.

On the edge of the yard usually sat Jojo, a lion-faced leper who crawled in and out of the bushes surrounding our house, to watch us as if we were a film show or something. He would sit there all day like a primitive sculpture and never make a sound, and then suddenly, when he saw something funny, he would come alive, laughing and clapping until his mutilated hands started to bleed.

Jojo made me laugh a lot, but my mother gave him and the other beggars alms to keep them away: USAID refined vegetable cooking oil, EEC butter, UNICEF milk, and all kinds of things that came free from the hospital. But Jojo kept on coming, what was left of his face now daubed in cooking oil.

One afternoon, when my spaghetti road had reached the edge of the yard, my mother came home from work to find Jojo tickling me with his leprous hands. There were pus and blood marks all over my favourite T-shirt. It made her so angry that she fired Ayene on the spot and sent her back to the hard life in her remote village in Ntcheu.

But nobody in the house was prepared to evict Jojo and he knew it. His leprosy was too far gone to be touched. He was never too bothered when Dad tried to shoo him off with a stick. He just came and went as he pleased.

Things changed, however, when Dr Richard Laws, a British medical volunteer returning home, left his two dogs with us. The big brown one had a bark that was so deep he sounded like the bass from the Nkhamenya Boys' Quartet. But he did not need to bark often to keep the intruders away because he panted constantly in the daytime heat, his mouth displaying a big red tongue and a set of razor-sharp zigzag teeth. His name was Caesar. The other dog, a little grey one who kept a low profile, looked like a fox posing as a dog. He just slept all day as if he had been bitten by tsetse flies. We called him Prince.

When Jojo the stubborn leper came out of the bushes and saw the unfamiliar canine duo, he made a U-turn and limped right back where he had come from. We never saw him again after that, but every now and then I would look up from my spaghetti road hoping that he had come out to play. Later on, Febe, the new nanny, would frequently find me lost in the bushes looking for Jojo. I thought I had seen his funny face peering from behind the tree beckoning me.

Bobo, whom I had not seen for ages, watched the new order from a safe distance, down the dusty footpath. And that's where the national campaign against rabid dogs found him, one hot afternoon. The notorious Mr Chimpeni took him out with one shot to the head. I can still hear the massive rifle bang today. I can also see so much blood oozing from a very little hole in Bobo's head.

3

The most exciting times in Nkhamenya were when my sisters took me to the *gule wamkulu* in the mud-hut villages surrounding our house. Emily told me that the masked characters in the dances were spirits that came out of the bottomless wells, but I doubted it, so I went there partly to prove her wrong.

The *gule wamkulu* legs were alien enough, splayed feet with heels so cracked you could fit a kidney bean in them, but they were human all right. Once I caught a frenzied *gule* looking at me, the one who had big greenflies perched on his gaping jaw like the dead Bobo. When our eyes locked for a moment, I pulled at Emily's arm and shouted, 'Look! Look! He has eyes in his mouth!' But Emily did not look. Instead she pulled me back into the ecstatic crowd with her hand over my mouth and immediately took me home. She refused to take me back to the dances until I promised to watch in silence.

My favourite *gule* was Makanja, the wicked wizard who came out to punish the people who were evil. I had seen his white wooden face on the Diptych. He wore a three-piece suit made from sackcloth and carried a blond ox tail to keep the tumbu flies away. When he appeared on the *bwalo*, the women and children took cover in the bushes and watched from a distance. Dancing on stilts, he was the most elegant of the dancers with his calculated routine; he almost touched the sky. They said he used black magic to stay up on his long legs but I did not think so.

On the way back from the *gule wamkulu*, I liked to stand on my toes and parade about like Makanja. Then one day I couldn't do it any more. The pain in my toes was unbearable. Several days later my feet were swollen and itchy and I could not walk. When Dad finally examined me he diagnosed jiggers, a nasty sand flea that was brought to Africa from Brazil by the slave traders back in the eighteenth century. My mother boiled her sewing needle and picked the jiggers out, telling my sisters not to take me anywhere near those natives again.

They were not going to: by the time I recovered from the jiggers, I had developed a bizarre phobia for the soil. Nobody could get me back in the playground to create those spaghetti highways with my brick bus, let alone take me to see some weird dancers at the end of the dusty footpaths. I now just wanted to sit high up on the chair, dangling my feet, keeping them clean. Dad had to order a pair of brown shoes from London to get me to play outside again. The order took so long, though, that when the shoes finally came they were too small. All the same, I was squeezed into them like the Chinese women on the Diptych. Dad said that it was the only way to keep the jiggers away.

Elson was not happy about my new shoes because he did not have any, although he had told Dad he had jiggers too. Now all he liked to do as we played together was look at my shoes, asking me if he could have a go; I let him but he kept bothering me for another go until my mother smacked him and told him to leave me alone.

One day as I played near our house, making echoing noises down the murky well, calling out 'Makanja', Elson crept up behind me and pushed me in. I hit the water head-long several feet down and then sunk deep into what felt like a pitch-black bottomless pit. When I dared to open my eyes, I saw a shining orange ball ahead of me. I swam towards it, excited because I had always wanted a bouncing ball to play with, but somebody grabbed my hand and pulled me out of the water before I could get hold of it.

It was a naked old man with eyes so glazed they were turning blue. He heaved me on to his lean shoulders and told me to hold on tight. Then, with his sinewy limbs stretched out to the walls of the well like a spider, he carefully climbed up with me towards the light.

Soon after that, my parents took me to the Church of Central Africa Presbyterian (CCAP), where I was christened with a new name, Samson, which the minister said meant 'child of the sun'.

4

In the year 1979, when Attati Mpakati, leader of the underground Socialist League of Malawi, had his fingers blown off by a parcel bomb in Zambia, Dad was promoted to clinical officer and transferred to Mulanje District. Before we moved he had come across a photographer who agreed to come to our house to take pictures of us kids. The natives called him Limwado. He was one of Dad's patients and he had just returned from South Africa, having taken early retirement after he had broken his back digging up diamonds at Kimberley. Limwado had brought back with him a camera that took colour photographs and he now went about the villages taking pictures of the natives.

He promised it would take less than a week to get our photographs.

We were excited. We prepared ourselves as if we were going to church, taking long baths and rubbing our bodies with Vaseline until we were shining like new shoes. My sisters put on their Alice in Wonderland dresses. My brother and I wore safari suits. We pranced about impatiently as we waited for the photographer.

Limwado walked with a slight stoop and had a face scarred by smallpox. Under his green cloth cap his Afro and sideburns were the most outrageous I had ever seen. He wore big pink sunglasses, a blue evening shirt with chitterlings (unbuttoned at the top to expose the gold chain on his sweaty hairy chest), red flared trousers and white platform shoes. When I saw Limwado I ran to the Diptych and brought back with me a copy of Dr Seuss' *The Cat in the Hat* and handed it to him to read, but before he could Dad took the book back.

Limwado must have been the coolest man in Nkhamenya because the natives followed him everywhere.

Having collected his deposit up front, counting the money several times over before stuffing it in his bulging back pocket, he lined us up on the veranda in front of the house and told us the secret of a good picture.

'When I say Cheese you say Cheese!' he said, exposing a missing front tooth. 'The natives look awkward in photographs because they do not know how to say Cheese!'

Limwado was right. Dad had showed us pictures of sad-looking natives on the Diptych, Chuma and Susi they were called, and so I prepared to give him the biggest Cheese! I could muster. I was ready, but when he took aim I noticed that the lens cap was still on his camera. That bothered me. Dad had shown me how to take off the cap before taking a picture so I came out of the line-up and reached up on my toes to take off the cap for him.

Limwado smiled away my toddler curiosity and put me back in line. He did not get what I was trying to do.

When I pointed at his lens he turned round to see what I was pointing at but there was nothing there, only the blazing afternoon sun.

'Your lens is not open,' Dad told him.

Limwado had no clue what he was talking about. He was already aiming his camera once more when Dad muttered 'Natives' under his breath, walked up to him and took off his cap for him.

Limwado gave him the thumbs up, beaming.

'A bit to the left!' he said. 'Back. Back. To the left again. Yeah! Say Cheese!'

'Cheese!' we said.

We were drowned out by Limwado's fans standing in the distance saying, 'Cheeeese!' as if it were their picture.

A week went by; a couple of weeks, three weeks . . . We were packed and ready to go but still Limwado was nowhere to be seen. Dad didn't trust any photographer for a long time after that, and he was not one to take his kids to the colourful photo studios popular with the natives, and so I have no childhood photographs.

MULANJE

1

The journey to Mulanje at the back of the big rackety Bedford lorry had been terrible. The road, a succession of broken tarmac and dust, was narrow and winding. For three days and three nights we bumped among the furniture and baked in a cloud of diesel and the sweltering tropical heat. I had a headache and felt queasy all the way. Caesar and Prince did not like it either. They vomited and defecated all around us.

But at least we discovered why Prince was dopey. He had worms.

2

I couldn't wait to learn how to read and write so I could send the boy to kill the Jabberwock in the plumbing system. The toilet seat in Mulanje was from the colonial era, an original Thomas Crapper, and it made this terrifying *gulu-gulu* sound when the cistern was refilling with water. Dad said it was the Jabberwock in there and installed a copy of Lewis

Carroll's *Through the Looking Glass* by the side of the toilet for my sisters to read. You knew whoever it was in the toilet was about to come out when they started reading out the poem. When the Jabberwock suddenly appeared they would flush the Crapper and send in the boy to kill it with the Vorpal Sword, usually the plunger:

> *One, two! One, two! And through and through!*
> *One two! One two! And through and through!*

The Jabberwock thus slain, the boy would come out of the plumbing system holding its head aloft, a hero covered in all kinds of slimy things, and my sister in there would congratulate him.

> *'And hast thou slain the Jabberwock?*
> *Come to my arms, my beamish boy!*
> *O frabjous day! Callooh! Callay!'*

I would be standing there outside the toilet, listening and imagining the drama, bedazzled and envious. I wish they'd said that to me when I shitted myself in Nkhamenya . . .

But killing the Jabberwock was a smelly business. I always made sure I was away from the toilet door when it opened.

I started school at Njedza Full Primary School near Mulanje *boma* as soon as my mother was convinced that my legs were strong enough to carry me the distance there. (It took over an hour to walk to school.) 'Full', because the school offered the full Malawian primary school education, which took eight years to complete. My uniform was a green short-sleeved cotton shirt and grey khaki shorts. With that, I wore grey socks and a new pair of brown Bata sandals, which we called 'Jesus'.

For my packed lunch my mother made me an egg sandwich, in a plastic container. She also made me a bottle-top counting necklace, which made a *cha-cha-cha* sound when I jumped up and down like the Maasai warrior on the Diptych.

That bright Monday morning, when I toddled along beside my mother on the way to school for the first time, remains one of the happiest memories of my life.

Njedza Full Primary School did not have enough classrooms for everyone. I started to learn the alphabet and my numbers on broken bits of slate sitting under a purple jacaranda tree. It took me some time to read the 'Jabberwocky', but within days I was able to make out the title of the Thomas M. Harris book, *I'm OK – You're OK*, by the side of the toilet. And so, in the meantime, that's what I said to tame the Jabberwock when it started coming through the pipes.

3

I made friends with the 'boy' whose uncle rented our servants' quarters. He had a dark clay face and permanent sleep grit in the corners of his yellow eyes. There were nits in his hair that looked like a scattering of trees in the Kalahari Desert. His stomach was swollen, as if he had kwashiorkor. His teeth needed braces: when he yawned, exposing a set of fiery red gums, he looked like the Jabberwock. I wondered how old he was because, at school, sitting there under the purple jacaranda tree, he was much bigger than any of us – like the Ugly Duckling, except that's what he really was.

When we asked him his name he replied, 'Zapa Zepe Zipi Zopo Zupu.' There was a lot of sexual innuendo in that answer because the playground word for sex was *zopusa*, which literally means 'the stupid'. We called him Zapa.

According to Zapa, the reason why there was so much poverty in Malawi was because it was the very spot where Lucifer had fallen when he was kicked out of the heavens. And that was also the reason why the country was called Malawi, which means 'flames'.

He knew how black people came to be, too: he said that, in the beginning, God created all people black. But when He asked them to go and bathe in the River Jordan, some of them were so lazy that they only washed the palms of their hands and the soles of their feet.

Zapa's favourite game was putting a piece of a broken mirror under the teacher's skirt as she walked among us checking on our work.

Zapa looked like the children in Oxfam appeals, but one day he came to school with a can full of coins and showed it to the girls. On our way home, he bought a packet of sugar and invited me for a party in the Chitakale tea plantations. We sat on the big boulder in the middle of a tea field and ate sugar to our fill, laughing.

On the way back home we passed though the market, where we came across Febe who sold doughnuts in the afternoon when my mother was back from work. We were getting a lot of free EEC butter and milk and USAID refined vegetable cooking oil from the hospital, so my mother decided to start making doughnuts to boost the family income. Trouble was, the natives were not used to so much milk and cooking oil, and they seemed not to like my mother's doughnuts much. They preferred *chikonda moyo*, a form of Irish soda bread, but my mother was not going to make that. It was too rustic for her status as a teacher and the *doctor*'s wife. And so she persisted with the doughnuts, which nobody wanted to buy, hoping that the natives would develop a taste for them. When we found Febe, looking bored, fiddling with the loose ends of the bamboo basket, Zapa showed what a true gentleman he was and bought all the doughnuts off her. He took off his shirt and filled it with the greasy doughnuts and suggested we go back to the boulder in the tea field to party some more.

'Are you coming, or what?' Zapa asked me.

I looked at Febe because I felt there was something wrong. Where had Zapa really gotten all his money from? He told me he had sold birds, but I did not believe him because birds were hard to catch.

'Go with him. I won't tell,' Febe assured me.

And so I followed Zapa back to the boulder.

In the evening, I was struggling through my supper when Febe called us to the kitchen window to see something strange happening under the starry night, in the middle of a distant field. A shadowy figure had this fire torch in his hands, with which he drew an array of patterns and shapes in the air. We were enjoying the spectacle when the figure suddenly stopped and started running towards our house.

'Help! I am burning up!' he cried. 'Kondwani's mother, help! I am burning up! Help! Somebody! Help!'

We all rushed outside of the house to have a look. It was Zapa being punished for stealing his uncle's savings and squandering them on my mother's doughnuts. His hands were tied together with sticks like a witch's broom and set on fire. The more he tried to put the flames out with all the waving, the harder the fire burnt. My mother ran to him with a bucket of water and put the fire out. When she took off what was left of the broom, Zapa's stubby fingers were covered with hundreds of little blisters.

That night, I could not sleep. I kept having nightmares

of the little blisters on Zapa's hands and I kept seeing the fire patterns and shapes in my head. I had to put them somewhere so I took a pencil and drew them in my exercise books until every page was filled with alien abstractions and everybody complained that they could not sleep with the lights and all the scribbling.

I never saw Zapa again after that.

4

At the end of that month Dad kicked Zapa's uncle out of the servants' quarters for not paying rent and when he sat down in the living room that evening unwinding with a newspaper, I interrupted him and asked him how black people came to be. He replied that it was because of Phaeton and he told me the story while flicking through his paper.

'He was the son of Helios the sun god but none of his friends believed him when he told them that. To substantiate his claims he asked his father to let him drive his chariot for a day. His wish was granted but he got carried away and lost control of the white horses that drew the blazing chariot across the sky. When the chariot swerved too high, the earth became very cold and when it dipped too low, the earth was scorched into a desert on the part that is now known as the Sahara; the skin of African peoples was burnt black and that, in a nutshell, is how black people came to be. As for Phaeton, Zeus struck him out of the sky with a thunderbolt to stop the wayward chariot. He fell headlong into the River Eridanus.'

Dad's explanation sounded made up, like Zapa's, so I abruptly left him alone to read his paper and went to the dining room where my mother was ironing his suit.

'Mum, how did black people *really* come to be?' I asked her.

My mother immediately stopped ironing and sent me to the Diptych to fetch her the Bible; the King James Version, she specified, because it was more true. She then sat me at the table and read me a passage from Genesis 9:

And the sons of Noah, that went forth of the ark, were Shem, and Ham, and Japheth: and Ham is the father of Canaan. These are the three sons of Noah: and of them was the whole earth overspread. And Noah began to be an husbandman, and he planted a vineyard: And he drank of the wine, and was drunken; and he was uncovered within his tent. And Ham, the father of Canaan, saw the nakedness of his father, and told his two brethren without. And Shem and Japheth took a garment, and laid it upon both their shoulders, and went backward, and covered the nakedness of their father; and their faces were backward, and they saw not their father's nakedness. And Noah awoke from his wine, and knew what his younger son had done unto him. And he said, Cursed be Canaan; a servant of servants shall he be unto his brethren.

Before she expounded the passage I rephrased my question:

'I mean how did we get the dark colour?'

'Oh, that is because of the sun,' she said, putting the Bible away.

'The *sun* sun?' I double-checked, pointing at the window.

'Yes, the sun, sun,' she confirmed, and resumed her

ironing, her face, behind the veil of white steam, looking very relieved. But I had already perceived the sour truth that she had learnt in the convent: that we were the cursed children of Canaan.

BLANTYRE

1

In 1983, when they finally managed to kill Attati Mpakati in Zimbabwe, Dad wrote a new affirmation in his diary:

A far more beautiful house than the one I occupy now is waiting for me. The house is big with all facilities in it and it is very beautiful. Its surroundings are very vast and it is enclosed in a wire fence. The surroundings are very beautiful indeed. Yes, it is a house to be proud of – much better than the present one! A time comes when this house shall be handed over to me and I shall be very delighted to shift into it. My salary will soon double up. A lot of money is on the way to me now! I shall soon be called to look after all clinical officers throughout the country and I shall lead them. I am subject to very rapid promotions.

He was soon promoted to senior clinical officer. We were transferred to the city of Blantyre and housed in a leafy suburb called Queens. The house was new and fully furnished by the government from the wardrobes in the bedrooms to the refrigerators in the kitchen. Our hospital beds were taken back to the wards.

Dad was also made the team doctor of the Malawi

national football team. Now that was really exciting. He got tracksuits and Puma football boots, which my brother and I took to the playground and tried out when he was not looking. During most international matches at Kamuzu Stadium we got tickets to sit in the VIP stand. We would sit there in the shade praying for an injury, so we could see Dad run on to the field and do his thing.

But all this was only cosmetic and temporary. Blantyre would soon prove a reality far removed from the picture Dad had imagined. To start with, Dad's new workplace, the Queen Elizabeth Central Hospital, was too big for him to have real influence in the way he was used to. One of the areas in which he must have lost influence was the hospital kitchen. We no longer got the free food, and so we struggled to eat a balanced diet. And Blantyre turned out to be an expensive city for my mother's and father's starvation wages, although their excuse for being perpetually broke was always 'school fees'.

2

I began to regard myself as an artist when I was seven years old, a few days after I started school at Chitawira Full Primary. We were learning how to read clock faces. In one arithmetic exercise, my answers were all wrong but my teacher still gave me ten out of ten because my clock faces looked good. She said I was an artist. I drew some more clock faces, but had to switch to boxers when everybody began to lose interest. From then on, I drew my way into almost everything on the playground, even more so when I appropriated Dr Hastings Banda's signature for my drawings.

Soon after independence in 1964, Malawi had become a one-party state. From that time all citizens of Malawi had been required to buy Malawi Congress Party membership cards every year. Those who did not comply were not allowed to travel, work, buy or sell anything. Those who refused were regarded as dissidents and risked being put in prison, exiled or forced to commit incest like the Jehovah's Witnesses in 1975. As for schoolchildren, those who did not own the card were sent home until they could afford to buy one. For many that meant never.

On the front of the card, which changed colour every year, was a portrait of Dr Hastings Kamuzu Banda, who by 1971 had been made the Life President of Malawi. Inside were membership pledges and the bearer's name and address. On the back was the MCP logo, the black cockerel, and Banda's fancy signature. I wished my signature looked like that so I copied it again and again until I mastered it and began to use it for my drawings so it looked like the Life President had done them.

The drawings were another hit in the classroom; everybody wanted to share their pocket money with me so they could lay their hands on them, but when my dad came across the work he took the little wooden axe he had inherited from his father off the wall and knocked my legs with the handle, warning me to stay away from politics. I tried to design my own autograph, but they all looked like Banda's, so I ended up adopting a dot for a signature. You could just make it out in the corner of the new drawings.

3

During the Independence Day celebration football match on 6 July 1984 – Malawi v. Kenya – Dad had no string in the waist of his tracksuit bottoms because I had used it to make a football, and had forgotten to put it back. When Kinnah Phiri was fouled, Dad's tracksuit bottoms fell about his ankles as he ran on to the field. The natives cheered him on like he had scored a goal as he pulled them back up. The president did not look amused.

On that particular day, I wasn't in the VIP stand because I was taking part in the Youth Rally and was sitting in one of the open stands carrying a set of cards that formed part of the giant stand-sized images of the rising sun on the Malawian flag, the MCP slogan – 'Unity Loyalty Obedience and Discipline' – Banda's portrait, and the black rooster with the word *kwacha* (dawn) under his feet. Sitting there, you had to be attentive so you could put the right colour in the jigsaw when called, but when Dad ran on to the field and dropped his tracksuit bottoms, I lost my concentration and forgot where I was. I put down the black card I had been holding over my head and stood up to have a better look.

'Sit down, *iwe*,' the MCP Youth Rally supervisor in khaki uniform on the edge of the stand ordered.

I gave him a defiant look.

'I say, sit down over there!' he bellowed, pointing his cane at me, but his orders were undermined by another loud cheer from the natives. Dad had finished his job on the field and was running off again holding his tracksuit up with one hand.

The kids around me put down their cards too and stood up to have a better look. They knew it was Dad on the field doing his thing because I had told them he was the team doctor.

The supervisor looked nervous and started hitting the tops of our heads with his cane, trying to put the president's eye back in.

'Sit! Sit! Sit! You idiots, sit!' he hollered, his face and armpits sweating profusely.

The boy behind me, under pressure from the domino effect behind him, put his hands on my shoulders. I tried to hold steady for him but my back hurt, so I leant on the fat girl in front of me. Unfortunately she moved to one side at that very moment. I crashed to the concrete seat, two rows away, landing on my front teeth. I heard them crack before passing out for a moment.

When they pulled me out of the heap of youngsters, my mouth was bleeding. I could not cry though, afraid my teeth would fall out.

They took me to the Red Cross tent under the stand where I thought they were going to turn me into meat for the crocodiles in Banda's swimming pool, but it was not to be: the Red Cross people washed my mouth out, asked me to bite on a piece of cotton wool and immediately sent me back to the president's eye on the stand.

Later that evening, as I went back home, biting on the same piece of cotton wool, my lips blown up like two balloons, my friends ran all over the place holding up their trousers like Dad, laughing.

4

One day Lucy got into a fight with the daughter of a midwife who worked for Dad. She beat the poor girl to a pulp when she said that Dad was crap at Caesarean sections; he was too slow; too many women were dying under his knife. Soon after that we were moved to Nkolokosa, a rough township across the river and fields from Queens, to make way for what they said was a 'real doctor' from England. The houses there were connected to each other like train cabins and had not been painted since colonial times except for the wall facing the hillside adorned with lights that said LONG LIVE KAMUZU. It was difficult to sleep, the first few days, because the sequentially flashing words on the hill beamed through the windows on to our faces throughout the night. But eventually we got used to it like everybody else.

One evening, soon after moving in, we were glued to the radio listening to the MBC seven o'clock news: three of Banda's cabinet ministers, Dick Matenje, Twaibu Sangala and Aaron Gadama, and an MP, David Chiwanga, had been killed in a car accident in Mwanza District as they tried to escape to Mozambique, allegedly to start an armed rebellion against Banda's regime. We took it with a pinch of salt. Word on the street was that the police had beaten them to death with hammers and crowbars for questioning the president's wisdom in parliament. Whatever the truth was, parts of the neighbourhood celebrated and thanked God for protecting Malawi from a civil war.

'We do not want a Biafra over here,' they said.

As usual Dad told us to stay away from politics.

When my mother went back outside to continue her

cooking, she discovered that her pot of kidney beans that had been bubbling away on the charcoal oven had been stolen along with the clothes that had been hanging on the line. And poor Prince had been poisoned to death. He was lying there, stone cold, with his hind legs up in the air, head twisted to one side, his tongue sticking out, black ants and flies crawling all over him. He smelt like roast meat with the heat from the oven.

We found Caesar under the lamp post, proudly pawing at a heap of clothes he had rescued from the thieves. But it was no good: the clothes, including my only decent khaki school shorts, were riddled with holes from Caesar's teeth.

My brother and I were thrown in together with the girls as our bedroom was converted into a storeroom. You couldn't leave anything outside in that neighbourhood.

5

The following night Joyce woke us screaming at the top of her voice and everybody woke up shouting, 'What's happening?' Someone thought there was a thief in the house and shouted, '*Akubaaaa!*' I thought the MYP (Malawi Young Pioneers) had come to kill us. Last time they had only managed to crack my front teeth, but this time they had come to knock them all out like they did for Muwalo and Gwede. My mother heard the pandemonium and came into the bedroom. When she put the light on, there was nothing there. The window was tight shut. Outside a famine-stricken neighbour's dog – his name Danger – bayed at the moon.

'What's wrong?' my mother asked.

'Somebody bit my toe,' Joyce said, feeling her toe with her index finger.

We looked at Chikondi, who slept on the other end of the reed mat.

'I didn't do it,' she protested, wiping the sleep from her eyes.

'She got the jigger,' I joked. It meant she had dirty feet and would be walking like a duck, like I did in Nkhamenya.

'Shut your mouth!' Joyce said. Her toe was bleeding a little. My mother examined it and shook her head.

'It was a rat. We will get a cat. Until then, kids, tuck in well.'

She helped us tuck in. By the time she left, the bedroom looked like a tomb full of Egyptian mummies. A little while later when Dad came into the room and found us looking like that, he laughed, went to the living room and picked out Sigmund Freud's *Moses and Monotheistic Religion* from the Diptych. With the book in hand he talked to us about Egypt, focusing on Akhenaten, the mysterious pharaoh who, he explained, invented monotheism as the world knows it today. It was an awkward night because it was the first time Dad had talked about God as ancient history.

Until the cat came, we kept waking up at night screaming 'Rat!' We missed our hospital beds. The rats returned whenever the cat was eaten by the starving dogs in the neighbourhood. My mother was not going to use rat poison. The one time she tried the rat died somewhere in the roof, and the whole house stank for weeks. As for the rat traps, they were too dangerous in a small house like that. Bond nearly crawled into one of them. He could have lost his fingers.

We went through so many cats in Nkolokosa: Donna

Summer, Mick, Tinkerbell, Tintin, Zarathustra, Haddock, Arm Pit (because she liked to lick armpits, that cat) and Alice.

6

Our diet went from bad to worse: wild blackjack leaves supplied by a toothless woman from the side of the hill that said LONG LIVE KAMUZU and the occasional kidney beans or fish on Sunday. Always eaten with *mgaiwa* (coarse maize meal which the Diptych said was fit only for swine). We kept at this diet until we couldn't stand it any more and started eating Caesar's bones, or leftovers from the plates of medical students, the only thing that Dad now managed to get free from the hospital.

Around that time, Dad had somehow been learning how to play golf, but one evening, on finding us kids helping ourselves to the dog food, he quit and gave us the golf balls to play with. From then on he started drinking a lot and would often come home after midnight. He stopped reading in his chair and treating his books like gems. He now only read for a few minutes at a time while sitting on the toilet and even moved his treasured Nietzsche volumes in there, where they could easily have been defiled by other aspiring philosophers within the house.

It was around that period that Dad got his mental diarrhoea and started dumping his knowledge on us. Often it was when he was drunk, but he would always deny it: 'A drunken man cannot stand on two feet,' he would tell Mum. 'I only want to teach these kids a bit of jive.' And that is how he got his name. The Jive Talker.

Ironically, it was Mum who had introduced Dad to Carlsberg Brown when they first met to make him talk more as he was a quiet, shy man when sober. But now she regretted it. When the Jive Talker was in full swing he was worse than a drunk and more like a madman. He would just suddenly come into our room in the middle of the night, a book in hand, and start jiving, like a storm or an eerie breeze, depending on the topic. He never put the light on. He jived with the moonlight seeping in through the curtains or the corridor light coming in from the open door. Sometimes I could not tell whether he had really come into the room or if I had been dreaming. When the girls complained that they didn't understand and wanted to sleep he would say that it was not necessary to understand jive, its main objective was to give us a *vision* because like Proverbs 29:18 had said: '*Where there is no vision, the people perish.*'

But what a terrible vision it was from the Jive Talker. His teachings came from a desolate landscape in which roamed a lonely philosopher called Zarathustra who carried the corpse of a tightrope walker on his shoulders, whom he later buried in a tree. The eagle, the serpent and a dwarf named Ego followed him everywhere. When Zarathustra encountered other people as he wandered (among them the joker, the last man and the last Pope who was black), he would tell them that God was dead and that if they were going to women they must carry a whip. He would also speak to them about Superman:

What is the ape to man? A laughing stock or a painful embarrassment. And man shall be just that for the Superman: a laughing stock or a painful embarrassment. The Superman is the meaning of the earth. Let your will say the Superman is the meaning of the earth!

Listening to the Jive Talker, I made up my mind that when I grew up I would be a real doctor, so I would not languish in a dirty township and go as crazy as Dad, or his favourite philosopher, Nietzsche, who obviously wasn't a real doctor either. After school I would often find myself going back to the posh house in Queens just to have another look. The house had an eerie silence like a ghost house but sometimes an ugly-looking dwarfish dog barked from the inside. The real doctor in there must have wondered, 'What kid is that, staring at my house, and climbing my trees all the time making monkey noises?' But I only wanted him to think I was a feral child, so he would take me in.

7

There was a huge termite hill at the back of our house on which the natives would gather during the rainy season to catch *ngumbi,* the big black flying termites. The Jive Talker did not like it because as the natives waited for the *ngumbi* to gather in their inverted pots, they would look through the windows to see what was happening in our house. But my mother told him not to worry because there could only be so many termites in one hill and the natives would soon disappear. Not that termite hill though. It churned out more and more flies week after week and when we had a go, it turned out that the whole family was allergic to termites. Dad had an itchy throat. My mother and the rest of us had skin rash. And so, amid protest from the neighbourhood, he bought two hoes and made us get rid of the termite hill. We found a two-headed albino snake when the ground was level, which finally convinced the superstitious natives that the anthill had to go. We thought that was enough, but Dad said that termites would not go away until we found the queen. So we dug deeper until we hit the waterbed and made a well. We were about to give up when the queen floated up in the water, white, fat and juicy.

My mother planted maize in the new ground. The crop did well but one morning we woke up to find a crop circle inside the field and it was not the Martians who had done it – the maize had been stolen.

'Serves her right,' I heard the skinny woman up the road say. Her kids loved to catch termites.

My mother made a blue agapanthus garden in the yard because there was no point growing anything else, the rainy season was over.

Coming back from her teaching one day, my mother picked up a dry reed on the bank of Naperi River and made it into a *nkangala*, an ancient Ngoni mouth bow, with two notes that sounded like a woman weeping in the distance. Late in the evening, when the neighbourhood was quiet, she would sit in her armchair and we would gather around her to hear her song; you could barely make out the words from the whining string:

> *Kulukulu nanjiwa mfumu ya likaso nanjiwa*
> *Kulukulu nanjiwa mfumu ya likaso nanjiwa*

One evening, as Mum played her song, the Jive Talker, who had been snoring in the bedroom, woke up and stood in the doorway in his underwear, listening. Most of us did not notice him because when Mum sang that song we were completely mesmerised. When she hit the last note, the Jive

Talker walked up to her, snatched her bow and broke it in two on his thigh without saying a word.

8

When the agapanthus had bloomed into a sky-blue yard, every afternoon after work my mother would sit down on the landing to tell us folk tales while looking out at the flowers. One of them told of a beautiful woman who turned down marriage proposals from rich men around the world but agreed to marry a mouse catcher. When the mouse catcher asked her what the catch was, she said that she only ate python eggs. This was no problem because out there in the bush the mouse catcher knew a python that laid delicious eggs at the top of a very tall tree. Every evening as he climbed the tree for a fresh supply of eggs for his wife, he would sing a song which Mum would ask us to help her sing:

MUM: *Ndala ndala ndala ndalira*
US: *Ndala ndalira*
MUM: *Ndala ndala ndala ndalira*
US: *Ndala ndalira*
MUM: *Ine Amayi Ndinakwatira*
Ine mkaziwanga
Nsima sakudya
Nyama sakudya
Nyemba sakudya
Koma afuna ndala
US: *Ndala ndalira*

One evening the Jive Talker came home to find us singing that song, gazing at the flowers in a complete trance, the neighbours listening intently. He fumed. Like a scarecrow come alive he went into the flower garden, flattened it out with his feet, and ordered us to stop singing that native song right away. When we asked him why, he said that the native song was the song of death.

'You hear that?' he shouted to the bemused neighbours also. 'The native song is the sound of death. If you want to live stay away from the native song.'

After that, my mother picked up her knitting and knitted furiously without looking up until late in the night, when we had no choice but to leave her alone and go to bed where Emily read to us from Madame d'Aulnoy about the *Yellow Dwarf*.

9

It was around this time that we secretly started to attend the St Pius Catholic Church on the other side of the river, but only for the communion wafers. We were not the only ones. The Eucharistic queue at St Pius kept growing, delaying the concluding rite, until one Sunday the priest shouted, 'No more! In the name of the Father, the Son and the Holy Ghost,' and started to use queue monitors.

My mother too wanted to go back to her original church, but for more substantial reasons. She said that the Roman Catholic Church was the only true Church. Didn't Christ give the keys of the Pearly Gates of Heaven to Peter? And were not Peter's bones kept by the Pope in Rome? What did the fact that Martin Luther had conceived the Reformation on the toilet seat say about Protestantism? But Dad wouldn't hear of it. He said he did not want any superstition or Platonism in his house. The one time she tried going, he banished her from the house. She came back from church to find her clothes in the street and the neighbourhood fighting with Caesar over them. She picked up what was left and went to stay with a friend in Chigumula.

Dad was strange that way. He never read the Bible or went to church himself – in fact, when drunk he preached that God was dead and had a book (in the toilet) called *The Antichrist*. But every Sunday he made sure that we all went to church: *his* church, the CCAP, where austere rituals, a chorus of snoring presbyters and a sorry hymn called 'Amazing Grace' made you go to sleep. When we reported this to him, he laughed, saying we were lucky to go to a church like that because a dozing presbytery would equip us better for modern life than the screaming Pope.

But at that time, I did not like to go to church any more because I no longer had a Sunday Best. In fact, we children now walked barefoot like the natives, except Emily, who Dad dressed like a model no matter how broke he claimed to be with the school fees. And he continued to buy new books for the Diptych, although he hardly ever read them from beginning to end.

10

When Mum was banished from the house and was in Chigumula my teacher asked me to sit up straight in class and I couldn't. She thought I was being rude so she called me to her table and struck my backside with a guava stick, four times.

'Now go and sit that little bum down!' she said.

But I didn't go back to my seat. I just stood there looking at her, holding my bum. The teacher told me to let go and turned me round to inflict some more punishment. As she was about to strike again, she suddenly froze in shock, when she saw blood and pus trickle down my legs. And that's how my secret was found out. My bottom had been wasting away: with Mum absent from home, hygiene standards had slipped badly and I had developed terrible sores on the buttocks. The teacher said the tumbu fly must have laid its eggs on my shorts and sent me home to wash myself.

Dad took me out of school for a while and during that time, my favourite hobby was sneaking out to catch tadpoles at the Naperi River. I put them in a large glass coffee jar, watched and fed them day and night in the hope that they would turn into fish, but they always turned out as frogs.

11

Then Mum returned from Chigumula when she heard that the Catholic Church would not be taking her back because she had not sought a dispensation before marrying Dad. When she heard what had happened to my bum she bought me my first pair of underwear. They were green Y fronts.

The first night I slept in my new underwear, I dreamt that Mum had sent me to the market to buy fish. On my way back I discovered that I was naked. I did not know whether to cover my crotch or the sores on my backside. I realised that I had two hands, and I could do both. So, with two fishes, one covering my crotch and the other my backside, I ran home. I now realised why those girls were laughing when I passed them on the way to the market.

When I awoke my new underwear was missing but thank God my bum was still healed.

I searched the house for my underwear for a couple of days but found nothing. Nobody in the house had seen my underwear. When I asked the kids next door, they looked puzzled.

'What's an underwear?' they asked.

'Panties,' I told them.

They burst out laughing.

'What's so funny?' I asked.

'Panties are for girls,' they said.

And sure enough, when I looked under Lucy's sleeping mat there were my green Y-fronts. Next to them was some Dandy Bubble Gum wrapped with a football card of Pelé doing the scissors-kick. I took the gum and the Pelé instead (panties were for girls anyway), and waited for the fallout, but Lucy didn't say a word. I guessed it was some sort of deal. I chewed and blew on that piece of gum for days, until it turned brown and my jaws hurt.

12

I was never good at football at school but I was an expert ball-maker. Whenever I turned up at the playground with my football, everybody wanted me on their team although I was rubbish. I could play to my fill, switching to any position I liked, and sometimes shooting at the goal I was closest to. But when the boy who looked like a giraffe on the playground came across my footballs, he insisted that I play only for his team, the best team, no matter how rubbish I tried to be. His name was Mabvuto but he called himself Mave, a play on the word *mavi,* which means shit.

Mave won every fight he got into, but he was always the one who walked away with a bleeding mouth. He suffered from scurvy like he was a sailor. Whenever you shared a piece of mango with him, he would leave blood on it, even a tooth at one point. One day after a game of football, Mave called me aside and asked me, 'Can you draw Bruce Lee?'

'Who is Bruce Lee?' I asked.

'He does this!' He clenched his fists and raised one of his dirty barefooted legs as high as he could, trying his best to hold the stance. His tight khaki shorts cracked. He crashed down to the ground.

'What was that?' I asked, helping him up.

'Kung fu, the jeet kune do,' he said. His teeth were bleeding. 'Bruce Lee can do it better. Come to the film show tonight and you will see. He is amazing!'

'My father won't let me go out at night.'

'Mine won't let me either. I go out through the window when he is asleep. Like a ninja.'

'I don't have any money,' I said, showing him the insides of my pockets.

'Don't worry,' he said, looking at my hands intently. 'Meet me outside the film show. *Enter the Dragon* begins at eight.'

And so that night I convinced Elson to join me and we ninjaed our way out to the film show to see Bruce Lee at the St Pius Catholic Church Hall across the Naperi River. We found Mave waiting for us there, under the darkness of the banana trees.

'Wait for me here until break time,' he said, and disappeared into the cinema hall.

My brother and I anxiously waited for him under the cold starry sky.

A big boy was stuck on the outside with us watching through the single hole in the curtain. As contagious fits of laughter came out of the hall the big boy shouted that Charlie Chaplin was eating his boot. But he wouldn't let us see when we didn't believe him.

Then Bruce Lee entered the *Dragon*. The watchers were ecstatic with whatever he was doing in there. The big boy came away from the hole several times to practise the new moves he was seeing. The *hiyas*! and the thumping inside the hall didn't stop until the rackety projector snapped for the interval. A group of watchers, among them Mave, came out to catch some air and relieve themselves behind the banana trees.

Mave took us to the yellow rays of light shooting out of the high windows of the projector room and gave me a black biro. He extended his hand and told me to copy the stamp on his palm with all the artistic might I could muster. I examined the stamp and copied it on my brother's palm and mine. Mave ran his hand over the stamps to make them fade away a little. You could never tell those stamps had just been hand drawn.

'Cool,' I said.

As soon as the lights in the hall were turned off for the next reel, Mave said, 'Come on.'

There was a bouncer dressed just like a ninja at the door, brandishing two shiny machetes. His shadow looked like the praying mantis. We flashed the stamps at him, and before he could adjust his cowl to say anything, we were in.

13

Soon after *Enter the Dragon* every kid at school was doing Bruce Lee. One kid hit me on the head with a nunchaku and I figured I had to make my own in case I was attacked again. Mum and Dad's beds had lots of springs and chains; I took off one of the chains and made a *nunchaku*. Mave advised me to use guava sticks because they were tough.

The night I took the chain, the Jive Talker got stuck in his bed and sprained his back a little. I braced myself for a good knocking on my legs with his wooden axe as we pulled him out because everybody said it was me, but instead he took out the big book of quotations from the Diptych and made me copy the whole section on Bruce Lee on to a sheet of A4 paper to give me a vision.

The key to immortality is first living a life worth remembering.

To see a thing uncoloured by one's own personal preferences and desires is to see it in its own pristine simplicity.

A fat belly cannot believe that such a thing as hunger exists.

Any technique, however worthy and desirable, becomes a disease when the mind is obsessed with it.

Pessimism blunts the tools you need to succeed.

Absorb what is useful, reject what is useless, and add what is specifically your own.

Self-education makes great men.

As long as we separate this oneness into two, we won't achieve realisation.

The function and duty of a quality human being is the sincere and honest development of one's potential.

Real living is living for others.

As long as I can remember I feel I have had this great creative and spiritual force within me that is greater than faith, greater than ambition, greater than confidence, greater than determination, greater than vision. It is all these combined.

If you love life, don't waste time, for time is what life is made up of.

Style is a crystallisation.

Dragons were being entered everywhere by would-be jeet kune do masters. Limbs were broken as children tried to master Bruce Lee moves. For a moment even football was out of fashion, the scissors-kicking Pelé forgotten. On the radio Carl Douglas's 'Kung Fu Fighting' was the most requested record. We fought each other all day at the playground. I documented it all in my school exercise books: dragons, ninjas, shaolins, Yukio Mishima, drunken kung fu masters, samurai, sumo wrestlers, you name it, they were all in there with Bruce Lee. Each one of them labelled in Chinese. My teacher went mad.

The St Pius Catholic Church Hall got rich with the

film-show project, loved it, and ordered some more Bruce Lees: Myron Bruce Lee, Bruce Li, Bruce Lei, Bruce Li Zine, until we could not tell which one was the real Bruce Lee, gave up and demanded James Bond instead. Guns were more effective anyway. And there was this tough Japanese bad guy in there who kept crushing golf balls with his bare hands and chopping off all these people's heads with his bowler hat, which we wanted to see. It was not long before we were also wondering who the real 007 was, but at least with the James Bond films it was easier to tell.

14

There was more than one way to escape the reality of Nkolokosa, thanks to the American evangelist, the Reverend Dr Robert Russell, who had pitched a huge tent in the neighbourhood that shone in the night like a giant gold bar from Fort Knox. This was one of those rare times parents would knowingly let you out in the night because Jesus had said, '*Suffer the little children to come unto me and forbid them not: for of such is the kingdom of God.*' The whole neighbourhood flocked to the shining tent, each for their own reasons. There was singing and dancing there, to a band with white people. The drummer whose hair looked like a lion's mane had an electric percussion instrument, a little black ball mounted on a silver metal stand that went *poom!* when he hit it, like in Anita Ward's hit song 'Ring My Bell' on the radio. The natives went crazy. Reverend Dr Robert Russell had a special song for it:

Take a leap into the water – poom!
Take a leap into the deep – poom!
Take a leap and sing with the angels
Praise the Lord Almighty! – poom!

When the Jive Talker heard us sing that song at home he said it was about the *leap of faith* but then things always meant too many things to him now.

Miracles: the lame could walk, the blind could see, those who walked in the darkness saw the light. Sometimes they gave out sweets. There were riches to be made if you gave one-tenth of your earnings to the Lord. But if you wanted to be really, really rich, you had to give all you had, like the woman who gave all to God in Mark 12:41–4. 'You know why Africa is poor?' Reverend Russell would ask, a wry smile on his face. 'Africans do not know how to give, that's why. Hallelujah!'

'Amen!'

If all that did not get you to give generously to the Lord, there was always Acts 5:1–10 to scare the hell out of you:

But a certain man named Ananias, with Sapphira his wife, sold a possession, and kept back part of the price, his wife also being privy to it, and brought a certain part, and laid it at the apostles' feet. But Peter said, Ananias, why hath Satan filled thine heart to lie to the Holy Ghost, and to keep back part of the price of the land? Whiles it remained, was it not thine own? and after it was sold, was it not in thine own power? why hast thou conceived this thing in thine heart? thou hast not lied unto men, but unto God. And Ananias hearing these words fell down, and gave up the ghost: and great fear came on all them that heard these things. And the young men arose, wound him up, and carried him out, and buried him. And it was about the space of three hours after, when his wife, not knowing what was done, came in. And Peter answered unto her, Tell me whether ye sold the land for so much? And she said, Yea, for so much. Then Peter said unto her, How is it that ye have agreed together to tempt the Spirit of the Lord? behold, the feet of them which have buried thy husband are at the door, and shall carry thee out. Then fell she down straightway at his feet, and yielded up the ghost: and the young men came in, and found her dead, and, carrying her forth, buried her by her husband.

'Hallelujah!'
'Amen!'
'Hallelujah!'
'Amen.'

You were never bored in Dr Russell's temple and he was paid in full for his efforts. By the time he left Nkolokosa for America he had replaced his shining tent with a magnificent new church called the Assemblies of God.

I went to the tent mainly to listen to the little black ball that went *Poom!*, to be mesmerised by Reverend Dr Robert Russell until I fell on my back, my arms and hands shaking uncontrollably, and to find out if these guys were in fact CIA. James Bond taught you not to trust anybody, especially in circuses like these. As Dr Robert Russell lifted his Bible, I peered inside his jacket to see if he had a gun.

My sisters went to the shining tent to meet up with their boyfriends.

15

One night, Lucy brought a chicken home from her date. She took a knife and ran it across a stone until it was as sharp as a razor, then beheaded the chicken. As she put the headless body in a bowl it ran off to the whitewashed side facing the hill that said LONG LIVE KAMUZU. By the time Lucy caught him, the headless chicken had splattered a section of the wall with his blood, making it look like the Jackson Pollock on the Diptych.

As if he had smelt the sizzling chicken, Dad came home from work in good time for supper.

'Where did you get this chicken from?' he asked, sitting at the table.

The household had not prepared an acceptable answer. Everybody had assumed a hungry man would not ask questions, especially before a sizzling chicken, so we just looked at him with greasy lips.

'Eh?' Dad asked once more.

My little sister Linda suddenly pointed at Lucy with a greasy chicken claw.

'You bloody natives!' Dad said, lifting his chicken drumstick as if it was a dead rat. He threw it out of the window where it landed on our new puppy, Sharp, but it was the bow-legged kids from next door who were soon fighting over it.

Damn! What is wrong with Dad? I wondered to myself.

That was another excuse for a night of jive. When he came back at dawn, he took his wooden axe off the wall and trashed every one of the china plates in anger, screaming, 'You bloody natives!'

He was so drunk that when he stumbled to the bedroom with the wooden axe to smash Lucy's legs he ended up thinking he was about to sleep and mistook her sleeping mat for his own bed. Lucy squealed, but the Jive Talker could not hear her. He was already snoring in her ear. We had to drag him out to his own bedroom.

From that day on when the girls brought home chickens from their dates we didn't tell Dad. As he was getting leaner and leaner from the blackjack leaves, we were getting pretty fat.

16

One of the most popular play spots in Nkolokosa was the huge, black, bubbling sewage pipe that lay high up across the Naperi River, joining Nkolokosa township to the neighbouring grounds of St Pius Catholic Church. It made an excellent vertigo sport. After school, there would always be a few urchins creeping across the pipe like ants, boasting of their ninja bravery as they went. Sometimes a few of the kids would lose their grip and splash into the murky river below, or crack their tender skulls like that unlucky boy, Dennis, who died there. It was Easter when I plucked up enough courage to become a sewage-pipe ninja. I went all alone and did the whole length without anybody cheering me on. When I made it to the other side, leapt off the pipe and was about to jump up and down in celebration, I saw a familiar pair of red flip-flops. The voice beckoned just above my head.

'Kondwani! Kondwani!'

It was my sister, Lucy, towering over me, hands on her hips.

'What are you going to do if I tell Dad you have been trying to kill yourself?'

'I didn't do it!' I protested, standing as if nothing had happened.

'I saw you. Look at the marks on your clothes. Do you want to come to church with me?'

I knew she meant the Catholic church because they were practically the only ones who kept praying throughout the week. The Assemblies of God at Reverend Dr Robert Russell's shining tent did the same but only in the evenings, so I shook my head.

'Dad said we shouldn't go there.'

'Then I am going to tell Dad what you've been up to.'

'I will come with you.' I couldn't give her my hand quickly enough.

'Good boy,' she said, putting her arm around my shoulders.

It was hot in the church. The air was thick but only one window was open; the one on the left-hand side of the chancel was guarded by a bunch of altar boys. As I walked through the aisle looking for a seat on the men's side, I noticed that some people among the sweaty congregation had swollen faces and wondered what was happening.

There was the traditional Easter play going on. In the corner a narrator with a swollen chin wiped his shiny face with a soiled hanky, opened his tattered Bible and moved the play to the Last Supper. He must have been short-sighted because he held the Bible very close to his nose.

'And the disciples did as Jesus had appointed them; and they made ready the passover. And now when the even come, he sat down with the twelve . . .'

Jesus, the man with the lightest skin on the stage, joined his ugly disciples at the table, opened his arms and spoke to them:

'Verily I say unto you, that one of you shall betray me.'

As the dusky disciples asked him, *'Lord, is it I?'*, I noticed a couple of wild bees flying among the congregation but everybody stayed put. Except me: when a bee zoomed past my ear I slapped at it vigorously. There was a momentary scuffle at the rear of the congregation as another bee hovered above my head like a halo; I waved that one off too but it stung my ear before it flew away. I could feel it swelling hot. I covered my ears with my hands, leaving just enough spaces between the fingers so I could hear the players onstage.

John, the disciple whom Jesus loved, wanted to say something but couldn't because he was suddenly stung on his forehead. He screamed, *'Ayi!'* crossed himself and walked off the stage. Somebody wearing a red robe at the back of the stage sent him back to the table immediately (I saw a hand push him). By the time they had the disciple settled in again at the table his forehead was all swollen. He looked like a gorilla. A child in the front pew laughed heartily, pointing a finger, but nobody else thought it was funny.

Jesus tried to calm down the anxious disciples by giving them a clue to the person who would betray him:

'He that dippeth his hand with me in the dish, the same shall betray me. The Son of man goeth as it is written of him: but woe unto that man by whom the Son of man is betrayed! It had been good for that man if he had not been born.'

It was no good because everybody at the table looked like they were ready to dip into the dish with him. That is why they had come to the table in the first place. Judas, looking fed up by Jesus' cunning, took a deep breath and bailed the disciples out of their misery. He almost thumped the table with his fist.

'*Master, is it I?*'

'*Thou hast said,*' Jesus answered him, still in doublespeak, and that did it for Judas. He gathered his robes and stormed off the stage in anger to get the police.

In the meantime Jesus blessed the cup, but as he was about to drink from it a killer bee hovered upon the rim. He tried to shoo it off but it was not going anywhere and the play was being delayed. When he tried to drink from the cup anyway the bee buzzed violently and stung his lip but he took it with good grace: he calmly sucked on his lip and gave the cup to Peter.

However, Peter was not as patient: when a wild bee hovered near him, he quickly put the cup down, took off his dirty sandal and thumped the table with it, killing the bee instantly. As he bent over to put his sandal back on a small mushroom cloud rose up from the table making some folk cough. Simon the Zealot grabbed the cup, covered it with his hand and shoved it under the table to protect it from the settling dust. Peter straightened up again only to find the cup missing.

By now a couple of children in the front pew were doubled up in hysterics but still the rest of the congregation did not look like anything funny was happening there. The narrator whispered 'Shush!' and the baffled Peter searched the table for the missing cup before planting a suspicious look on his innocent Master.

The bees seemed to have left the church and all was calm until the play reached the part where Jesus carries his cross to Golgotha: a bunch of altar boys keeping an eye on the open window suddenly screamed in unison: 'They are coming!' Jesus turned to have a look, his upper lip all swollen, sweating buckets. The cross must have been too heavy for him; it took him for ever to turn. When he saw thousands of merry African killer bees streaming into the church in the purple rays of the setting sun, he threw down his cross with lightning speed and ran out of the church through the aisle. The whole congregation and the wild bees followed him.

I looked for Lucy among the scattered flock but she was nowhere to be seen. I found her by the roadside, searching for me among the crowds coming from the church. Following her like a dog was a cool guy in a white shell suit who looked like Lionel Richie.

'What happened? What happened to your ear?' Lucy asked.

'The bees bit us. The play is finished.'

Lionel Richie looked disappointed, but after I promised Lucy not to tell, he took us to the Apollo, the big cinema in the city instead.

There was nobody else in the cinema; hundreds of red velvety seats, all for the three of us. Lionel Richie must have been a very rich boy to afford a place like that. He bought us popcorn and bottles of Coke, and we sat back and watched *Footloose* with Kevin Bacon on the biggest screen I had ever seen. You had to turn your head left to right and back again to see all the action.

From that day on, I started to dance whenever I could, and whenever I did folk asked me, 'Have you ever seen Michael Jackson?' and did funny things with their feet. I took it as a compliment, so I wanted to see *Footloose* again, to see if I could learn more dance moves. Lucy wouldn't take me though; she said that she had broken up with Lionel Richie. But I think she was lying because I kept seeing her with him in the darkness beyond Dr Russell's shining tent. He was easy to see with his white shell suit.

17

I made up my mind to make my own money by selling birds like the fat man I had seen at Dr Russell's shining tent one day. He displayed the birds in a big basket and he sold them to the stocky builders working on the new church, making all this money which he shoved into his greasy pockets.

There were lots of birds in Njamba Forest – carmine bee-eaters, paradise flycatchers, lilac-breasted rollers, cattle egrets – and I was going to catch them all and ask my mother to fry them up for me. I had calculated that if I sold fifty of them, that would be enough to buy a ticket to *Footloose*.

I knew how to catch birds, because I had seen Zapa do it back in Mulanje. He would use a knife to tap the milky liquid from the *khadze* tree and then boil the stuff in a tin to make a sticky gum. He then covered a long wire with the gum, put it in the tree where the carmine bee-eaters loved to perch and waited. When birds came they'd get stuck on the wire and then he would take them home and roast them.

Tapping the *khadze* tree in Njamba Forest turned out not to be as easy as I thought. First, the tree was hard to find, because I could not remember what it looked like. Then when I finally found it the trunk was so hard that I had to climb up the tree to try the softer branches. I successfully made a big cut into the branch above me but the milky stuff took for ever to come out. I was perched in the tree for hours and the sun was setting. Then when I checked the tin for one last time a huge blob of milky stuff dropped into my eyes sticking the eyelids together as I tried to wipe them clean. I dropped the table knife and the little tin and climbed down the tree, blind.

I found my way home by following the choruses coming from Dr Russell's shining tent. I crawled past the tent on the right, edged my way down the slope, followed Caesar's bark and I was home. I told my mother I had been looking up in the trees and the milky stuff had just dropped in my eyes and glued them together. When she examined them it wasn't milky stuff at all.

'What is it then?'

'It's bird shit, love.'

'Really?'

'Really. You can open your eyes now.'

18

A couple of days later a Coca-Cola truck came through the neighbourhood, parading gleaming bicycles that could be won if you found all the components of the bicycle hidden in the Coca-Cola bottle tops. It was great news. If I won that bicycle, I could sell it and use the money to go and see *Footloose* as many times as I wanted; I still hadn't given up on it.

In the weeks after the truck's passing, the kids next door, my brother and I visited every bottle store, collecting all the tops we could find, but the same thing kept coming up: the chain. Sometimes you would find the handles and maybe a wheel or the frame, but never the saddle, the missing piece in the jigsaw. I figured if I looked even harder than anybody else maybe I could find it. So at night my brother and I ninjaed our way to the Mai Nyagondwe Bottle

Store in Chitawira on the other side of the Naperi River. We would sit there in the dark, watching the natives drink and dance to the rumba on the shiny jukebox till the early hours of the morning. When they were either too drunk to care, or too distracted by the women with red lips and big bums, they threw the bottle tops to the floor and we would swoop down on them like hawks from the darkness.

Still no saddle, just more chains.

One night, we hung on at Mai Nyagondwe's until closing time to search through the bottle tops that were swept into the rubbish pit. When the cleaner had gone we were on them. I was the first one to get in. I stepped on a broken piece of glass and cut my foot. When Elson came to see what was wrong he stepped on the glass too and did the very same thing. We dragged our feet home, bleeding profusely.

When we were crossing Naperi Bridge, a drunken man turned around and barked, 'Who is it?'

It was the Jive Talker on his way home from his drink. Before he recognised us, we ducked out of sight and over-took him.

We reached home just before sunrise.

NKHOTA-KOTA

1

In 1984, they sentenced Orton Chirwa and his wife Vera to be hanged for treason. Orton Chirwa was one of the founding members of the Malawi Congress Party who fell out with Banda soon after independence when his leadership had suddenly turned autocratic. It was said that Chirwa and his family had been lured back from exile in the United States, Britain and Tanzania by the Malawian Secret Service.

What had they come back here for? I wondered when I heard the rumour. There was nothing in Malawi. I wished I were grown like the Jive Talker. Then I would have taken my jive against Banda straight to the marketplace using a megaphone like that of Reverend Dr Robert Russell: Why did you have to crack my teeth in your eye at the stadium? I can't drink cold water any more. What's this all about, naming everything around here after yourself? Kamuzu Stadium, Kamuzu Barracks, Kamuzu Mbumba, Kamuzu Academy, Kamuzu Bridge, Kamuzu International Airport, Kamuzu Dam . . . You think you own this country, don't you? Why do you paint our houses only on the side facing the hill that says LONG LIVE KAMUZU? We can't sleep at night with the blinking lights and all. Think of all the people you have fed to the crocodiles, Mr President. Look outside your bedroom window at night and see them calling out to you for a swim in the blood red pool under the moon-light. Muwalo and Gwede's corpses hanging in your wardrobe saying 'Good morning' every time you open the doors to get your suit. The cabinet ministers you battered to death in Mwanza District waiting to have lunch with you in your dining room, crowbars still embedded in their heads like dreadlocks. Don't you fear or feel anything? You said it was a car accident that killed them, so how come the only thing that was broken on the car was the bumper? Oh yes, we have seen the car in Chileka and we don't believe you. People are hard to kill, you know. They scream, shake and gasp . . . It's not like in the movies where they just drop dead like flies with a single bump . . .

Then I would cut and run, heading for the Mozambique border. From there I would walk to South Africa and then take a boat to America, the land of the free, and that would be it. The Americans knew the Life President 'supped with the Devil' and they would grant me freedom and I would live in a big house, eat delicious food, watch *Footloose*, *The Jungle Book* and *A Fistful of Dollars* as many times as I wanted.

I was imagining all these horrors and musing over this plan one night when the Jive Talker walked in, going on about Nkhota-kota, a remote district in the Central Region, and its wildlife and I knew that we would be moving again soon.

'Nkhota-kota District is mostly a game reserve but you should not go beyond the barbed-wire fence. Trespassers are prosecuted and thrown in jail. They won't think you are on a safari for a minute. The game reserves, kids, are but extension of Western zoos. Who among you here has ever seen an elephant, a lion, a leopard beyond the Diptych?

'Do not swim in the lake. You might catch bilharzia. Quicksands might swallow you up when the tide is out. Crocodiles might crunch you to death in the marshy areas. The bite strength of their jaws dates back to the dinosaurs and the crocodile is the only animal beside man who can play dead. Do not touch him. But do you know something? Crocodiles are only good at closing their mouths. They can hardly open them when there is the slightest resistance. Should you ever find yourself in trouble with one hold those jaws shut with the last remaining strength in you. That's your only chance of survival. But if I were you I would be more scared of the hippopotamus. They are the biggest man-killer after man. Do not stand in her way when she is trying to get back to the lake. She only runs in a straight line and sweats blood, which functions as suntan lotion on her skin. That's why she looks all red in the pictures when not covered in mud. Hippos have to resurface out of the water every three to five minutes even when they are sleeping . . . It's all automatic for them. The hippopotamus may come to your rescue when the crocodile is attacking you because she hates the crocodile to her guts. But I wouldn't bet on it if I were you . . .

'Do not walk in the bushes at night. The puff adder likes sleeping on warm paths with enough venom in his jaws to kill four or five men. But the bite itself is strong enough to shock you into paralysis . . . Pythons might constrict you to suffocation and swallow you whole. She will stay docile for weeks while she digests you if need be . . . The spitting cobra will make you blind. She can spit with pinpoint accuracy from up to two metres when cornered. Actually she doesn't spit despite her name, but rather sprays the venom out of her glands through muscle contraction . . .

'Be careful of the tourists at the lake, most of them are spaceheads, the last of the hippies looking for Malawi Gold. You know what Malawi Gold is, kids? Marijuana, the stuff that will make you laugh when there is no joke. Don't smoke it, it makes you too laid-back for anything. A spacehead can only go so far . . . You need that raw drive to get you places in this world. Ever since Bob Marley commented that Malawi hemp was the best he'd ever smoked lots of people from around the world have been flocking to Nkhota-kota to get some. It's the hemp capital of the world now. The Americans, the Dutch, the Germans, the French, the British, the Australians . . . they are all there. So, stay away from the backpacker and don't let the tourist take your picture, next thing you know, you are in an Oxfam appeal . . .'

2

Nkhota-kota might have sounded like *The Jungle Book* but it was better than Blantyre for us because Dad was the boss once more. We got our hospital beds back and the other things that came free from the hospital. Our home was along the black tarmac road that serpentined through the Bush Line to the blue waters with the foamy white waves in the distance below. Fine beach sands, mango, banana, pawpaw and avocado trees surrounded the house. The place was an oasis. The catch was that the trees dropped a lot of dry leaves and rotten fruit at night, which attracted creepy-crawlies from miles around into the yard. To keep those away the nanny had to sweep up the whole yard every day, leaving behind a huge sandstorm as she went along.

A few days after we arrived, my younger brother and I were helping the nanny out, sweeping up our own sand-storm, when Caesar and Sharpe ran past us, tails between their legs, hissing and urinating as they disappeared around the other side of the house. Shortly after them, a very big red dog appeared in the settling dust, gently flicking its tail from side to side, leaving unusually large footprints on the finely swept sands. He headed towards the water tap and started licking it with his big tongue.

Watching the dog with its huge sharp teeth, everything felt like a dream. My hair stood on end. I weed myself. I could feel the warm piss trickle down my legs. I wondered where the nanny was.

'Muuuuuuum!' Bond called. 'Come and see Clifford!' (Clifford was the big red dog on the Diptych.) He had his hands stretched as wide as he could to show the size of the dog. His eyes were popping out of their sockets.

Mum came out and looked around.

She suddenly swooped on us like a chicken protecting her little ones from a hawk and gathered us into the house, locking the door behind her. She then took a deep sigh of relief, crossing herself.

'Phew! That's a lion,' she said.

'Don't they have the big hair, though, the mane?' My knees were shaking.

'That's a lioness, kid.'

I sat myself on the sofa.

The lioness roared once, shaking the whole house. By the time we looked out of the window she had drunk her fill and was gone, leaving the puddle beneath the leaking tap blood red.

3

Linga Full Primary, the Anglican Church school, was a collection of very basic but tidy building blocks inside a stone fence. The gate, the doors and the windowpanes had long since disappeared. The name Linga meant refuge and the school had been so named because it had been built near the huge baobab tree under which David Livingstone had negotiated, albeit unsuccessfully, to end the slave trade in the region with the Arabs. It is said that the Arabs were so cavalier with the errant Englishman (Livingstone's preferred identity on his travels because it had more bite) that after the meeting they offered him a couple of female slaves to accompany him on his further explorations. The Christian missionaries that followed in Livingstone's footsteps had to bring more than the Gospel with them to fulfil his wishes.

Francis, my new friend at Linga, was the son of the Anglican minister, Reverend Gota, who ran the little Gothic cathedral near the school. Like a typical pre-teen, Francis tried his best to look and behave like his influential father: while *pushback* (a bastardised pompadour) was the hairstyle in fashion, Francis's hair was evenly cut short which made him look uncannily like his father since they were almost of the same height. His shirt was always buttoned up around his neck; you could tell he was dying for a dog collar. In class, he sat at the front and was always quiet and attentive, his left hand crossed over his chest while the right one stroked an invisible beard on his chin. Whenever the teacher made a good point he nodded his head in approval. There were always a couple of biros neatly tucked in his breast pocket although only one of them worked. His handwriting was a bit too big but always neat: he wrote slowly, like he was laying down a rope across the page. He never forgot to date the work, always used a ruler and rubbed out incessantly. He would always be the first to volunteer to distribute the exercise books but couldn't collect them because he was always one of the last people to finish. He contemplated his work too much: you had to stand there and tell him to hurry up so you could collect his exercise book or rub out the blackboard. He never carried a school bag but preferred to walk around with his exercise books pressed against his heart the way his father carried the Bible. Yet unlike the rest of us his exercise books were never dog-eared. My own pre-teen traits would manifest themselves a little differently as I prodigiously absorbed and parroted the surreal world of the Jive Talker and the Diptych: they were already calling me 'Big Head' at school.

When I found out that Francis was a Tonga I under-stood his obsession with cleanliness: the Tonga ultra-hygienic habits were legendary and well known far and wide. The Tonga men had a proud history of fighting alongside the British in the King's African Rifles during the two world wars and it is said it was from them they learnt to stay clean all the time. Perhaps the Tonga had taken the washing too liter-ally, but during the colonial times when Nyasalanders went to Rhodesia or South Africa to look for work as housekeepers and garden boys, they would tell the white employers there that they were from the Tonga tribe to get the job quickly.

On the way to the lake for the first time, when I brought up the Tonga legend, Francis told me that in fact the average Tonga tribesman took a bath five times a day.

'Why five times?' I asked him.

'Because white people like clean people.'

'Really?'

'Really.'

'How come they like to explore the jungle?'

'I don't know,' he said.

When the lake began to reveal itself in the distance, Francis pointed at a collection of mud huts along the dusty footpath, which led down to the beach on the other side of the lagoon and shouted: 'There they are!'

'Who? The Tonga?'

'No, the Yao! That's them! Stay away from that side!'

There were lots of other tribes along the lakeshore.

'What is the problem with the Yao?' I was curious. Francis gave a predictable answer:

'They are Muslims, you know. They don't believe in Jesus and they wipe their bottoms with their hands when they go to the toilet. They carry around a pot of water. Imagine that.'

His mouth was twisted in disgust.

Nobody liked the Yao much. They were originally from Mozambique and had been converted to Islam two hundred years before Livingstone 'discovered' the lake. Back in the days when the slave trade was thriving along the lakeshore, the Yao had collaborated with the Arabs to catch other Africans from the weaker tribes for slavery, claiming they were Kafirs and Kafirs did not have a soul and therefore were not human but beasts of burden. It was easy to catch the natives then in raids they called *chifwamba* because most of them had no clue what a gun was. The slave raiders would surround the targeted village in the night and start shooting their muskets in the air: Bang! Bang! Bang! Then they would wait in the shadows. In no time the so-called Kafirs would come out of the mud huts wondering what the strange thunder was, only to be captured by the raiders. The weak captives, the sick, the old and the cripples, were usually slaughtered on the spot to inspire total submission. The selected ones were sold to the Arabs who packed them in dhows and shipped them across the flaming lake to Zanzibar and Mozambique. There they would be sold again to merchants from Asia and America. Some of the men were castrated because eunuchs fetched the highest price.

As we got closer to the beach the roaring sound of big blue waves hitting the shoreline filled us with excitement. Francis acted out his exhilaration by running ahead of me towards the beach, but he suddenly stopped halfway and held on to his crotch like the Yao had castrated him or something.

'What is wrong? Are you OK?'

'I am OK,' he assured me, waving me off.

I doubted it. He looked in pain. To make him feel better I told him something that would make him love the Yao more.

'You know what Muslims say about Jesus Christ? They say he cannot be God because he went to the toilet.'

'Jesus? No way!' His eyes lit up.

'That's right. It's written in the Koran. I think they have a point because Jesus could be a son of a Roman soldier and Mary could have claimed the child was from God to avoid being stoned to death. I've always wondered why Jesus looks different from his disciples in the pictures.'

Francis was lost in thought for a moment, stroking his invisible beard.

'That cannot be true,' he said abruptly.

'Why not?'

We had reached the beach and Francis was too excited to answer. He hurriedly took off his clothes, folded them into a neat pile and ran towards the waves and took a dip. He stayed under water for what seemed like for ever. When he finally came up for air like a dolphin he answered the question, which I thought he had long forgotten:

'Because he walked on water!'

'They say he was a magician!' I shouted back, but there was nobody there, only a big blue ripple.

Back on the beach, Francis did something bizarre: he carefully dug a finger-sized hole in the warm sand. At first, I thought he was going to talk to me about the little boy who tried to drain the whole ocean into a hole in order to illustrate the mystery of the Holy Trinity to St Augustine, but instead he inserted his penis in the hole and lay flat over it. When he had made himself comfortable he indicated that I should sit next to him facing the shimmering lake. He then continued his tirade against the Yao with new verve:

'You see that grass compound over there with the red flag, on the other side of the lagoon? Stay away from anything that has a red flag along the beach. The Yao have their *jando* in there. If you go too close to the grass huts and see the initiates inside, you have to be initiated too, by force if necessary. They strip you naked, shave your hair to the bone and paint your body with ash. Then they cut your foreskin with a blunt knife and put it in your breakfast porridge. When you cry they beat the drums hard so nobody will hear you:

> *Aliku*
> *ali kulumba*
> *kulumba*
> *kulumba mbale*
> *mbale*
> *mbale katete*
> *katete*
> *katete mbuga*
> *mbuga*
> *mbuga kaini*
> *kaini*
> *kaini ngadya*
> *ngadya*
> *ngadya kambwe*
> *kambwe*
> *kambwe ganula*
> *ganula*
> *ganula chikanga*

chikanga
chikanga leza
leza
leza ng'ani.

'You must learn this song just in case you are caught. They will think you are initiated and let you go.'

'What does that mean?' I asked, because it was certainly not Chichewa.

'Nothing,' Francis replied. 'It's the Devil's chant to prepare you for sin.'

With that he pulled the mound of sand, which he had used as a drum to sing the Devil chant, closer to his chest, dug his chin in it and continued speaking through clenched teeth, looking like a crocodile:

'After the song they tell you about women and make you sleep with the girls to practise sex.'

'Really?'

'Really. Yao girls are the best in the world at doing sex because they are taught everything at *nsondo*. They cut their bit and put it in their porridge to make them strong and sweet.'

'Which bit?'

'The bean.'

'The clitoris, *waaah!*'

'It makes them behave. Then the mentors invite toothless old men to teach them how to have the sex. They make the girls lie on their backs and lift their hips upwards while gyrating gently this way and that way: "From now on you are women and not mortars for pounding. Meet him in mid-air and swing with him gently right there until he comes. Do this to your husband and he will never leave you for another woman." They are crazy. For discipline the toothless old men place sharp knives under the girls' bottoms as they practise. They have to keep their bums up there.'

'You are kidding me?'

'Not kidding. You know how to have sex, don't you?'

'Yeah.'

But Francis suspected that I did not know so he told me how:

'You go under the bean but with Yao girls you don't have to go under the bean. Before you do it to her, you have to shake her hand first to find out if it's hot or cold. If her hand is hot, stay away from the girl. She is visiting the moon. Strange things happen if you sleep with a Yao woman visiting the moon. You urinate fish with spiky fins trying to swim back into you. Can you imagine the pain?'

'What do they do at the moon?'

'They come blood.'

'You mean the period!'

'When her hand is cold then she is good to have. You push her back. Her breasts, you know. Here, all over here. You keep doing it until she falls on to the mat.'

'That's called foreplay.'

'Foreplay?'

'Yeah. You know, like James Bond and Pussy Galore.'

'No. They don't do it like that. You push her back. If she falls down with her legs wide open she wants sex.'

'Really?'

'Really. That's the truth. Don't sleep with the girl if she does not want to. She will burn your penis down to a charcoal stick . . . Do you know how to tell if a girl has a big hole? Look at the gaps between her toes.'

With that Francis stood up and went to the rocks to have a pee. I followed him and challenged him to see who could pee the furthest. His urine was a blood-red arch.

'Francis, you are sick!' I shouted but he ignored me.

'You are just a baby, Big Head,' he said, examining his penis. 'What do you know about going to the moon? Come, I will teach you how to swim.'

I hesitated, so he left me standing there, my mouth open in disbelief. As I watched the blood-red urine trickle down into the lake, my mind wandered home, straight to the Diptych.

Schistosomiasis: a parasitic tropical disease, caused by any of three species of flukes called schistosomes, and acquired from bathing in infested water. The larval form penetrates the bather's skin and develops in the body into adult flukes, which settle in the veins of the bladder and intestines. Eggs laid by adults provoke inflammatory reactions; there may be bleeding and ulceration in the bladder and intestinal walls, and the liver may also be infected. The first symptom is usually tingling and an itchy rash where the flukes have pene-trated the skin. An influenza-like illness may develop weeks later, when adults produce eggs. Subsequent symptoms include blood in the urine ... .

The sensible answer to Francis's invitation for a swim would have been a resounding 'No!' but the wide blue lake was too tempting. Besides, the Jive Talker also said that tropical parasites were our friends – they saved us from the ruthless European settlers who wiped out whole indigenous peoples in the other mildly infested parts of the world.

I followed Francis to the other side of the rock where there was no red urine in the lake. He jumped into the water feet first and again disappeared for what seemed like for ever. I thought about the schistosomes, then the hippo and the crocodile, but I was now more afraid of drowning, as I had never swum before. He resurfaced, waving his hands, shouting, 'Jump in, Big Head! Jump in! It's very shallow here. See.' He was waist-deep in the water. I looked around and slipped out of my clothes. I held my crotch just in case Yao girls were looking and jumped in. It was bottomless but I was determined not to drown. I kicked and splashed with my hands and feet for dear life until I realised that I was floating with half my stomach full of water. Francis was now sitting on the rock shouting, 'You can do it! You can do it.' I paddled to the rock feeling like a little dog, crawled up and vomited in his face, claiming it was an accident.

On the way back home, we passed through a village called Phangwa where a group of men smartly dressed in army fatigues danced in their ranks to the rhythm of a big double-sided drum, wiping their faces with snow-white hand-kerchiefs. It was the dapper Tonga. After the war there was nothing else to do with their military skills so they had transformed their parades into *beni*. The traditional harangue against the Tonga was that they were lazy. They did not like working in the field and if they were not ironing their uniforms, dancing, washing in the lake, or cleaning a white man's house in Salisbury or Joburg, all they liked to do was to sit in the shade like the British, drinking tea and playing *bawo*.

Impressed by the elegant spectacle, I spoke to Francis out of the blue.

'I bet they wouldn't call themselves lazy though. They'd say they are gentlemen, gentlemen of leisure.'

'What?'

'Nothing.'

4

My coffee-jar fish bowl filled with fish in Nkhota-kota. Only two of the tadpoles turned into frogs, and I returned them to the stream behind our house. While I was at it I found a bullfrog eating a mouse; he swallowed it whole. I named the frog Bolo after my favourite bad guy in the kung fu movies – the big fat guy who always gave Bruce Lee the toughest time. I would listen to Bolo croak in the night like a lullaby. I slept to images of kung fu fights with people shouting Bolo! Bolo! Bolo!

Bolo never fought for more than a minute. Before you knew it he had broken your leg and snapped your spine, lifted you up above his head like a log, thrown you sky high like a rag doll. You were dead.

When Dad saw my fish, he bought a fishing net and rented it out to the fishermen at the lake who paid him back in fish. We lived like the hippo now. Fish for everything, breakfast, packed lunch, dinner. The house smelt like a fish market.

'We will be turning into mermaids soon,' Joyce complained.

A game poacher who called himself Mr Meat and cycled around with a toothpick in his mouth came to our rescue and began to sell us all kinds of meat from the game reserve at good prices: elephant, antelope, hippo, crocodile, impala, eland – he had them all in the huge basket behind his boneshaker. One day, he sold us what he had described as revolutionary meat because he had cut it from a new kind of antelope that had just evolved in the game reserve. The animal hadn't even been named yet, although they were working on it. I had a bad reaction to the new meat. My hair got itchy and when my mother shaved it there were sores all over my scalp. Dad put GV (a blue antiseptic) on the wounds, which made me look all spotty like a hyena. Everybody was laughing at school so I skipped school by feigning diarrhoea and spent lots of time in the toilet dipping into Dad's books and notes.

One evening I was picking out obscenities from Georges Bataille's *Story of the Eye* when I heard Dad from somewhere in the house speaking in surprise:

'Emily, what are you doing here?'

Emily? She was supposed to be boarding at St Mary's Secondary School in Zomba. I rushed out of the toilet and followed the voice to the sitting room. My brothers and sisters were crammed at the door, peering inside from a safe distance. I squeezed past them into the danger zone. Emily, who now looked like Diana Ross, was sitting at the table gazing at an open Bible. Dad was sitting opposite her resting a clenched fist on the table, brandishing his little wooden axe with the other hand. He only brought it out for serious punishment, that axe.

What was happening here?

'Why are you back from school in the middle of the term? Has the school run out of food? Are you sick? Is it politics?' Dad threw all these questions at Emily but she had no answer. Instead she began frantically to flick through the pages of her Bible looking for something. When she found it, she ironed out the page with her hand, and started mumbling an emotional prayer, which in no time changed into tongues. It sounded like baby talk to me: *dididi mmamsshakkaatata ha mam litkitatu tatt agagag guu lali hek haha shah mmammma. Looo mulo lo o mama momii ala ali. Dimilili lo la didi ma* . . . that sort of thing. Dad raised his wooden axe to strike, but lowered it when Emily suddenly stopped, raising her hand to protect herself. She looked pitiful. Bond giggled.

Then Emily began to read from her Bible. It was the well-known John 3:16: *'For God so loved the world, that he gave his only begotten Son, that whosoever believeth in him should not perish, but have everlasting life.'*

Joyce and Lucy put hands on their mouths trying hard not to laugh. Dad threw us a devilish glance. We stampeded backwards, but regrouped at the door in no time.

'Emily, I have to know why you are back from school.' Dad tried a more friendly approach. Still, she gave no reply, only another frantic search through the Bible and a smattering of tongues under her breath.

Dad gave up for the day and left for jive. Emily gave a big sigh of relief and closed her Bible.

In the night the Jive Talker gave us a lengthy lecture on the relationship between Alcoholism and Born Againism, saying that there was no difference between the victims of the two great European narcotics. Neither could face reality, and wanted to escape by getting high and so on and so on until the girls began to yawn, resting their heads on the table – in the case of Emily, the Bible.

As soon as he left us and went to bed the rats in the ceiling resumed their evening play and everybody came back to life listening intently.

Then there was the long-awaited metallic snap! Febe the housekeeper climbed on the table to check on the rat trap in the ceiling. There she found yet another giant rat stuffed with fish. It was dinner time for Bolo. I took the fat rat and a torch and headed for the stream with an entourage of curious siblings. They had heard of Bolo's big appetite. Emily followed us and stood at the door.

'Drop that evil!' she shouted. 'Don't you people know that rats are agents of the Devil who brought the plague to the Egyptians? That frogs are demons?'

She flicked through her Bible and read from Revelation 16:13: '*And I saw three unclean spirits like frogs come out of the mouth of the dragon, and out of the mouth of the beast, and out of the mouth of the false prophet.*'

She looked like an angel standing in the light of the house, and I felt like Beelzebub leading the children of Israel astray, standing outside in the dark. I dropped the rat and wiped my hands on the sides of my shorts. Sharpe picked the rat up and disappeared into the darkness with it. Febe grabbed the torch and together with the rest of my siblings they followed the dog.

For a moment I didn't know what to do. Then I walked back into the light of the house and showed Emily that my hands were clean.

'And what is that on your hand?' Emily asked, noticing the parallel lines I had drawn on the back of my hand. I went to the Diptych, picked out a paperback, it was *Gulliver's Travels*, and showed her the bar code on it. I was into bar codes now, because they were all over the new paperbacks. I didn't know what they were used for. I just thought they looked cool.

'It's 666,' she said and sat me at the table to explain. She began by reading to me from Revelation 13:

'*And I beheld another beast coming up out of the earth; and he had two horns like a lamb, and he spake as a dragon. And he exerciseth all the power of the first beast before him, and causeth the earth and them which dwell therein to worship the first beast, whose deadly wound was healed. And he doeth great wonders, so that he maketh fire come down from heaven on the earth in the sight of men, And deceiveth them that dwell on the earth by the means of those miracles which he had power to do in the sight of* the beast; saying to them that dwell on the earth, that they should make an image to the beast, which had the wound by a sword, and did live. And he had power to give life unto the image of the beast, that the image of the beast should both speak, and cause that as many as would not worship the image of the beast should be killed. And he causeth all, both small and great, rich and poor, free and bond, to receive a mark in their right hand, or in their foreheads:

And that no man might buy or sell, save he that had the mark, or the name of the beast, or the number of his name. Here is wisdom. Let him that hath understanding count the number of the beast: for it is the number of a man; and his number is Six hundred threescore and six.'

She expounded the prophecy: '666 is already here. The three pairs of longer lines you see in the bar code are 666. The separation of goats from sheep, the wheat from the chaff has already begun. Any time now the last trumpet will sound and Christ will appear in the clouds.'

I looked closely at the bar code and indeed the longer lines made the whole thing look like the Devil's pitchfork.

Scared like hell, I rubbed out the lines on my hand and ran off to the bedroom where I tore out the pages in my exercise books on which I had obsessively drawn bar codes. The Jive Talker had shown me hell on the Diptych; the inscription on its misty iron gates had read, 'Abandon every hope, Ye that enter,' and I did not want to go to a place like that.

Emily followed me into the bedroom and found me standing there with all these crumpled bits of paper, full of 666s.

'What can I do?' I asked her, quoting Nicodemus.

'You must be born again,' she said, quoting Jesus. 'Read the Bible and pray to God for the forgiveness of your sins'.

'Reading gives me a headache,' I said.

'That is because you read too much Devil stuff.'

'How about the natives? They can't read.'

'They are going to Hell.'

'Granny in Ntcheu, she can't read either.'

'You must enter the Kingdom of Heaven like a little child.'

'I am a little child.'

'Do you want to go to Heaven or not, little devil?'

My mother came in to have a look and told us it was time for everyone to go to bed.

5

That night when I woke up with my bladder bulging with piss, I saw the flash of a flaming black cross on the window that made my heart jump, thinking it was the Constantine omen from Jesus Christ. But I decided that it was only a car passing the house because I remembered that Constantine had seen the vision in broad daylight. Still, it made me afraid to get out of bed and go to the toilet as the light switch was far away, across the room, near the door. I found myself breathlessly listening to Bolo's demonic croak carried into the room by the din of the stream. It sounded like the names of the devils on the Diptych recited backwards:

> *Succubi – devils that live in caverns . . .*
> *Satan*
> *Pluto*
> *Neptuni – devils that live in water*
> *Minos*

Mephistopheles
Mellialta
Malebranche – mischief-making devils
Luciferani – devils that live in the underworld
Lucifer
Incubi – devils that live in caves
Dusi – devils that live in woods and forests
Culicchia
Ciriatto
Cerberus
Carontes
Calcabrina
Cagnazzo
Bocco
Berlic
Belphagor
Belial
Beelzebub
Beelzebub
Beelzebub
Beelzebub

. . .

Thus I drifted back to sleep and dreamt that I was on top of a big blue mountain with thousands of people watching the crucifixion of Christ. I wanted to find out what Christ looked like but because I was small, jostling with all these people for a better view, the only part of Christ I managed to see were his feet, pierced together by a huge iron nail, and they were completely covered with blood dripping down from the upper part of his body. I couldn't tell what colour he was. He bled so much that the whole place was covered in a sticky layer of purple blood. It was hard to move your feet.

Then he cried, '*Eli, Eli, lama sabachthani!*' and gave up the Ghost. At that moment the sun dimmed and there was total chaos. A purple haze descended on us, making everything difficult to see. I still badly wanted to go to the toilet, and I thought this was an opportunity to do it. I pushed my way to the Bad Thief to wee against his cross but he spat on my head through the mist.

'Get off my fucking cross, man!' he bellowed.

That thief had his hands pinned to the cross with the biggest nails I had ever seen but he still managed to show me the finger. I left him alone and headed towards the Good Thief, who was kind enough to let me wee against his cross. He even smiled down on me as I relieved myself.

'Does that feel better now, kid?' he asked.

'Yeah, much better now, thanks,' I said and gave him the thumbs up.

'No problem, kid.'

When I woke up, I had wet the hospital bed.

6

Now I knew that Jesus couldn't be God because he went to the toilet but I decided to take a 'leap of faith' and be a Born Again because I wanted God to protect me from the demons lined up between my bed and the light switch. I did not want to wet my bed again and have the house laughing at me or die of a bursting bladder like that Danish astronomer who wore an iron nose on the Diptych, his name, Tycho Brahe. I promised Jesus that I would help his mission by finding the Antichrist to atone for my sinful obsession with bar codes and thinking that he was a bastard.

The following evening, I headed to the stream and stoned Bolo to death while singing the Poom! song from Dr Russell's shining tent:

> Take a leap into the water – poom!
> Take a leap into the deep – poom!
> Take a leap and sing with the angels
> Praise the Lord Almighty! – poom!

Emily found me there, said I was a good boy and baptised me properly by ducking me into the stream. She said that the sprinkled baptism I had on my head as a baby was not valid as Jesus was not baptised that way.

Then I began to read the Bible day and night, looking for the Antichrist. I illustrated the monsters of the books of Daniel and Revelation and studied them closely to find clues. When Emily realised that I had a special gift for writing from the Holy Spirit she asked me to transcribe her tongues, so we could find out what God wanted us to do. We filled a whole exercise book with them. That was the hardest job I have ever done and I was glad when Emily went back to school after serving her suspension. I called the exercise book *Emily's Book of Tongues*.

There had indeed been one setback that was a test to my young faith from the beginning: a few days after I had become a Born Again, a letter from St Mary's Secondary School arrived saying that Emily had been suspended from school for three weeks after she had been caught out of bounds late at night. She was spotted climbing the perimeter fence of her boarding school and they believed she was on her way to the disco at Chancellor College, where her boyfriend waited. Part of me suspected that she had become a Born Again merely to protect herself from Dad's wooden axe, but listening to her tongues carefully I decided that she was truly born again. It sounded like jazz.

7

When the rainy season came, every time there was thunder and lightning I remembered Matthew 24:27 and trembled with fear, thinking it was Judgement Day: *For as the lightning cometh out of the east, and shineth even unto the west; so shall also the coming of the Son of man be.*

I was afraid that Jesus would return before I found the Antichrist and I would not be able to enter the Kingdom of Heaven. I had tried everything and looked everywhere for clues, from the Bible to *Emily's Book of Tongues*, but still I couldn't find him. I even made friends with a Born Again at Nkhota-kota Secondary School named Jim, ten years my senior, so he could lend me tracts on the Antichrist in exchange for my father's philosophy and self-help books, which he wanted to exorcise again and again, but there was still no plausible Antichrist to be found.

To make up for my failings, I aspired to be like a saint I had come across on the Diptych named Simon Stylites. He was an ascetic who lived atop a column in a desert for thirty-seven years, '*until shit flowed down from his loft like wax drips from candles,*' as the book put it. But the demons around me would not let me be like my hero.

When I painted a beard on my face and spoke in tongues for a whole day my mother said I was mad and needed to be taken to a psychiatric hospital and put in a straitjacket. When I fasted, my father said that an African fasting must be kidding and subjected me to more jive. I had to put my hands over my ears so I could not hear the evil. At school when the teacher came across *Emily's Book of Tongues*, she decided that I had mental problems, and when I took a vow of silence, she caned me for being rude. Back at home my mother refused to give me any food until I promised to answer the teacher, telling me that a closed mouth never gets fed.

But the demons did not come to me only through people. One Sunday afternoon, while I was singing 'El Sheddai' on the veranda, a black mamba fell out of the mango trees and began sliding towards me in the sand like a sidewinder. I ran into the house and shut the door with a bang.

'What is it?' my mother asked.

Before I could answer her she opened the door and saw the black mamba now sliding across the concrete floor towards us. She quickly walked over to the snake and killed it by stomping on its head with her foot. She looked like the Virgin Mary doing that but I had never seen her so angry as when she looked up. Once I came across the effects of black-mamba bites on the Diptych I understood her extreme reaction.

> paralysis of the tongue and jaw
> swollen eyes
> slurred speech
> mental perplexity
> dilated pupils
> respiratory distress
> loss of muscle control
> coma
> death within an hour

The black mamba was the work of the Devil himself.

8

A few days later I returned to the lake with Francis. With the great expanse of shimmering blue waters unfolding before me, I realised that I had indeed been born again. Everything looked and felt different.

The sounds of the waves were the hosts of Heaven: seraphim from Isaiah 6:2; cherubim from Ezekiel 1:5–24, 28:12; thrones, Revelation 20:4; dominions, virtues, powers, principalities, archangels, angels, Job 38:1–7 and the saints. In the distance a white ship was approaching the jetty. It looked like Jesus Christ walking on water as in Mark 6:45–56, with the Holy Ghost on his shoulders, Matthew 3:13–15.

They called the ship *Ilala*, after the place in Zambia where Dr Livingstone's heart had been buried. Another two boys joined Francis and me on the jetty to watch. As the ship got bigger and bigger, Francis took off his clothes and jumped into the water, waving his hands to welcome it. I joined him, praying that I could walk on water to show them that I was filled with the power of the Holy Spirit but I sank straight to the bottom. When I resurfaced, everybody had come out of the water. They were watching me paddling like a dog, laughing at me. Francis was calling me out, pointing to something floating in front of my nose. Was it a hippo, a crocodile? No, it was a chunk of human excrement. I jerked myself back and swam round to the edge of the jetty, gulping in a few pints of the desecrated water along the way. As I crawled out of the water, the shrieking urchins ran away like naked little demons, pointing fingers at each other like the disciples at the Last Supper.

I did not think it was funny. I sat on the rock disgusted,

clutching my clothes, spitting the dreadful contents out of my mouth. I did not want to hear what Francis sitting next to me was blubbering about as he tried to suppress his laughter. My dad had cured this guy of his bilharzia and this was his way of saying 'thanks'. I pushed him aside.

'Get thee behind me, Satan!' I shouted and sat there thinking about ringworm, tapeworm, cholera, dysentery, giardiasis, typhoid fever, hepatitis A, hepatitis E, dracunculiasis, echinococcosis, polio . . . The sun was scorching my back. I thought about Hell.

Then, in defiance, I watched the waves washing the piece of shit towards the other side of the lake, towards Mozambique where there was a civil war going on: capitalists versus communists.

The lifeboats from the ship landed on the jetty. Three white girls with hair that danced in the breeze arrived with the multitude of black passengers. They looked like angels. My eyes followed them and watched their sandals make footprints in the sand. I wished they would take me with them to the finer sands of the tourist beaches, where nobody shat in your face.

Francis quickly put his clothes on and ran after them. I followed him. 'Give me money! Give me money!' he begged the girls. They stopped to listen to his incredibly rude English, smiling. '*Ndalama palibe*' (There is no money), they answered him back in Chichewa, which was disappointing because I liked to hear the English. I whispered to Francis, 'Say please.' I could not beg myself because Dad had told us not to beg like the natives, not directly anyway.

'Please! Please!' Francis said, extending his sad little hand. Still nobody was giving out their money, so I decided to intervene and try something different.

'Where do you come from?' I asked the girls.

'Scotland,' answered the blonde one, her silver sunglasses sparking off stars when she looked at the water.

'Is that in England?' Francis asked.

'NO!' the girls protested in a chorus.

'United Kingdom, you . . .' I said, pushing Francis behind me. 'Will you be my pen pal?' I asked the blonde one.

She briefly looked at the other girls for approval as she tucked her hair behind her ears, then she tore out a piece of paper from her rucksack, pressed it on her tanned thigh, and wrote her address with the pencil she'd retrieved from her breast pocket. Then she took out her camera and indicated that we should stand before the shimmering part of the lake on which dugout canoes fished in the shadows, including the urchins who were just joining us. I didn't like it so I stood apart from them, upright like a gentleman. I was not going to look like one of the natives. But my prospective pen pal did not like my pose and lowered her camera. She looked at my shining black Bata shoes, which Dad had just bought me for being top in my class, and shook her head.

'No shoes,' she said, 'and join the group.' I looked at my shoes.

'His shoes are brand new,' Francis, now lost among the urchins, said.

I nodded my head to that. And I was not going to take them off. Next thing you knew they would be using your photograph in an Oxfam appeal. The blue-eyed girl (for she had now pushed back her silver glasses on to her hair) seemed to sense that I was not going to take them off, so she raised her camera to take the picture, smiling like the Good Thief in my dream who made me wet my bed. But she couldn't fool me. We had studied the pinhole camera at school and I knew that light travelled in a straight line: she was cutting me out of the picture holding the camera at a weird angle like that. I moved closer to the bunch of urchins to get into the picture but still she was trying to angle me out of the frame. I finally gave in to her. I took off my shoes, kicked them away and joined the ragged group. She gave me the thumbs up as I posed with hands on my hips. I was trying to get one over on her, figuring that she couldn't use that picture for an Oxfam appeal because a hungry person wouldn't look so full of himself.

9

Have you not heard of that madman who lit a lantern in the bright morning hours, ran to the marketplace, and cried incessantly: 'I am looking for God! I am looking for God!'

As many of those who did not believe in God were standing together there, he excited considerable laughter. Have you lost him, then? said one. Did he lose his way like a child? said another. Or is he hiding? Is he afraid of us? Has he gone on a voyage? or emigrated? Thus they shouted and laughed. The madman sprang into their midst and pierced them with his glances.

'Where has God gone?' he cried. 'I shall tell you. We have killed him – you and I. We are his murderers. But how have we done this? How were we able to drink up the sea? Who gave us the sponge to wipe away the entire horizon? What did we do when we unchained the earth from its sun? Whither is it moving now? Whither are we moving now? Away from all suns? Are we not perpetually falling? Backward, sideward, forward, in all directions? Is there any up or down left? Are we not straying as through an infinite nothing? Do we not feel the breath of empty space? Has it not become colder? Is it not more and more night coming on all the time? Must not lanterns be lit in the morning? Do we not hear anything yet of the noise of the gravediggers who are burying God? Do we not smell anything yet of God's decomposition?

Gods too decompose. God is dead. God remains dead. And we have killed Him. How shall we, murderers of all murderers, console ourselves? That which was the holiest and mightiest of all that the world has yet possessed has bled to death under our knives. Who will wipe this blood off us? With what water could we purify ourselves? What festivals of atonement, what sacred games shall we need to invent? Is not the greatness of this deed too great for us? Must we not ourselves become gods simply to be worthy of it? There has never been a greater deed; and whosoever shall be born after us – for the sake of this deed he shall be part of a higher history than all history hitherto.'

Here the madman fell silent and again regarded his listeners; and they too were silent and stared at him in astonishment. At last he threw his lantern to the ground, and it broke and went out. 'I have come too early,' he said then, 'my time has not come yet. The tremendous event is still on its way, still travelling – it has not yet reached the ears of men. Lightning and thunder require time, the light of the stars requires time, deeds require time even after they are done, before they can be seen and heard. This deed is still more distant from them than the distant stars – and yet they have done it themselves.'

It has been further related that on that same day the madman entered divers churches and there sang a requiem. Led out and quietened, he is said to have retorted each time: 'What are these churches now if they are not the tombs and sepulchres of God?'

10

My faith was constantly under threat from jive but it was really the arrival of the Reverend Dr Kaleta from the Middle

East that dealt it a fatal blow. He was a recent graduate of the University of Tel Aviv, where he had spent many years studying biblical archaeology. During his sermons he did not talk about Heaven or Hell like the minister before him but instead gave lectures about the Holy Land. He had all these posters, diagrams and maps of his excavations there that he showed the congregation at every opportunity.

'This, here, is Golgotha, the place of the skulls, the very place they crucified Christ,' he would say, pointing at some dusty patch of land with a stick. It didn't look like the gigantic blue mountain I had seen in my dream. I wondered why Christ would have chosen to die in such a miserable place – you would think that after his ordeal in the manger he would choose someplace more uplifting than that.

'That is Gethsemane, the olive grove where Jesus Christ was betrayed by Judas. Down there, Gehenna. You see what we now know as Hell was in fact a garbage dump outside the walls of Jerusalem. They had to keep the refuse burning to minimise the stench.

'This is Mount Sinai, the place where Moses received the Ten Commandments from God: somewhere around here anyway . . . we don't really know the exact peak.'

'Ha?' somebody in the congregation would always interject as he spoke, and I knew what they were thinking: Is that the famous mountain? How could Moses have disappeared on that little hill for days on end? Sinai was but an anthill compared to Mount Mulanje. The wilderness of Judaea in which John the Baptist had heralded the coming of the Messiah could have passed for an oasis in the Sahara. The streets of Jerusalem were not golden at all, they looked like some dodgy alleyways in Limbe.

When the minister pointed out that the only thing that grew in the Holy Land was olives, I wondered how was one supposed to survive an eternity on olives? No wonder the place was full of lunatics. The last time I had been on a fast and saw the Devil, Dad had jived that visions and ecstasies were caused by a weakened cerebral valve, the result of inadequate vitamin supply to the brain, common in the people of the Dark Ages and arid places such as that.

The Dead Sea was interesting, you could lie on the water on your back and read a book, but it was only a drop in Lake Victoria . . .

The Diptych had lied about the Holy Land; none of it looked like the Michelangelo or the Rembrandt, let alone the El Greco. Reverend Dr Kaleta's maps and posters of the real Holy Land made the grand narratives of the Bible sound absurd. In fact, the minister was aware of this problem because one day he explained that the Bible was not history but rather *mythos*. This did not mean that it was a lie; it only meant it was written in an 'Hellenistic style': the truth was exaggerated or twisted for dramatic or poetic effect with the objective of teaching the people about a particular way of life, not to inform them . . .

So, that was the reason why most of the ideals in the Bible shrank when measured against harsh reality? I was pondering this thought on my way from church one day, when I suddenly felt peculiarly light, like I could fly. Well, I still couldn't so I ran all the way home like a cheetah instead, and when I got there I locked myself up in the toilet for a long think. When I finally flushed I decided that I no longer believed in God. Nietzsche was right. God was dead.

Thanks to the Jive Talker, I had been aware of Contingency for some time but it was only after listening to Reverend Kaleta's lectures that I felt confident enough to embrace it and this is perhaps what had made me feel like the burden of millennia had been lifted off my shoulders coming back from church that day. Without God there was no need for Reverend Kaleta to feel embarrassed or be on the defensive about the Holy Land; it was just another part of history. There were no demons on the way to the light switch because with the death of God came the demise of all the other worldly beings that came with Him: the white girl at the lake was not Lucifer for forcing me to take off my shiny shoes; she was just a horrible woman trying to make me look like a native. There was no need to get too worked up about it and start speaking in tongues. As for me, all I wanted by taking off my shoes was to have my picture taken so I could shine too, just like the rest of the urchins. There was no need to feel like I had sold my soul to the Devil for a bit of flash. (And anyway, when I told Mum that story, she said that people are supposed to take off their shoes on the beach.) Zapa's blisters were not a punishment from God. He was just unlucky to have an uncle like that. My brother was not Cain for throwing me in the well in Nkhamenya. He was only a child and he wasn't possessed by Beelzebub. Bolo wasn't a demon either – he had never asked for much, only a dead rat every now and then; he kept the food chain going that way. There was no need for Salvation – man hadn't fallen from anything but a tree in Olduvai Gorge. Africa was not the spot where Lucifer fell when he was kicked out of the Heavens, and Africans were not the children of Ham or Canaan destined to be *drawers of water and hewers of wood* for Asian and European folk. They were children of Zinjanthropus. Religion was just a human creation . . .

Thus I realised I had taken the *leap of faith* all right but that there was neither the height there nor the depth to take me anywhere for my purposes. I felt silly like Charlie Chaplin in *Modern Times*, mistaking the shimmering puddle outside his shack for a deep river. Contingency was much more beautiful and forgiving than God, much more mystifying even. So, like a samurai warrior who cuts down the Buddha obstructing the path to his destiny, I walked past the bleeding feet of the crucified Christ I had seen in the dream. I now just wanted to be part of the *higher history* that Nietzsche's madman was harping on about. And I thought that I knew what it was.

Ironically it was at that moment that I felt I had finally found the Antichrist but it was too late now. God was dead.

11

Reverend Kaleta's sermons attracted large numbers of people. You had to get there very early to get in at all. But the minister did not last long; he died in a mysterious car accident one day, coming from the Middle East with some more maps, diagrams and posters. They were sure it was the Criminal Investigation Department that had taken him out, because when they found him, stripped naked, lacerated and dead in the ditch, one of the maps of the Holy Land had been shoved up his bottom.

Soon after Reverend Kaleta's demise, Dad was given another promotion. He was now Chief Clinical Officer, and a couple of months later we were moved to Thyolo, a district known for growing tea and bananas in the Southern Region.

To celebrate becoming 'Chief' Dad bought a car, an old 1972 Toyota 180B. To start it up, he had to pour some petrol into the carburettor and ask us to push him. He always parked it on slopes, just in case there was nobody around to push him. The brakes were not to be trusted either, so the car rested on a stone that he kept in the boot. Once Dad bought that car, he did not want to walk to work again. For insurance he had made a bizarre arrangement with the District Chief of Prisons: whenever his engine broke down, a group of prisoners on hard labour would come to our house and push him all the way down to work, and back up when he knocked off. We realised quickly why the car developed a new problem every time he took it to the garage – the mechanics were mutilating it of spare parts the same way they did other cars to fix ours.

In the end driving the car was as good as walking, considering the hard work that went into keeping it on the road. On our way to Thyolo, we had flat tyres in Salima, boiling in Lilongwe, another flat tyre near the Mozambique border in Ntcheu, which was pretty unnerving because that war between the communists and the capitalists was still raging on (we heard the AK-47 gunshots in the distance). Then we ran out of fuel just before we reached Chingoni Village, where we were stopping to visit our maternal grandparents, who had just come back from Zambia. The natives pushed us the rest of the way.

12

Grandad was lured back from Zambia by George Green, an English miner, who fished him out of the copper mines and asked him to work as his right-hand man as he looked for gold up and down Malawi. They found nothing and parted company, but it was too late for him to return to his old job, and anyway the Zambian copper market had crashed. Looking at his limited options, he decided to go back to his home village to try farming.

Grandad had built one of the few tin-roof houses in Chingoni Village and bought all the neighbouring farmland, except that which was owned by the Nzama Catholic Parish. Grandad's hope was to get it back for free one day, for he claimed bitterly that it had been unlawfully taken from his father. At the back of the house was a large kraal with grass thatching, incessantly cleaned although there were no cattle in it.

Like most of the young villagers, my aunts and uncles had moved to the city except Uncle Humphrey, the last but one of their nine children still living with the grandparents. Humphrey was laid-back and funny; I suppose he needed a sense of humour to survive the boredom of living in a deserted village like that.

We had taken them by surprise. They had no money and there was nothing for us to eat in the house. Granny, however, had an idea. She went to the UNHCR refugee camp in Kaloga, where Chingoni Village was split in two by the Malawi–Mozambique border. There she queued up with the refugees and received free portions of maize flour, kidney beans, sugar, salt, and cooking oil.

While the meal was cooking, Granny went into the corner of the sitting room where she had set up a shrine to the Virgin Mary to confess her sins, and to my surprise she did it in Latin:

'*Confiteor Deo omnipotenti, beatae Mariae semper virgini, beato Michaeli archangelo, beato Joanni Baptistae, sanctis Apostolis Petro et Paulo, omnibus Sanctis et vobis fratres, quia peccavi nimis cogitatione, verbo, et opere mea culpa, mea culpa, mea maxima culpa . . .*'

I noticed that the centrepiece of the shrine, a blue-eyed

figurine of the Virgin, was flanked by posters of Robert Powell and Madonna the pop star. I wondered what was happening. When she finished her prayers, I found out.

'That is not Madonna, *Agogo*,' I told her.

'Oh yes it is. What do you know, Lucifer?' she said, reaching up to remove a spot on the picture.

'That's Madonna, the singer from America, not the Virgin.'

Uncle Humphrey, who was sitting on the veranda polishing Grandad's gun, started laughing.

'It doesn't matter which one, does it?' he retorted.

'Diabolus! Is that so? How about that one?' Granny asked, taking down the poster, pointing at Robert Powell.

'That's Jesus Christ all right,' I said.

After the meal, Granny put on some music to show off her new tape recorder, a donation from the Vatican to the Nzama Catholic Women's Choir, in which she was the head chorister. It was haunting Gregorian chants. Heathens or believers, we all gathered around to listen. If not for the music, it was for the machine. Cassette players were the in thing but Dad hadn't come round to buying one yet. We took it in turns to press the control buttons: Play, Fast Forward, Rewind, Stop, Pause and back again.

Humphrey seemed amused by all the fuss. He had already seen lots of cassette players in Zambia. When the music slowed down to a demonic distortion, he took the batteries out and warmed them in the sun. When he put them back in, and encouraged us to have a go again, the tape played overzealously and snapped.

Uncle Humphrey fixed the tape but when he put it back the hymn played backwards like the Beatles' song that said 'Paul is dead' on the radio.

'Now the gentlemen sing properly,' Grandad said, examining his polished gun on the veranda. He was ready to go for his evening bird shooting in the fields.

Uncle Humphrey, Dad, my brother and I went with him, leaving Granny complaining about her cassette. Humphrey said he would fix it later and the girls were happy because they wanted to listen to the demons.

There was nothing on Grandad's farm except acres and acres of yellow grass, but he did not see it that way, as we waded through them towards a better shooting spot.

'The fields of gold,' he said.

'How is that?' Dad asked.

'I am switching to cattle farming.'

Suddenly the empty kraal that stood in his backyard made sense.

He continued: 'I have been applying to the Farmers' Club to lend me some money to buy cattle to chew these fields of grass into gold for three years now but the natives won't let me have the money. They keep asking where I was during the fight for independence, which is rather odd because there was no such thing as a fight for independence in this country. You remember what happened, don't you? During one heated political demonstration in Blantyre a colonial police officer stepped on a native woman's bare foot with his boot, sending her limping all over the place in excruciating pain. When that news of colonial police brutality reached Westminster the MPs doubled up laughing and Malawi was granted independence out of pity. Hahahaha!'

I couldn't believe my ears.

'Is that true *Agogo* or are you just taking the mickey?'

'That's a true story, kid. Mai Phombeya, the woman was called. But of course you won't find that in the official history books.'

'It might be a while before you get your loan. I don't see any other government around the corner,' Dad joined in, the familiar uneasiness whenever he talked about politics etched on his face. I suspected he was just trying to stop me from asking any further questions.

'I will wait,' Grandad said, squinting hard as he scanned the sky for birds. 'Who knows what is round the corner? There is no point growing maize, the hybrid seed can't cope with the weather. There is either too much rain or not enough of it. That seed can only grow in a test tube; every year we have to beg the government for new seed. Besides, I am too old to hoe.' He was aiming at a bird circling in the sky. There was loud bang, which echoed against a huge boulder on the edge of the field.

'Every good philosophy should answer the gun . . .' he said, reloading the gun, an enigmatic smile on his face. Dad agreed, nodding his head in contemplation.

Uncle Humphrey ran to pick up the bird.

'It's a fish eagle!' he shouted, raising the bird in the air.

ARTHUR'S NUCLEAR BUNKER

1

I spent the first night in our new home with a searing toothache and a splitting headache. Shrouded in my blanket like a mummy, writhing and perspiring in agony, I cried all night. To relieve the pain, Dad prescribed me some aspirin. When that didn't kick in my mother stuffed the rotten cavity with crushed aspirin and even prayed to St Apollonia, the patron saint of toothaches, for me – still nothing happened. But somehow I made it to the following morning and the tooth was extracted at Thyolo District Hospital. The dentist also booked me in for an appointment to go to the Queen Elizabeth Central Hospital in Blantyre to have another tooth filled.

My cheek was still swollen from the tooth operation when I started at Nachipere Full Primary, a twenty-minute walk from the dusty road that separated the Bush Line from the neighbouring villages. As I took my allocated place, a boy with a long neck like an ostrich began to laugh hysterically at my swollen face, until he was hit by the teacher with a little blackboard pillow full of chalk dust and the whole class laughed at him as a little white cloud hovered above his head.

His name was Arthur and he couldn't be bothered to do his work. Instead, with his ostrich neck bending over the desk and his tongue sticking out from the corner of his mouth, he drew things on pieces of paper ripped out from the middle of his exercise book. He then made fancy aeroplanes out of the drawings and flew them across the room when the teacher was not looking. He was not a bad artist. The drawings were weird torpedo things, all of them labelled at the bottom in the crudest handwriting I had ever seen: *SS-6 SAPWOOD, R-7/8K71, SS-7 SADDLER / R-16, SS-8 SASIN / R9, SS-9 SCARP, SS-11 SEGO, SS-17 SPANKER, SS-18 SATAN / R-36M2 / Voivode, SS-19 STILETTO, SS-24 SCALPEL / RT-23, SS-25 SICKLE / Topol, SS-27 / Topol-M . . .*

Back at home when I looked up the names, the Diptych said they were Soviet intercontinental ballistic missiles. The boy was a psycho and needed help. Urgently. I drew the two US ICBMs that I had come across on the way to the Soviet ICBMs, the *Minuteman I* and the *Minuteman II*, so that I could take care of him the following day. I drew ten, both of them five times for contingency.

I wanted the missiles to be delivered in an equally eccentric way. I had a go at butterflies, starships, hummingbirds, dinosaurs, rhinos, but my origami skills were not up to scratch – I couldn't even manage a decent aeroplane. So I screwed up the drawings into nasty little balls and put them into a plastic bag.

I unleashed the hydrogen grapeshot on Arthur when he attacked me during the last lesson, but the deranged boy was ready for Mutually Assured Destruction, having spent the whole day drawing ICBMs and folding them up into fancy Tupolevs again. For a moment the whole place looked like the screaming Picasso on the Diptych, before melting away into nothing.

In the aftermath Arthur and I found ourselves in detention, in Siberia, clearing up radioactive debris not only in our cell but also around the whole campus. Upon being released, at the end of the decade, Arthur wanted to show me his nuclear bunker so I went with him to his house, which was just a stone's throw away from the detention centre.

The bunker was actually a concrete tank in the ground with a makeshift plastic roof, part of a government sewage project which had been suspended due to lack of funds. We clambered down the wobbly wooden ladder left behind by the builders. There was nothing inside the bunker except a couple of bricks to sit on and an old battered magazine that said *Plain Truth*. I picked it up and sat myself in the corner. As I thumbed through the magazine I found myself automatically following the sentences underlined in an incisive red biro in the feature article. They were the effects of a nuclear war.

ghostly shadows upon the walls and stones
blindness
shrapnel wounds
severe bleeding from every orifice
vomiting
skin rashes
skin fray
unquenchable thirst
hair loss
destruction of all plumbing systems
destruction of all electrical appliances

'We have been bombed!' I shouted, looking up from the magazine. Arthur, who was busy gracing his bunker with new graffiti, unleashed an impish laugh. 'You finally got it, bubblehead, you finally got it!' he said. Then turning back to his drawing he murmured and whistled a twisted rendition of the Black Death song.

Ring a ring o' roses
A pocketful of neutrons

A fission, a fusion
We all fall down.

He was working on a fat Russian hydrogen bomb in charcoal. He had just labelled it *The Tsar* when we were shaken into stillness by distant lightning and thunder. Then there was a sudden downpour outside the bunker. The plastic roofing leaked terribly and caved in on us. In no time we were drenched to the bone, but we remained in the bunker doing some kind of rain dance, singing and laughing ourselves to death.

Ring a ring o' roses
A pocketful of neutrons
A fission, a fusion
We all fall down!

After the rain I headed home, wet like a bird, shivering. The next day I was sent home early from school because I was still shivering despite the scorching sun. By midday I was basking on the veranda like a crocodile. In the evening, Dad reckoned it was malaria and prescribed me chloroquine. At night, my body burnt like it had never done before. My blanket was soaked with sweat. I had nuclear war nightmares. For the next three days I lost my appetite and threw up some yellow stuff. My head felt like a splitting pumpkin and my glands were surely poisoned. My mouth salivated like a mangy dog; I itched all over, as if overrun by ants. I scratched and scratched. Dad said I had become resistant to chloroquine and put me on Camoquine, a new drug that made the floor under my feet move like I was on the sinking *Titanic* – but it helped. My temperature improved and I was on my way to full recovery when three days later my little sister Linda gave

me the piece of mango at breakfast which caused the diarrhoea that kept me glued to the toilet on and off for the
whole morning.

2

Around midday, when I wiped myself, my bottom felt
bruised; I had wiped myself too many times with the *Malawi
News*. When I flushed the toilet the whole house shook. The
cistern screamed like a demon, the toilet bowl welled up,
and spewed its malodorous yellowy-brown liquids to the
floor. It trickled around my bare feet and seeped into my
father's Nietzschean volumes. When I peered into the bowl
a stern black-and-white portrait of Dr Hastings Kamuzu
Banda stared back at me: a grave-looking old man clad in a
striped three-piece suit and homburg hat. In his hands he
carried a walking stick and a blond flywhisk. I shuddered
with dread. Any portrait of Kamuzu Banda filled you with
dread and it was everywhere: on money, in the shop, in the
headmaster's office, in the classroom, on covers of newspaper and magazines, on textiles, in my father's office, on
my mother's traditional dress, on the calendars, on clock
faces, in my school exercise books:

Q: When was His Excellency the Life President Ngwazi
   Dr Hastings Kamuzu Banda born?
A: 14 May 1906 . . .

That was his official birthday but nobody knew for sure
when he was born. Some said 1898, others 1896, 1900, 1902

or 1904. It was all kept mysterious by the Ministry of Information. But there was a more interesting Banda on the Diptych:

He was a Chewa and was born the son of peasant farmers in Chiwengo Village, Kasungu District. They named him Kamuzu, meaning 'root', because it took a root from a witch doctor to induce his birth. His earliest education was at a mission school run by the Church of Scotland, in Mtunthama. By the age of eight he had mastered the Gospel according to St Matthew and so he was made a teaching assistant, his salary two pence a month. His secondary school education was in Chilanga but he was disqualified in his final exams for cheating. He claimed he had only been trying to see the blackboard as he was a small man. He left for South Africa on foot, when he was only twelve years old, and made a stopover in Zimbabwe where he got a job as a medical orderly at Hartley Hospital in Chegutu.

He was thus a child prodigy, like John Stuart Mill and Mozart. I felt perplexed but knew the first thing I had to do was plunge the president down the toilet and flush him away as quickly as possible, before the Malawi Young Pioneers could see me. I felt the familiar Camoquine-induced dizziness as I reached for the plunger. My mouth was dry; I was dehydrated and needed to get back to my salt-and-sugar solution in the bedroom quickly. Or maybe it wasn't dehydration or the Camoquine at all. I wondered if Banda himself had sent me a curse to finish me off for wiping my bottom with his face. You never knew. He was said to be a witch doctor, able to radar what every one of his subjects was doing through his flywhisk, and there was no witch doctor in the country who could undo the magic in it because it came from overseas where he had spent many years studying.

Reaching South Africa he worked as a compound clerk at Witwatersrand Deep Mine at Boksburg. In July 1925, under the sponsorship of the American Bishop Reverend William T. Vernon of the Methodist Episcopal Church, he left South Africa for a formal education in Xenia, Ohio. He made a stopover in London where he visited the grave of Dr David Livingstone at Westminster Abbey and promised him that he would help realise his dream of bringing civilisation to Africa. He was around thirty years old when he started his secondary school education at Wilberforce Academy, where he claimed he was treated better than other black people because he was not a Negro. He went on to study law at the University of Chicago, where he experienced the gangster culture of the Depression time championed by the likes of John Dillinger and Al Capone. Upon completion of his law degree he moved to Meharry Medical College in Nashville, Tennessee, to study medicine. While there, he witnessed the lynching of a black man, which left a deep impression on his consciousness. He graduated with an average of 90 per cent in his final exams and was highly commended for his surgical dexterity. He then applied for a medical job with the British government back home in Nyasaland, but was turned down on the grounds that the British did not recognise American-trained doctors.

The fly on the high window, rejuvenated by the fresh stench of sewage in the air, had finally managed to get into the toilet and buzzed around my face as I plunged the toilet.

> *'One two! One two! And through and through!*
> *One two! One two! And through and through!'*

Light brown, dispersed blue-grey patches on the thorax, dark grey on the posterior part of the abdomen. Yellow face and legs . . . It was the nasty tumbu fly that had laid its eggs on my shorts in Nkolokosa and given me boils loaded with fat maggots. I stopped plunging immediately and picked up one of the soggy paperbacks on the floor and chased the tumbu fly across the room, splashing slimy sewage all over. I needed to get that nasty pest. I opened and closed the book on the fly with all the strength I could muster. There was a sharp crack, a big smelly splash, and then nothing.

He left for Scotland to study for a British medical qualification at the University of Edinburgh, where he was made an elder in the Church of Scotland. His part-time job was teaching missionaries Chichewa before they left for Nyasaland, although later on, when he returned to Africa, he claimed to have forgotten the language and used a translator, mesmerising audiences with his effortless command of the Queen's English. After graduating, he took a two-year course in tropical medicine in Liverpool, on completion of which he tried for a job once again back home. He was turned down once more, this time because the white nurses refused to work under a black doctor. In 1945, he opened a clinic in London where he practised as a highly respected physician. His house became a meeting place for some of the most prominent future African leaders such as Kwame Nkrumah, Seretse Khama and Jomo Kenyatta.

In 1953, he ran into trouble for having an affair with his secretary, a white woman, and the wife of an army major. His reputation ruined, he left for Ghana, where more controversy surrounded him when he opened an abortion clinic in Kumasi. In 1958, he was invited back home by Nyasaland Nationalists who wanted him to lead the fight against colonial rule. He was welcomed back as 'the Messiah' by thousands of people at Chileka Airport but was soon jailed in Gwelo Prison, Northern Rhodesia, when his impassioned speeches sent the natives rioting throughout the country. Upon being released in 1960 he formed the Malawi National Congress Party and continued the struggle. On 6 July 1964, Nyasaland became independent under the name of his own choosing, Malawi, with him as its prime minister. Malawi alluded to the allegedly prosperous Maravi Kingdom, which was situated in the area before the Arab slave traders and the British colonials came along and reduced it to rubble. In 1965, a rebellion broke out among his cabinet ministers in protest at his autocratic leadership, the slow pace of Africanisation, and his alliances with apartheid South Africa and Portuguese colonies in a foreign policy he called 'supping with the Devil'. The rebellion was easily suppressed when it failed to take root in the rural areas where his big-man image was more popular. In 1966, Malawi became a republic with him as its first president. He headed an autocratic one-party government, which championed Victorian ideals. He had his opponents executed or jailed, often indefinitely, telling them to rot! rot! rot! in jail while stamping his foot. In 1971 he was made Life President by the Malawi Congress Party, his full title: His Excellency, the Life President of the Republic of Malawi, Ngwazi Dr Hastings

Kamuzu Banda, MD, LRCP, LRFP &S, FRCS, FRCP (Edinburgh), PHB, Hon. DSc, Hon. LLD (Massachusetts), Hon. LLD (Malawi), Hon. LLD (Wilberforce), Hon. LLD (Indiana), DOF (Destroyer of the Federation of Rhodesia and Nyasaland), Father and Founder of the Malawi Nation.

3

What did we do when we unchained the earth from its sun?

For a moment I thought I saw Zapa. He was standing there in the sun scratching his big belly with blistered little fingers, laughing; but no – it was a warthog wallowing in the mud, trying to keep himself cool. *'Perhaps laughter will then have formed an alliance with wisdom, perhaps only gay science will then be left,'* he said. When I flicked through the soggy paperback, the dead tumbu fly dropped to the floor, shuddered its wings and metamorphosised into an even bigger tumbu fly with a pink head of the Greek philosopher Socrates, who spoke to me while flying around my face, his voice a deep constant buzz like that of an electric transformer:

'What if, some day or night, a demon were to steal after you in your loneliest loneliness and say to you: "This life as you now live it and have lived it, you will have to live once more and innumerable times more; and there will be nothing new in it, but every pain and every joy and every thought and sigh and everything unutterably small or great in your life will have to return to you, all in the same succession and sequence – even this spider and this moonlight between the trees, and even this moment and I myself. The eternal hourglass of existence is turned upside down again and again – and you with it, speck of dust!" Would you not throw yourself down and gnash your teeth and curse the demon who spoke thus? Or have you once experienced a tremendous moment when you would have answered him: "You are a god and never have I heard anything more divine!" If this thought gained possession of you, it would change you as you are or perhaps crush you; the question in each and every thing, "Do you desire this once more, and innumerable times more?" would lie upon your actions as the greatest weight! Or how well disposed would you have to become to yourself and to life to crave nothing more fervently than this ultimate eternal confirmation and seal?'

I had never seen a jive-talking tumbu fly before, so when Socrates was finished with me and flew out of the toilet I followed him to see where he was going. He headed to the living room and then towards the Diptych, which opened up as the fly came closer, revealing a bright light. I had to squint to protect my eyes as I watched the tumbu fly dissolve into the light with a rustle. I didn't know that the Diptych was a secret doorway to another place so I entered to have a look around.

I found myself in an empty white room strewn with two thousand shiny green apples that seemed to have been sprinkled out of the red columns of typed words on the walls. When I examined the columns closely they were made up of all the words of Genesis 3, the Fall of Man, rearranged into alphabetical order. And that's when I realised that I was not alone. Dancing among the apples further down the room was a Pre-Raphaelite barefoot woman from the Diptych, wearing a white dress and a band of daisies in her hair. She danced with a pink rosebud in her hand to the Pink Floyd song on the radio called 'Set the Controls for the Heart of the Sun'. I watched until the song had finished, when she spoke to me, breathless.

'My name is Beatrice and I am a hippy. Welcome to the summer of love.'

She then invited me to recite the words from Genesis, pointing at the walls, like a teacher. She used her rosebud for a cane and the whole room smelt like a garden. With every section I completed, she picked an apple, rubbed it on her bosom and gave it to me to eat. I read out the words quickly and eagerly because the apples were luscious:

A

ALSO

AND

AND

AND

AND

AND

AND

AND

AND

AND

AND

AND

AND

AND

AND

ANY

APRONS

AS

BE

BE

BE

BEAST

BOTH

BUT

DAY

DESIRED

DID

DID

DIE

DIE

DOTH

EAT

EAT

EAT

EAT

EAT

EAT

EVERY

EVIL

EYES

EYES

EYES

FIELD

FIG

FOOD

FOR

FOR

FRUIT

FRUIT

FRUIT

GARDEN

GARDEN

GARDEN

GAVE

GOD

GOD

GOD

GOD

GODS

GOOD

GOOD

HAD

HATH

HATH

HE

HE

HER

HER

HUSBAND

IN

IN

IS

IT

IT

IT

KNEW

KNOW

KNOWING

LEAVES

LEST

LORD

MADE

MADE

MAKE

MAY

MIDST

MORE

NAKED

NEITHER

NOT

NOT

NOT

NOW

OF

OF

OF

OF

OF

OF

OF

OF

OF

OF

OF

OF

ONE

OPENED

OPENED

PLEASANT

SAID

SAID

SAID

SAID

SAID

SAW

SERPENT

SERPENT

SERPENT

SEWED

SHALL

SHALL

SHALL

SHALL

SHALL

SHALL

SHE

SUBTIL

SURELY

THAN

THAT

THAT

THAT

THAT

THE

THE

THE

THE

THE

THE

THE

THE

THE

THE

THE

THE

THE

THE

THE

THE

THE

THE

THE

THE

THE

THE

THE

THEM

THEMSELVES

THEN

THEREOF

THEREOF

THEY

THEY

THEY

TO

TO

TO

TOGETHER

TOOK

TOUCH

TREE

TREE

TREE

TREE

TREES

UNTO

UNTO

UNTO

UNTO

WAS

WAS

WAS

WE

WERE

WERE

WHEN

WHICH

WHICH

WISE

WITH

WOMAN

WOMAN

WOMAN

WOMAN

YE

YE

YE

YE

YE

YE

YE

YEA

YOUR

When I woke up I was in my bed, propped up against a pillow, sweating profusely. My mother was giving me a salt-and-sugar solution for my diarrhoea. My brothers and sisters were looking at me with question marks hovering above their heads.

'What were all those words for?' somebody asked.

'Huh? The sun is God!' I said, quoting the J.M.W. Turner on the Diptych.

'Do you want to get stoned?'

4

When my appointment day for tooth-filling at Queen Elizabeth Hospital arrived, I was loaded into a Thyolo Hospital Land Rover ambulance full of TB patients. I could tell they were TB patients because they were all skeleton-thin and they spent the trip coughing and spitting into little plastic containers. I was afraid of catching the TB, so I took off my shirt and wrapped it around my head, leaving only space for the eyes like the Bedouin Arab on the Diptych. When the patients saw me doing that they laughed, their chests wheezing, until they began to choke. I was not taking any chances, though.

Emily had just come back home from school again, but this time it was because she had been diagnosed with TB and had to go to the hospital for an injection and a fistful of tablets every day. She had quit Born Againism, and picked up a new high just like the Jive Talker had predicted. Now all she liked to do was hang out with her new boyfriend from Blantyre, coming home late at night through the window, very drunk, nursing her hangovers on the sofa the following day, with a Daphne Du Maurier, reading out to the whole house, 'Last night I dreamt I went to Manderley again.'

The queue at the Queen Elizabeth dental clinic was long and smelt like a dead rat. I wondered how many of us had toothbrushes and toothpaste at home. The little girl in front of me looked like she had marasmus and had a swollen cheek full of rotten molars. Her foul mouth was forever wide open except when a fly tried to get in. I could tell by the crusted lines on her cheeks that she had been crying all night. The old man behind me – tall and stooped, resting his smiling, half-blind head on a walking stick – I guessed had come to have his last tooth extracted. He looked like he had wasted his teeth eating children. Sucking on his tooth-less gums he gave me a tip on keeping my teeth healthy and long-lasting, saying that I should give them a thorough mouthwash with my wee every morning, which I did not think was a good idea.

The dentist was an English man, so I guessed that he

was a real dentist. That relaxed me a little bit. Two young men waited on him. I thought the fat one looked like a hippo, and the other smaller one, a rat. All of them were clad in white coats and blue surgical masks.

'What is your name?' the dentist asked as he drew himself close to the chair. The smell of tobacco and sweets leaked out of his surgical mask.

'My name is Samson!' I said loudly, like we did in Standard 1. I was nervous. I told him my Christian name because I didn't feel like giving a Chichewa lesson. And I was beginning to like that name since meeting Beatrice the dancing hippy in the dream.

'That's an interesting name,' the dentist said, tilting back my head. My eyes watered and shed some tears as they frantically searched the room for where the nasty jabbers might be. 'And where is Delilah?' he asked, his blue eyes glinting. I was so tensed up I missed the joke entirely.

'Judges 16!' I shouted.

The hippo and the rat man laughed hysterically, their shoulders shaking. The rat man had the jabbers. He was preparing a nasty-looking little syringe.

'Right, Samson, say aaah,' the real dentist said.

'Aaaaaaaaah!' I said, before I realised that he meant I should open my mouth. They must have concluded that I was a half-illiterate native by now because nobody was laughing.

The dentist poked and counted my teeth, speaking some dental gibberish to the young men, and then left the room.

The students suddenly looked anxious and transformed into some dodgy tooth-drawers from the Dark Ages. The face of the hippo was sweating profusely when he bent over to look into my mouth. The sweat from his forehead dropped into the corner of my eye, but I dared not blink. I could feel his amphibian eyes down my throat. I tried to swallow them but they stayed there, looking.

The rat man, dark as night, lifted the syringe and squirted some of its contents into the sink. My body shuddered as a peculiar scene flashed in my head: the crucified Christ, still nailed to his cross, brought into a white room like that in my dream, and laid on the rack; a lone dentist working on his teeth.

The rat man approached the hippo, offering the syringe. The hippo moved away from him and said, 'You go first.'

'Oh no, you go first.'

'You go first.'

They chased each other around the room until I opened my mouth and noisily cleared my throat. I just wanted them to get on with it.

'Say aaaaaah,' the rat man finally gave in. I shot him a stern glance to indicate that my mouth was already opened.

'Er . . . wider please,' he said, as he peered inside my mouth, the syringe shaking in his hand. Afraid that he might drop the needle in my eye, I closed it quickly. I wasn't even sure whether he had injected me or not because I felt nothing, except for the bitter liquid going down my throat. My hands were completely wet with nerves.

The rat man passed the syringe to the hippo who gripped my head tightly with his rubber hand like a vet. I stretched my toes hard and froze in terror as he dived into my mouth with the syringe. I could feel it slowly piercing the back of my throat, the needle coming out the back of my neck. When he withdrew it, I swallowed whatever was stuck down my throat and watched him squint his eyes into nasty little balls once more, selecting another target. When he struck again, I swear that through the corner of my eye I saw the needle briefly come out of my left cheek.

My mouth was thoroughly done. I had no clue where it was any more. My head felt like a bouncing ball.

As the rat-faced one mixed some gooey-looking stuff on a small silver palette, the hippo got hold of my head once more. Sweating and breathing heavily, he scraped and drilled at my tooth until there was the familiar power cut around the hospital. For all I know, it could have been from the maximum-level drilling the hippo was doing on me.

'I think he's ready,' he announced in the dark, as he waited for the emergency generator outside to kick in.

Twenty minutes later, I was a disabled person. I could no longer close my mouth. Whatever it was that the rat man had filled my tooth with, he had used a mountain too much of it, and the hippo was not happy. Taking turns, the wretched students tried every tool and technique in dentistry to scrape off the mountain, but to no avail. As one worked on the tooth, the other one paced about the room, keeping a nervous eye on the clock hanging on the wall.

When the real dentist finally walked back in, I breathed out for the first time in what seemed like for ever.

'Right, how are we doing, lads?' he asked, examining the bloodstained silver tools in the hands of the students.

'Aaah ah,' I said, calling for help from the rack.

The real dentist peered into the remains of my mouth and gave his verdict: 'This is a zero, boys,' he said.

5

'Did they at least use a new needle?' Dad asked back at home after he had absent-mindedly listened to my nightmare day. He was sitting in his armchair flicking through a new blue *Medical Gazette*.

'I don't know.'

'Always insist that they use a new needle when you go to the hospital. There is a deadly virus going around.'

'You should have told him that before,' Mum said.

Dad shrugged his shoulders and continued reading.

When he was finished with the *Gazette* he at first put it in the Diptych but on second thoughts removed it and took it to his bedroom, where I found him burying it among other junk journals in the drawers.

'The dentist said I should get a new toothbrush,' I interrupted him.

'Wait until the month end,' he answered, without turning round to look at me.

But I couldn't wait for ever, for that's what 'month end' usually meant with Dad. I couldn't afford another rotten cavity. I was going to do anything to avoid another appointment with those tooth-drawers. An idea came to me to write to Claire in Scotland and ask her for a toothbrush.

Now, I was not the one to beg so I took out the book on the birds of Southern Africa and drew her a carmine bee-eater. I told her she could have the bird if she sent me a toothbrush. The envelope had no stamp on it, only the words BY AIRMAIL. She would have to go to the post office and get the letter herself. I thought that the carmine bee-eater covered for that too.

On the way to the post office I had to stop when I heard a peculiar metallic squeaking sound coming from behind the wire-and-reed fence, five houses away from our house. Checking that there was nobody in sight first, I pulled the reeds apart to have a look inside. It was a white girl with golden hair on a swing, her head looking like a shooting star. I wanted to speak to her right away although I had no idea about what.

'Hello!' I called out anyway. 'Hello there!' I was too nervous for anything else.

When she located my eyes in the fence, she dropped off the swing, went into the house and brought out a banana, which she passed to me through the hole and went back to her swinging.

I regarded the banana for a while, decided that I was actually a little bit hungry and ate it on the spot. I still wanted to talk to her though, so with a mouth full of banana, I called out to her once more.

'Hello!'

Once again, the girl dropped out of the swing, went to the house and got another banana for me. I ate that one too.

When I said 'Hello!' for the third time, the dogs began to bark.

A frightening red-eyed native with a panga, the watchman or something, came out of the boys' quarters and ordered my peeping eyes to move on. I went away reluctantly. I was already totally in love with Alice. I never came to know her name and so I called her Alice. I wanted her to be my girl-friend so I could touch her golden curls whenever I wanted, push her sky high on the swing and watch her head go me-teoric . . . anything. I just wanted to be with a girl like that.

After the post office, when I went to Arthur's bunker and told him what had happened, he doubled up laughing.

'What's wrong?' I asked.

'*Ada*, are you that ugly?'

'What do you mean?'

'Her giving you the banana and all, Romeo. You must have looked like a gorilla in the zoo.'

'But *she* was inside the fence.'

'Yeah, but that was your fence. You said that Africa is like the zoo, with all those tourists high up on safari trucks looking down on us.'

Arthur laughed, telling me that he was only joking. He

added that in fact he thought I was a handsome fella and advised me to write Alice a letter, which I immediately did sitting in my favourite corner. I signed the letter Zorro because I knew she had only seen my eyes. But enclosed with it was my full two-page profile, stating my real name, school, star sign, hobbies, favourite music and books and so on. I folded the letter and the profile into a square and put them away in my breast pocket until the day when I would see her again on the swing.

During that time, as I anxiously waited for my lucky break, I had a recurring dream that I was a sailor on the slave ship on the Diptych. The big black ship was neatly packed with a cargo not of Negro slaves, as might have been expected, but of an army of giggling Barbie dolls winking at me. My job was to make sure the Barbies remained neatly in their ranks as the ship rocked this way and that on the mighty green ocean. Feeling incredibly happy, I would wake up laughing. But each time I returned to the wire and reed fence and peered inside, Alice was never there – only the same annoying Rhodesian ridgebacks, barking me away from the peephole.

I got lovesick and went off my food. My mother wondered if I had anaemia until Celenia, the new housekeeper, found the now worn-out love letter and profile in my pocket as she did the laundry and handed the two documents to my sisters, who completely embarrassed me by reading them out aloud to Mum. They called my letter an 'epistle' and the profile a 'CV'. From that moment on, I vowed never to write another love letter as long as I lived in that house.

But I didn't give up on Alice. I force-fed myself all the food put before me, strapped my weight on and went back to the fence with Arthur and the reluctant Caesar to talk to her again, this time like a real man. I was going to say,

'Hello there! What is your name? Can we talk for a minute?'

That Sunday afternoon, however, Alice's house appeared deserted except for two bony stray dogs copulating on the veranda. Alice's family must have moved out.

We unleashed Caesar, who grunted gratefully and ran back home as quickly as his ageing legs could carry him, climbed up over the fence to have a look around and found that the house was indeed empty.

Going through the big cardboard box left on the landing in the backyard I found an orange Wembley ball in pretty good condition and that made my day. I left the rest of the contents in the box – hangers and other bric-a-brac – to Arthur. I couldn't believe my luck washing the ball clean under the tap. I would probably be the only kid in the neighbourhood with a bouncing ball.

But I couldn't bring myself to play with the ball for fear of damaging it. Instead, I took it to Arthur's nuclear bunker where I found myself totally immersed in jive as soon as I had carefully lowered myself down into the dim concrete chamber.

6

God is dead. God remains dead. And we have killed Him. Who will wipe this blood off us? With what water could we purify ourselves? What festivals of atonement, what sacred games shall we need to invent? Is not the greatness of this deed too great for us? Must we not ourselves become gods simply to be worthy of it?

★   ★   ★

As I gazed at the ball, deep in contemplation, Arthur, who was sitting in the opposite corner of the bunker, thumbing through a pile of glossy magazines, interrupted my ensuing transfiguration, taunting me: 'Hey, *Salvatore Mundi*, you know how to break bread but do you know how to make it?'

'No. What do you have there, Satan?' I was only half listening.

'A recipe, "How to Make Bread". Ever wondered how?'

Arthur was fond of trivia. By the time he had dramatically cleared his throat and made himself comfortable on the brick, ready to read out the recipe, I was back staring at my bouncing ball but as I listened to him read I suddenly saw the ball being plastered with pages of the Holy Bible, one from each book, until its shiny surface was completely eclipsed with the Word.

'*Measure part of the flour into a bowl, and add any other dry ingredients or flavourings.*'

'Genesis, Exodus, Leviticus, Numbers and Deuteronomy!'

'*Make a depression, or well, in the centre of the flour, and add the dissolved yeast and other liquids.*'

'Joshua, Judges and Ruth!'

'Are you listening or what?'

'Yes, I am listening, go on!'

'*Beat well to combine.*'

'1 Samuel, 2 Samuel, 1 Kings and 2 Kings!'

'Ha, you are crazy, Rasputin.'

'No no no, go on! I am listening, Nicholas, I am listening. *Beat well to combine.*'

'That's right. *Gradually add the rest of the flour until the bread dough becomes difficult to stir.*'

'1 Chronicles, 2 Chronicles, Ezra, Nehemiah, Esther, Job, Psalms and Proverbs!'

'At this point, flour your work surface and dump the dough out of the bowl on to the floured surface. Begin kneading the dough.'

'Ecclesiastes, Song of Solomon, Isaiah!'

'To knead, turn the dough over several times, gathering any stray particles. Fold the dough in half towards you, and push away with the heels of your hands.'

'Jeremiah, Lamentations, Ezekiel, Daniel, Hosea.'

'Turn the dough one quarter turn, and repeat this process until the dough is smooth, elastic, springy, and no longer sticky.'

'Joel, Amos, Obadiah, Jonah, Micah, Nahum, Habakkuk, Zephaniah, Haggai, Zachariah and Malachi!'

'This will take from five to ten minutes. Doughs made with bread flour typically require more kneading than those made with all-purpose flour.'

'Matthew, Mark, Luke, John.'

'Grease a large mixing bowl lightly with shortening. Place the smooth, kneaded dough into the bowl, turning it over so the top is greased as well. This step makes sure the dough doesn't dry out as it rises. Cover with a clean cloth and place in a warm spot. An electric oven with the light turned on, or a gas oven with the pilot light are perfect places for rising.'

'Acts, Romans, 1 Corinthians, 2 Corinthians, Galatians, Ephesians, Philippians, Colossians, 1 Thessalonians!'

'Let the dough rise until double in bulk. This means the dough increases in size, and when you press your fingers into the top, the indentation remains when you remove your fingers. Punch down the dough, and turn it on to a floured surface. Shape according to the recipe.'

'2 Thessalonians, 1 Timothy, 2 Timothy, Titus, Philemon, Hebrews, James!'

'Place the dough in greased loaf tins, or on a greased cookie sheet for free-form loaves. Cover and let rise again until double in size. This second rising will take less time, because there is more yeast in the dough.'

'1 Peter, 2 Peter, 1 John, 2 John, 3 John, Jude and Revelation!'

'Lunatic! What was that?' Arthur retorted, putting aside the magazine, looking relieved that he did not have to read any more.

'The Holy Ball! *Translated out of the original tongues and with the previous translations diligently compared and revised.*'

'And what would that be?'

'A football plastered with the pages of the Bible for exercising and exorcising! Step one: take a football, PVA glue and loosened Holy Bible pages. Step two: plaster the Bible pages on to the ball, one by one, until completely covered. Step three: allow the Holy Ball to dry before any exercises and exorcisms.'

'That's blasphemous, Lucifer. Seriously, you cannot turn the Word of God into a football.'

'If that's the case blasphemy is the beginning of any religion.'

'You are starting a new religion?'

'Not quite, Your Holiness – I am just reviving an old one: sun worship. I have given it a new funky name though – Holyballism.'

'Holyballism. That sounds kind of cool. But why worship the sun? It's only a ball of fire.'

'But what a fire! We wouldn't be here without it.'

'I know, I know, Galileo. Still, what has the sun got to do with footballs plastered with the pages of the Bible?'

'Everything!' I dropped the ball on the floor. I had to stand up to jive that one. The ball bounced twice before Arthur suddenly stood up too and smashed it hard with his instep sending it ricocheting around the bunker. The scheming little devil had been trying hard to make me let go of the ball for the whole afternoon and now, somehow, he had finally succeeded. He controlled the ball down to the floor with glee and was dribbling and kicking it about, shielding it from my reach as I spoke to him.

'Your Holiness, the Holy Ball is the funeral of God. God too needs to be buried so He cannot haunt us in the aftermath of His passing.'

'But God can never die.'

'Of course He can and has done, Longinus. *God is dead.* Cast your spear in his side and see. That's why he is but a football now. But no need to worry because there is no longer any need for us to believe in God. God has become too crude an answer to the fundamental questions of our existence: *Whence do we come? What are we? Whither are we going?*' like Gauguin has asked on the Diptych. Everybody knows that there is no God with a white beard up there nor Hell below us; a simple telescopic scan of the Heavens by Galileo proved Copernicus right and the Bible wrong: the sun and the heavenly bodies do not revolve around the earth; the earth is but a speck of dust in the Big Bang.'

'But how did it begin, though? All by itself, My Lord?'

'Who said it began, Adam? Since we are here it makes more sense to say it never began. Things may become but they never begin.'

'Whoa! That's deep, Lemaître.'

'Yeah. But of what use is the formula of water to a drowning man? You see, for most people the death of God means depression, escapism or even suicide because life has lost its meaning. They lose interest in life and live like zombies . . . They become alcoholics, drug addicts, passive nihilists, unbridled consumers of stuff, they become fatalistic . . . The ghost of God haunts them, if you know what I mean. God comes to them and sucks out their life force like a vampire. They are the last men. But for us the death of God is Good News and that is why we are not afraid to take part in His funeral.'

'Tell us the Good News then, Galileo! It's about time!'

Arthur passed me the ball. I scooped it up and smashed it against the wall.

'Your Holiness, history has turned a full circle here – call it the Second Coming if you will. The superior man who invented monotheism, the first known individual in history, the Egyptian Pharaoh Akhenaten, worshipped the sun as the one true god: he learnt from the sun the meaning of life. The death of God marks a return to that attitude through self-expression and this historical atavism will be enacted in the making and the destruction of the Holy Ball through exercises and exorcisms: Akhenaten represented the sun as a solar disc, we represent it as a ball but for us too the meaning of life is to shine like the sun; to be aware of our mortality and affirm it rather than live in denial; to take life and spend it with passion and style because this is the only life we will ever know, the life that recurs eternally for us.'

'*Amor fati!*'

'That's right, Your Holiness. *Set the controls for the heart of the sun* and *become who you are*. We live and die with the sun. The one lesson we can learn from history is this: Moses should have looked no further than the sun because beyond the sun there is nothing and nothing is beyond God. The Holyballist vision therefore is the complete return of the sun as the paramount provider of life and its meaning, the day when all Holy Books of the world shall be made into Holy Balls exercising and exorcising people into everlasting happiness.'   *bollocks*

'*Amor fati!*'

'*Amor fati!*'

A kicking and smashing frenzy ensued in the bunker at the end of which I climbed out for some fresh air, but when I saw the distant horizon drenched in a majestic purple sunset, I grabbed an air guitar, stood before the huge red sun in the middle and started singing George Harrison's 'Here Comes the Sun', which I dedicated to Alice. Arthur, who had given up keeping up with me, poked his bemused head out of the bunker, a hand over his eyes, watching my performance. For the 'freakout', I twisted and hopped around like a hippy at Woodstock until the sun disappeared on the horizon.

When I jumped back into the bunker, Arthur said that I was crazy but I didn't care now that I felt exhilarated like I had been on a trip driving Helios' fiery chariot across the sky for the first time. I was shining.

7

Do we not hear anything yet of the noise of the gravediggers who are burying God?

By the end of that year, I had made the Holy Ball, dropped the name Kondwani and chose to be called Samson, because it meant 'child of the sun', which I thought was cool. I then developed what I called *The Holy Ball Book of Exercises and Exorcisms* on whose first page was the Holyballist prediction: *A day is coming soon when all Holy Books of the World shall be made into Holy Balls exercising and exorcising people into everlasting happiness.* The rest of the exercise book was full of drawings of riotous angels, demons, dominions and saints that I had seen in my dreams after ripping my Bible apart to make the Holy Ball. Among the drawings were some of the 144,000 from the Book of Revelation which I had encountered when I went to Heaven to explain myself to Elisha, the short-tempered prophet who set two wild bears on a bunch of little boys for laughing at his bald head in 2 Kings 2:23–5. The 144,000 stood in a large hallway, waiting for their day, and none of them moved, except for the occasional flapping of wings, because they all had their halos plugged in. I took the exercise book to Arthur's nuclear bunker where I used it to analyse my unconscious mind.

8

It has been further related that on that same day the madman entered divers churches and there sang a requiem. Led out and quietened, he is said to have retorted each time: 'What are these churches now if they are not the tombs and sepulchres of God?'

Around Christmas, when I heard that Gelena CCAP Church was going to put on the Sunday-school nativity play, I dressed myself in my Sunday Best and took the ball to the church in my school bag to proclaim my brand-new religion, if not to the whole congregation then at least to the stubborn Sunday-school teachers. Jesus was twelve years old when he first had a go at the rabbis – I was going to take my chance at eleven years old, which I thought was a good age for a philosophy based on a ball.

Before I ascended the flight of stairs that led into the church I plucked off the huge sunflower in the garden and held it in my other hand as a symbol of the basic message behind Holyballism: look no further than the sun. I thought flowers were a fitting testimony, the way the petals curved in and out of the circle like the fire arches on the magnetic face of the sun.

For a while, during the progression of the play, I remained in my seat either paralysed with nerves and wanting to go to the toilet or distracted by Dingiswayo, King Herod's General. He had the whole congregation in stitches every time he appeared onstage. Clad in a black army beret, well-pressed khaki trousers and shirt, painted moustache and a pot belly made up of rags, he uncannily resembled an MYP officer. Whenever King Herod called him on to the stage, he shouted, 'Bwana!' (boss) but pronounced the word in such a loose manner that it sounded like *mbwanda* (bean) which alluded to the pussy. And when he saluted his boss, who was a chubby little man, his bow was so swift and low that he hit the top of his turban with his forehead like a sledgehammer, every time. But when 'The Massacre of the Innocents' had reached its climax with Rachel bewailing her children in Rama and not being comforted, I hurriedly took the Holy Ball out of the bag, stood up and approached the stage to interrupt the players. I wanted to start exercising and exorcising the congregation by telling King Herod that there was no need to go on killing those children because God is dead (Long live God!), the Second Coming is here, the Kingdom has come. I was going to quote Malachi 4:2: *'But unto you that fear my name shall the Sun of righteousness arise with healing in his wings; and ye shall go forth, and grow up as calves of the stall.'* But before I could do it, the soldiers saw the ball and knocked it out of my hands, shouting 'Bouncing ball!' and started having a kick-about. The shepherds, angels, Joseph and Mary all joined in as chaos spilt out of the church following the ball as it proclaimed DA! DA! DA! DA! . . . on *deaf* ears.

'Bouncing ball! Bouncing ball!' they shouted.

'It's a Mosaic eclipse!' I said but nobody paid attention.

King Herod's General, who was the biggest lad among the players, pushed his way through the melee like a bulldozer, grabbed the now ragged Holy Ball, peeled it to the orange like a grapefruit, bounced it off the ground once and kept it for himself. He didn't even realise it was the Bible he was tearing off.

When I protested, he gave me a kick in my stomach. I lashed him in the face with the sunflower and headed back to the Bush Line running. He just stood there stunned like a blinded Cyclops, rubbing his eye, but holding on tightly to the ball. His soldiers ran after me until the deacon ordered them back to the play.

I was totally devastated.

9

Back at the nuclear bunker, I had nothing to show but a big dirty footprint on my favourite shirt and a dishevelled sunflower; Arthur advised me to forget Holyballism for a while and resort to pugilism to get my ball back. He volunteered to teach me how to box like Muhammad Ali: float like a butterfly, sting like a bee, that sort of thing. We filled a sack with sand to make a punchbag, hung it on a tree, and started working out. Every afternoon I was under that tree punching like the madman Mr Window.

In the meantime Arthur renamed his nuclear bunker the Catacomb after I had messed up the walls with graffiti from my new religion. The walls were riddled with sun symbols from around the world that I had come across on the Diptych.

One wall had the quotation by J.M.W. Turner, *The Sun is God*. Opposite *The Sun is God* was a simple yellow rhombus at whose cardinal points were the names of the four pivotal icons of Holyballism: Akhenaten, who conceived God as the sun; Moses, who eclipsed the sun with the Word; Christ, who perceived the Word as man; and Nietzsche, who brought back God, the sun as the meaning of the Word. Below the yellow rhombus was the single most important commandment of Holyballism (based on the sound of a bouncing ball): *DA!* Adjacent to these two was a large drawing of Alice (copied from *Alice's Adventures in Wonderland*) with the Holy Ball in her hands, as a bemused Yellow Dwarf in an orange tree bearing the Holyballist slogan, *Exercise And Exorcise*, watched on.

Across from Alice and the Yellow Dwarf was the most prominent piece in the bunker, my rendition of Frida Kahlo's painting, *Nuclear Sun*. In place of Akhenaten's solar disc, the *aten*, I had a large orange circle, surrounded by the names of some of the major heroes and villains from history that Frida Kahlo put in her painting; all in different luminous and rioting colours, shooting out like the rays of the sun. Starting with Akhenaten there followed: Kukulcan, Gukumnatz, Coatlicue, Quetzacóaltl, Tezcatlipoca, the Canteotl, Tlaloc, Brahma, Nefertiti, Marx, Paracelus, Epicurus, Freud, Buddha, Genghis Khan, Gandhi, Dr Hastings Kamuzu Banda (just in case the MCP were to discover the nuclear bunker), Lenin, Stalin, Osiris, Horus, Zeus, Apollo, Venus, the moon, Jehovah, the Virgin Mary, the Trinity, the Devil, Zarathustra, Christ, Jan Lievens, Alexander the Great, Tamerlane, Caesar, Mohammed, Martin Luther, Napoleon and Hitler.

After days of working out when I felt the six-pack was ready and my knuckles were hardened into iron ball bearings, I looked for Dingiswayo for a showdown. We found him playing keepy-uppy with the ball at the school play-

ground, surrounded by hangers-on. He was a superstar now
with the bouncing ball. There were scores all over the dusty
place. And it looked like he had grown a couple of metres
taller since the last time I had seen him. Standing there, he
looked like Charles Atlas.

I nudged Arthur with my elbow to show Dingiswayo
the scroll with the Jack Broughton rules of pugilism we had
prepared as part of a trick to guarantee a win but he couldn't
do it. His hands were shaking as if he had Parkinson's disease.
Anyway, I had already taken off my shirt and secretly re-
inforced my fists with stones. I was ready to fight and there
was no turning back now. No turning back. Arthur whispered in my ear instead:

'May the Yellow Dwarf be with you.'

I stepped on Mr Atlas's score marks.

'Get off my marks,' he said, cracking his knuckles.

'I want my ball back!' I said. My voice was already shaky.

'What do you need a ball for? You can't kick a thing.'

'It's my muse.'

'Get a girlfriend,' he said flexing his neck. He approached
me arms akimbo, like a prizefighter, *Raging Bull* or something. My knees clicked and wobbled.

Dingiswayo pulled me off his score marks by the ear. I
wanted to punch him in the stomach but I was afraid that if
I did anything more to upset him, he would rip that ear off
like St Peter did for the Roman soldier. Instead of punching,
I grabbed his hand with both of mine to ease the pain on
my ear. When he saw the stones fall from my fists, he let go
of my ear and kicked my backside with a dirty foot. I ran
home for dear life, useless Arthur trailing behind me.

Back at the Catacomb once again, Arthur suggested that
I get magic from a witch doctor. I told him that if *khini*
worked, Malawi would have won the World Cup. I was
leaning towards letting the ball go anyway. My mother said

jive was driving her crazy, and I definitely didn't want Mum to go crazy and turn into a zombie like the mad Nietzsche. So much for famous child prodigies like Rimbaud. So much for meeting Alice again, and showing her what I did with her ball.

'Man, I am not going to lose an ear over this,' I told Arthur. 'Dingiswayo can keep the damn ball. Holyballism is a state of mind.'

MULANJE II

1

Banda used to complain about his country to his closest friends: 'What did we do wrong to deserve such a wretched place on God's earth?' At some 94,000 square kilometres Malawi is relatively tiny and landlocked to suffocation by her giant neighbours: Mozambique, Zambia and Tanzania. Located within the Great African Rift Valley, she is shaped like a piece of colon. Her rocky, unruly savannah landscape makes her bad for large-scale farming. She is simply too hard to hoe (Grandad had not given up on her for nothing). When the erratic rains do come, she leaks all her nutrients into Mozambique, frequently flooding the giant country with untold miseries. Yet unlike most African countries, Malawi has no precious minerals or crude oil to make up for it, and is thus a special case when it comes to poverty. With life expectancies that now stand at thirty-six years for women and thirty-four for men, she is one of the poorest countries in sub-Saharan Africa. Had it not been for the hostile borders most of the nomadic tribes imprisoned in that little hellhole would have moved on long ago. It is for this reason that Banda was able to justify his 'supping with the Devil' foreign policy.

In September of 1986, Samora Machel, the Communist President of Mozambique, accompanied by Prime Minister

Robert Mugabe of Zimbabwe and President Kenneth Kaunda of Zambia, came to Malawi for a crisis meeting with Banda. When he stepped out of his presidential jet, a heavily bearded man in army fatigues, he walked up to a grim-faced Banda, waiting at the end of the red carpet, and pointed an angry finger at him, accusing him of harbouring and funding the capitalist Renamo rebels who had been wrecking his country since 1975.

His accusations were well founded. For years Banda had teamed up with apartheid South Africa to fight against Machel's Communist government in the hope that after victory, Malawi would be extended to the Indian Ocean, gaining access to some precious natural resources and an international harbour along the way.

But it was shocking, nonetheless, the way Machel cast his judgement. He should have been more diplomatic. We had never seen anybody point a finger at the Life President like that in public; something had to give. The following month when we heard that Comrade Machel had died in a plane crash in South Africa, nobody was surprised.

But in typical fashion, Banda was the first head of state in the world to fly the national flag at half-mast and send his condolences to the people of Mozambique. During the following two weeks, any form of entertainment was banned and the MBC radio aired nothing but classical music in honour of Comrade Machel. The sombre DJ at MBC played not only Chopin's Funeral March and Beethoven's Eroica but a whole load of them: sonatas, concertos, symphonies, mazurkas . . . I guess classical music did not sound like entertainment to him. Or was it Banda's wicked sense of humour? Either way, to this day, whenever classical music is played to most Malawians, they bow their heads thinking there is a funeral.

When the last composition had been played – Handel's

Fireworks Music, I think – the neighbourhood sprang back to life. I woke up to a stereo pounding out Paul Hardcastle's '19':

> *In 1965 Vietnam seemed like just another foreign war*
> *but it wasn't*
> *It was different in many ways, as so were those that*
> *did the fighting*
> *In World War II the average age of the combat soldier was 26*
> *In Vietnam he was 19*
> *In ininininin Vietnam he was 19*
> *In ininininin Vietnam he was 19*
> *In ininininin Vietnam he was 19*
> *n n n n nineteen*

We had new neighbours next door. There was a showy boy whose family had just come back from the UK, where his father had been studying. He wore blue tracksuits and red Adidas sneakers and there he was, once again, break-dancing and body-popping on the veranda. He called himself Darwin because he knew he performed like an ape. That was his style. When he was not spinning on his head, wind-milling, worming or moonwalking across the floor, he pranced about and beat his own chest like King Kong. All the kids in the neighbourhood gathered around to watch him dance. I was so jealous because he was stealing my shine. Before him I was the man: the kid who could draw like Picasso, speak English like a *Negro*, philosophise like the Messiah himself and who was always top of class at school.

I watched him from my bedroom window, thinking of ways to battle him down to size. I had a couple of dance moves myself, but without a boom box in the house and a pair of cool Nike sneakers how was I to show my moves? So instead, I fished out a stringless box guitar I had made from a USAID cooking oil box, rolled a papaya leaf joint, and jammed to Bob Marley's 'Time Will Tell' with Arthur, out on the veranda, trying to sabotage Darwin. We had to shout real loud to be heard over the top of his Kenwood stereo, telling him what he took for heaven was actually Babylon but it did not work. Nobody was looking at us. Emperor Haile Selassie, King of Kings, Lord of Lords, the Conquering Lion of the Tribe of Judah, a direct descendant of King Solomon through Makeda, the Queen of Sheba, had long been deposed from his throne and buried under a toilet; Ethiopia had starved to death, the Rasta had breathed his last through Lovers Rock and now everybody wanted disco and all that boogieing stuff. Darwin's fame was spreading like bush fire.

Then one evening, the projector at the film show of the Thyolo District Council Hall was replaced by something called a video monitor. For the first time, you could watch the whole movie uninterrupted, albeit in tiny images and missing whole portions if you went to the toilet. The first thing we saw on that video was Michael Jackson's *Thriller*, which included his electrifying 'Billie Jean' performance at the Motown 25th Anniversary. I memorised the choreography from start to finish because they had to play the performance over and over again that night and the days after that. We couldn't get enough of it. The following day, I polished my battered school shoes, cut my Sunday Best trousers a couple of inches above the ankle and I was on my way. I still needed a boom box, though, so I opened the radiogram, which had been dead for years now, to see if I could bring it back to life. I connected the rat-eaten wires – green on green, red on red, yellow on yellow – and, by some miracle, the radio was resurrected. And boy was it loud – like an archaic sleeping giant that had suddenly been awoken. Having no cassettes was no problem for me; I used a simple trick on the radiogram to fool the neighbourhood kids into thinking we had a Kenwood stereo in the house. I signed up my sister Joyce to be my DJ as I faced off Darwin on the veranda, creating my new image as the neighbourhood Michael Jackson. Joyce would turn up the radio when a good song was playing, and it was funky stuff only, no native stuff was allowed:

Alan Namoko and his Chimvu River Dance Banda: OFF
Madolo: OFF
Madolo: OFF
Ricky James: ON
Michael Yekha: OFF
M'bilia Bel and Tabu Ley Rochereau: OFF
Papa Wemba: OFF
Mahlathini and the Mahotella Queens: OFF
Madolo: OFF
Prince: ON
Chic: ON
Musical Youth: ON
Kasambwe Brothers Band: OFF
Roots: OFF
Songani Swing Stars: OFF
Michael Jackson: ON
Donald Kachamba: OFF
Madolo: OFF
MBC Band: OFF
Madonna: ON
Rose Royce: ON
Ethel Kamwendo: OFF
Run DMC: ON
Madolo: OFF

But by the end of 1986, before I was finished with Darwin, we were back in Mulanje.

2

Our house was the same old colonial mansion on the blue slopes of the big mountain. It was getting old now and there were cracks in the foundations. When we opened the empty house, a snakeskin blew across the dining hall as the wind rushed in through the front door. And then came the baby black mambas.

They slipped in and slept in the shadows of the furniture, always one baby snake in each shadow. They looked territorial. Late in the evening, you would be sitting at the table, lost in a book, when something slimy would zigzag underfoot and suddenly you were back on your toes. You would take a closer look and find a squashed baby black mamba, only half dead. To finish it off you had to mash up its head with a heel of a shoe, because a snake did not die until his head was mashed.

You would wake up at night, switch on the light, and there would be a couple of baby black mambas curled up and sleeping under your bed.

I felt sorry for Celenia the housekeeper, who slept on the floor in the pantry.

At school, the same old Njedza Full Primary, my teacher, Mr Dziko, had a lot of trouble keeping me awake in his class. He thought I had sleeping sickness. 'Where did you come from? The Gambia?' he would ask, before whacking my hand with his notorious guava stick.

Bruce Eliason, a new friend of mine, from a remote village in Mimosa, said he knew herbs to keep the snakes away. He came over to our house, one afternoon, on an ancient boneshaker called Humber, bringing with him a spiky green plant called *mpunga bwi* which he applied to all the cracks in the house, making the whole place smell like farts. The black mambas came up from the foundations in droves for the following few days. We killed twenty-seven of them before they stopped.

On the day when Bruce came to check on the situation, I offered to cycle him home, to show my gratitude. We were already past level ground and speeding down the Bush Line when he told me that there were no brakes on the Humber. The green Mulanje landscape was laid out before us, tea plantations dotted with smoking factories and workers' villages for as far as the eye could see. Then there was nothing, only the rushing wind and a dizzying green. I held on to the boneshaker and prayed for the best. We crashed into the iron gates of Bandaga Tea Factory but Bruce was nowhere to be seen. My knees and elbows badly cut and bruised, I picked up the wobbling Humber and hobbled back to the road. I met Bruce halfway, grinning like a Cheshire cat. He had jumped off the carrier on the back of the bicycle long ago.

He helped me to the hospital.

I dared not visit the outpatients, where they gave you aspirin for everything and the queues lasted for days. Instead, I braved it out and went to see Dad, who was never happy about his children visiting him at his workplace. I told him that I had fallen on the high steps that led up to our house from the hospital. What was I to do? Surely I was bleeding to death? Dad groaned and assigned me to a nurse who stitched my wound up and gave me some colourful capsules. When I showed them to Bruce, his eyes lit up with envy.

'Can I have some for my cough?' he said.

'What cough?'

He drew on his windpipe long and hard and spat a mountain of saliva on to the side of the road. It looked like a healthy spit to me but I gave him all the pills anyway. Since he had rid our house of the baby black mambas and I had just wrecked his boneshaker, giving him a few pills seemed like the least I could do as compensation. But I was also curious to see if the medicine would work on him as placebos if he was really sick. The Jive Talker said he had treated lots of complicated illnesses using vitamin pills.

3

Caesar was very old now. He was losing his hair, coughing up crazy stuff and had withered away to skin and bone. The neighbourhood was getting superstitious, so my mother asked me to take him to the vet so they could put him down. When I let him off the leash to give him his last taste of freedom, he disappeared into the bushes beyond the backyard and was gone for ages, so I followed him there to investigate. I found him with his head up the skirt of a madwoman who picked wild flowers in those bushes. The natives called her Mama wa Chifufu (Mama the Epileptic) and she'd worked at the hospital as a midwife, until she'd gone crazy on the job. Caesar was licking the darkness between her legs and she was giggling, as she sang the familiar Black Death nursery rhyme:

> *Ring a ring o' roses*
> *A pocketful of posies*
> *ah-tishoo, ah-tishoo*
> *We all fall down.*

It was a small creepy world. Not only did her song remind me of the surrealism of Arthur's nuclear bunker, but this glade was also the very spot where Zapa had stood a few years earlier, hands ablaze, drawing fire patterns in the air.

'Caesar! Enough. Let's go!' I shouted out to the dirty dog.

He reluctantly followed me down the road wagging his tail. We faded away to Mama wa Chifufu's song:

> Ring a ring o' roses
> A pocketful of posies
> ah-tishoo, ah-tishoo
> We all fall down.

The vet, a grey-haired man with skin as wrinkly as Caesar's, gave him a single shot in the leg.

'That's it,' he said.

As I made my way back home Caesar followed me but the vet did not try to stop him. He just stood there with an enigmatic smile on his face, watching us go up the road. Then suddenly, Caesar dropped dead. Only then did the old vet come to carry his body to the office.

The following morning, before I limped to school, still recovering from the bicycle crash, I went to check on Mama wa Chifufu's spot. She was already there in the morning mist, gathering wild flowers and singing 'Ring a Ring o' Roses'. When she caught sight of me, she showed me the darkness between her legs, inviting me over. As I contemplated the situation (not that I was going to do anything), a topless sweaty muscular man, carrying a big tree trunk on his shoulders, came down the mountain path. When he saw what was happening, he laid down his burden, wiped his brow and told me to go home. I pretended to go and hid behind a blue gum tree to see what he was going to do. He carried the giggling Mama wa Chifufu off from her glade, laid her on the big rock nearby and started to do it to her. The madwoman smiled, laughed and cried at the same time. But I had to limp on to school where on arrival Mr Dziko whacked me hard for being late. I didn't feel the crack of the whip, though – my mind was back in the woods, with Mama wa Chifufu and the tree-trunk fellow.

4

Khumbo Lungu, the nephew of the field manager of Chitakale Tea Estate, was a Seventh-Day Adventist. Khumbo was already well into his teens, as he had grown up in a remote village in the north and started school late. When he saw me going to church one Sunday, he stood in my way and told me not to go, saying that those who worshipped on Sunday were the children of the Antichrist – the Pope, the destroyer of the true Sabbath. A day was coming soon when Sunday rest would become compulsory (I guessed for the Seventh-Day Adventists, Muslims and other such dissidents), and all those who kept the Pope's Sabbath would be branded with the mark of the beast on their foreheads or right arm, ready to be checked into Hell. When I curiously asked him how he knew the Pope was the Antichrist, he picked up a stick and wrote in the sand the official name of the Pope, Vicarius Filii Dei. He then showed me how to add up the letters so that you ended up with the figure 666.

5 (V) + 1 (I) + 100 (C) + 1 (I) + 5 (V) + 1 (I) + 50 (L) + 1 (I) + 1 (I) + 500 (D) + 1 (I) = 666

It was the same Melanist trick I was familiar with. I had lots of examples like that which I had accumulated while searching for the Antichrist back in Nkhota-kota. I replied by showing him how to find 666 in the names of Emperor Nero, Louis XVI, N'Appollione (Napoleon's Corsican name), Martin Luther and Ronald Wilson Reagan.

'See, you can never really tell who the Antichrist is,' I told him. 'There are simply too many possibilities. And if we were to follow St Augustine's doctrine, *There you have the Antichrist – everyone that denies Christ by his works,* anybody who comes after Christ is condemned to be the Antichrist. Two thousand years of history have shown us that a Christian is impossible. Christianity with its denial of the fundamental driving force behind every human character, the *will to power*, the will to consolidate ourselves, merely serves to alienate people from themselves, from life.'

'Why are you going to church, then?'

'For the drama; some of these ministers draw like Picasso.'

'So you are an atheist?'

Khumbo looked like he had just discovered something he had been looking for for a long time. His eyes were glinting with excitement.

'I don't believe in God or any other supernatural deities, but I wouldn't call myself an atheist. I have a natural god, the one that keeps the earth in orbit, the one that sustains and gives meaning to life: the Yellow Dwarf. For me, an atheist is anyone who denies this only God possible for us. In this case, you are the one who is an atheist, Khumbo, being a Christian and all.'

5

The following Saturday I found myself at the Seventh-Day Adventist Church. For the drama. I had just discovered that the name of the founder of the church, Ellen Gould White, also added up to 666 in Roman gematria. Khumbo was still praying for the miracle of my conversion, or at least I thought so. I had always been curious about Ellen G. White because she too was a child prodigy like Jesus. She was only nine years old when one of her schoolmates hit her in the face with a stone, which sent her into a coma for three weeks. She came out of it with temporal lobe epilepsy, which gave her visions from 'God', visions that have inspired the Seventh-Day Adventist Church to this day. She was a bit of a hypocrite though, urging her followers to become vegetarians while she herself ate turkey and chicken in private. Anyway, I was curious to see how her project was faring, so I went with Khumbo to observe the true Sabbath for a change.

The church was new but still needed a door and windows, so I was not surprised that the sermon was about tithing. No drama there. More intriguing was Khumbo's niece, Ivy, an ebony-smooth, buxom girl who sang like an angel. Her four brothers accompanied her a cappella and together they looked like Five Star standing there. When the congregation said Amen! at the end of her song, the men drowned out the women for a change.

On the way home from the church, after I had shown Khumbo how to find the Antichrist in Ellen G. White, he surprised me when he asked if I would like to go out with his niece. I told him yeah, why not; so one afternoon he arranged a date with Ivy for me in the Chitakale tea fields at the bottom of Mulanje Mountain.

Khumbo put Ivy in a glade somewhere in the tea fields, fed me some *thubulo*, an aphrodisiac laced with rhino horn and sent me to look for her like I was a dog or something.

'When you find her, fuck her, OK? Fuck her real good,' he said.

He was talking dirty all of a sudden like he had Tourette's syndrome. There was sweat on his brow and he flared his nostrils like a rhinoceros.

'With all the stuff you have taken you have to do it, or you will end up wanting to do dogs,' he said.

'What do I do?' I asked him, because I had never fucked a girl before.

'Fuck her. Fuck. You don't believe in God, do you? A fuckin' sun worshipper. What are you afraid of? Fuck.'

He splattered my face with drops of saliva when he said fuck.

'What does a girl look like?' I asked, wiping my face with a shaky hand.

'A cowrie shell. You mean you don't know? All that grown-up crap you talk about and you don't know what a woman looks like. How old are you?'

'Twelve.'

'I thought you were fifteen . . . Come here.'

He pinched my nipples. One of them was swollen stiff from puberty.

'You are a man,' he said, feeling the pebble. 'Go and give it to her!'

I nodded involuntarily.

'Fuck,' he spat on my face again.

There was a huge banana at the wet patch on his shorts when he sent me on my way.

Ivy and I lay on our backs in a clearing among the tea

trees, staring at the clouds. We had nothing to say to each other. Against the awkward silence, I heard many dogs barking in the distance and I wondered if I was falling for the bitches, with all that *thubulo* Khumbo had given me. When I looked at Ivy's pink-and-green flip-flops the spaces between her toes were gaping wide. Somewhere in the distance I thought I could hear Khumbo cracking on. 'You are an atheist, aren't you? Fuck her. Damn it!'

'Let's fuck,' I suggested to Ivy.

'OK,' she said.

She slipped out of her underwear and raised her blue cotton dress to her tummy.

For all my knowledge about cowrie shells and women, for all the nudes I had seen on the Diptych: Botticelli's *Birth of Venus*, Titian's *Venus of Urbino*, Velázquez's *Rokeby Venus*, Count Balthazar Klossowski de Rola's *La Chambre*, Manet's *Olympia*, Albert Moore's *A Bathing Place*, Pierre Auguste Renoir's *After the Bath*, Edgar Degas' *After the Bath III*, William Bouguereau's *Baigneuse* . . . I didn't know girls had pubic hair. I felt my hair stand on its ends like I was looking at a ghost.

'Fuck. You will go crazy . . . I mean pregnant,' I told her retrieving my breath, pulling up my shorts. 'Dress up, we will do it another time.'

'OK,' she said.

I tucked in, she dressed up and we continued to gaze at the sky on our backs. But it was all a bit weird for me now. The clouds looked like patches of Ivy's pubic hair. Then I realised it would soon start to rain and had to hurry back home.

I was wading through the tea fields, towards the foot-path to the Bush Line, when I thought I heard Ivy laughing at me from the glade and wondered what was funny. It seemed to me that we had parted amicably.

I found Khumbo under the purple jacaranda tree at the edge of the tea fields, deep in onanism. He was way into it and didn't even notice me standing there.

'Fuck her, you little devil! Fuck her!' he said to his little devil.

There was thunder and lightning as I slipped away. As I crossed the stream hopping from one stone to another, a big black mamba with a raised head stood in the middle of the path on the other side watching me intently, but it slithered away when I jumped with fright.

I arrived home to find the wild Emily back from her secretarial college in Blantyre, her tummy all swollen. She was pregnant by some random guy she had met in one of the nightclubs.

6

Whenever I saw my pregnant sister, I felt nauseous and got visions in my head. I would see her lying there stark naked, legs apart like a frog, head turned to the side like St Teresa, all hairy like Ivy, and this big sweaty man would be lying on top, doing things to her. And she would be crying like she was sad or hurt, yet loving it like Mama wa Chifufu on that rock. I hated her for giving me all these thoughts that were driving me mad and tried to avoid her all the time.

For a while, I played a lot of football after school, but had to quit because there were rumours in the playground that I didn't know how to fuck. So instead I went to the library to read.

One day I followed Bruce to his village in Mimosa, to ask him stuff about women. I wanted to tell him about Mama wa Chifufu, Ivy and my sister, but I just couldn't. The words wouldn't come out of my mouth.

Bruce's home was a one-room mud-brick hut with grass thatching and they all slept in there together around the fireplace; his father, mother, two brothers and three sisters. I wondered how his mother and father could fuck in a house like that. When Bruce's sister, the one with the big bottom, realised I was the doctor's son who had cured her brother's persistent cough, she whispered something into Bruce's ear.

'Ruth would like some cotton wool and methylated spirit,' Bruce translated.

'What for?' I asked.

Ruth looked at me like I was a fool and laughed.

'For her going to the moon,' Bruce said.

'Oh. I will see what I can do.'

Ruth left the suffocating room looking happy and spread the rumour around the village that the doctor's son was in residence and was promising people medical supplies.

Soon there was a long queue of ailing natives outside the hut.

A man wearing a *chitenje* like a woman walked in, legs wide part and stinking like rotten meat. He carried a ripened pawpaw in his hands, which he handed to me as a gift. After introducing himself as Bruce's uncle, he lifted his skirt to show me his manhood as if I was a nurse. He smelt so bad I had to pinch my nose. There was milky yellow discharge coming out of his penis. It dropped on to the mud floor, making a black patch with a white dot in the middle. His scrotum was swollen into two huge purple pears. I thought it was gonorrhoea. I knew all about venereal diseases now. I had read about them while looking for real female crotches in the medical books in my parents' bedroom, after the embarrassing encounter with Ivy.

'I need some capsules, *bwana,*' the man said.

I told him that I would see what I could do, just to make him go away.

A woman breastfeeding a baby knelt down before me and popped out her other breast to show me a lump. She said the hospital and the witch doctors hadn't been able to cure it after a long time trying and asked me for some capsules. I promised to get some for her, although I knew that what she really needed was a mastectomy, and very soon.

They all needed capsules: the boy with a deep gash above his ankle, the woman with goitre who really needed to eat more fish, the anorexic woman who asked for contraception. All except a witch doctor, who asked for a syringe and a stethoscope, 'that listening horn', as he put it.

Why capsules? I wondered, as Bruce cycled me home on his wobbly Humber.

7

They were colourful, that's why. I realised this quickly after coming across my father's medical supplies in his bedroom; the pills were full of promise. The native was a sucker for colour as if he was a hippy. I should have known. The Diptych said the native would sell his brother for the multicoloured Venetian beads and other such bric-a-brac in the days of slavery. And then there were the markets full of colourful African prints, which my father said were not really African at all, but Dutch. The Dutch had imported the textiles into Europe from Indonesia, but couldn't sell them because the Europeans thought they were too outlandish. When they tried them in Africa though, the natives loved them.

Here was something interesting to do with all those capsules in Dad's bedroom: play a medieval quack doctor from the Diptych for fun. There were lots to choose from and all were remarkable artists: Mantacinni the Italian who travelled around Europe in a golden coach drawn by a pair of white horses, promising to raise the dead at will. The night before he went to the graveyard to do his thing, people would visit his hotel, bribing him to leave town, as most of them wanted their loved ones to remain in their graves. And at dawn, he would move to the next city and start all over again. He got rich that way – by understanding human nature and preying on it. Then there was Dr Valentine Greatrakes (also known as the Irish Stroker), a gynaecologist who claimed he could treat any woman's disease by stroking them . . . He collected testimonies of the women he had cured and put them in a book called *Wonders if not Miracles*. Not forgetting Dr Lionel Lockyer, an Englishman who sold 'sunshine pills' claiming that they contained the sun, and just like the sunshine, they would heal all kinds of ailments. Somehow, they worked on most of his patients . . . This was my chance to play Dr Lionel Lockyer for the natives and see what would happen.

I selected the most colourful capsules and gave them to Bruce to pass on to my patients back in the village. I convinced myself they would work like Dr Lockyer's placebos, since the native believed in colour like *khini*. I took the massive *Manson's Tropical Diseases* and made a list of all the diseases I was treating, prescribing the capsules according to colour so I could be consistent with my future diagnosis. It was called 'Dr Lionel Lockyer's Prescription Chart':

DISEASE	COLOUR/COLOURS
Dermatitis	black and white
Schistosomiasis	red and yellow
Multiple sclerosis	pink and grey
Epilepsy	black and white
Cestodes and trematodes	grey and white
Sickle cell	red and white
Breast cancer	purple
Measles	blue and black
Chickenpox	gold
Heart diseases	red
Bilateral facial oedema	purple and pink
Sties	lavender and white
Conjunctivitis	turquoise and red
Malaria	yellow and black
Diarrhoea	brown and orange
Miasmas	grey and pink
Kwashiorkor	green and gold
Paracoccidioidomycosis	pink
TB	red
Typhus	purple
Yellow fever	yellow
Influenza	white
Dysentery	silver and pink
Mumps	pink and white
Retinoblastoma	black
Parkinson's	blue and white
Alzheimer's	white
Elephantiasis	grey
Endemic goitre	purple

| Gonorrhoea | green and orange |
| Syphilis | cream |

Somehow most of the natives were getting healed and they came for more. Very few died. Bruce would explain the symptoms of the person who needed capsules back in the village, I would look them up in *Manson's Tropical Diseases*, consult my chart and decide what capsules to prescribe. Soon I was making a lot of pocket money from the sunshine pills.

8

Every Sunday afternoon there was a disco at Mulanje Community Hall and that's where my personal accountant, Thokozani, and I would hang out under the sparkling disco ball, with other rude boys, gangsters, villains and creeps, drinking Coca-Cola and exchanging the latest break-dance moves we had seen at the video shows. I never kept the money from the sunshine pills at home to avoid raising suspicion although Dad did wonder if there was a rat in the house gorging at his supplies.

When the DJ announced that there would be a disco-dancing competition I put all the money into having a Michael Jackson leather suit made. I bought a piece of black vinyl and went to see the big-bellied tailor on the veranda of Mr Manyumba's Grocery. They called him Kachembwe, and he was the best tailor in town. He could turn blouses into shirts, shirts into Chinese shirts, skirts into trousers, flies facing left to face right, bell-bottoms into turn-ups, jackets into double-breasted jackets . . . there was no limit to what he could do when sat behind his greasy Singer, pedalling away.

I showed him a magazine clipping of Michael Jackson wearing the 'Billie Jean' leather jacket and asked him to make that for me. He said he would have to charge me extra because he had never worked on that kind of material before. I said there was no problem, as long as the suit was ready by the end of the week. And it was, just in time, albeit leaving his fingers all bangaged up like a mummy.

To finish the outfit, I helped myself to my mother's Jheri curl kit, and bought a pair of black plastic shoes called Gondolas. I would soon find out why they were called Gondolas.

I wanted sunglasses like Michael Jackson had worn at the Grammys and a black fedora like he had in 'Billie Jean', but there was no chance of getting those in the remote district of Mulanje, so I settled for 'geek chic', like Buddy Holly, John Lennon and Woody Allen, which could easily be arranged: I told Dad that I couldn't see anything any more when I read. He sent me to Mr Bimphi, the hospital oculist who sometimes doubled as optometrist. I tried my best to fail the eye test by staring at him blankly and squinting my eyes before the eye chart. He nodded his head thoughtfully and prescribed me some second-hand, thick-rimmed women's glasses because he said the hospital had run out of men's glasses. The glasses crossed my eyes for real and made my nose bone tingle, but I soon got used to them. I looked like a girl in them, but I wore them anyway. It was a very good excuse to adopt the androgynous look, which had fascinated me ever since I read about Akhenaten on the Diptych and I also liked David Bowie. For the fedora, I got a wicker hat from the market and covered it with black glossy paint.

Mulanje Community Hall had no air conditioners but was packed to the hilt. I was sweating profusely in my vinyls before I even took to the dance floor to compete. I went by the name the First Knight of the Order of the Yellow Diamond because the name of the game was to shine at all cost and my style was too hot for the natives to handle.

My 'leather' suit shining and my moonwalk flawless like I was dancing on black ice, I was easily picked out of the crowd for the finals. I had to compete with a guy, Smith Phiri, who called himself H.M. because he said his style showed no mercy to the natives either. He got his moniker from Henry Morton Stanley, the notorious Welsh explorer who, having found the long-disappeared David Livingstone, entered East Africa with 300,000 rounds of ammunition and came out of the mouth of the River Congo in the West without a single bullet left. Like H.M. Stanley, H.M. believed in giving any native who dared to cross his path a good run for his money.

H.M. wore a tight yellow T-shirt, which said 'Brazil' in green, across the chest, and denim hot pants because he couldn't afford trousers. His left ankle was bandaged but I soon realised it was not mere fashion like my bandaged right hand (I was unable to secure a white glove, let alone one studded with diamonds). When he took to the stage to the Ricky James, body-popping and windmilling all over the place, the outer side of his bandaged ankle began to bleed steadily. You could see the red dot getting bigger and bigger with every move he made. Instead of watching his performance the audience and the judges were more fascinated by the red dot on his ankle. By the time he finished the white bandage had turned red. I felt sorry for him and told myself to remember to give him some free capsules for the wound.

I danced to Michael Jackson's 'Billie Jean' whose Motown

25th Anniversary choreography I knew so well I could dance it in reverse. When the opening drum sequence came on, I grabbed my crotch with my bandaged hand and *broke it down*. As I threw my legs this way and that, one of my Gondolas flew off and hit the wall making a black dot on the plaster. I let it pass as a good omen. But to my surprise there was a hole in my sock as well, which was strange because those socks were brand new. To hide the hole, I stood on my toes like the mad Nijinsky on the Diptych. The audience went crazy as I pulled towards the shoe on an invisible rope and put it back on robotic-style. I spun round and threw my hat directly at Thokozani in the audience so he could keep hold of it for me. Throw your hat to any random native in the audience and you could bet that you would never see it again. Moonwalking back to the centre of the stage, I spun round and ended up on my toes once more, sending an electric wave across my arms, up my belly; I wiggled down like jelly . . . I couldn't wait for the song to come to an end though: the vinyl suit was boiling me in my own steaming sweat, which condensed and gathered in my plastic Gondolas together with the water which I had poured on my head to enhance the Jheri curl before coming on. When I finished my routine, it was like I had just stepped out of a Venetian canal. I couldn't wait. I took off the damn Gondolas right there onstage and drained them. The sweat puddle made a little mirror on the surface of the dance floor so that when I took a bow it was like I was bowing down to my own image reflected in the wet patch. The whole house was feeling me and even the judges clapped their hands and they hadn't clapped for H.M., only felt sorry. I was not surprised when Yellow Diamond triumphed as the 1988 Disco Dancing Champion of Mulanje.

9

My glasses seemed to work wonders. At one point I took them to the library and sat at a huge table while reading the *Lord of the Flies*. I wanted to tap into the myth that people who wore glasses were clever but I quickly forgot my intentions as I followed Ralph and Jack around the desert island. Thirty minutes later, when I looked up, I got a fright. The whole table was occupied by a bunch of native kids, open books in front of them, their heads turned towards me, like the disciples at the Last Supper, waiting. The little kid sitting opposite me had his face half drowned to just below his eyes by the huge volume of the *Complete Works of Shakespeare*. He was looking at me like I owed him something.

'What are you looking at?' I asked the kid.

'I want to read,' he said.

'That book is too big for you. Try *The Very Hungry Caterpillar* or something.'

I pointed him to the children's section, but he was not interested. He was staring at my reading glasses enviously.

'Do you want to have a go?'

The kid nodded his head, as the rest of the table raised their hands and screamed, 'Yes!' I told them to be quiet; everybody was going to have a go.

The glasses were too big for the kid. He had to hold them up using his hands as he moved his head side to side across the Shakespeare, feigning to read.

I asked the kid to be kind and pass the glasses around, while I went back to my reading.

Some folks were taking too long to read their *Don Quixotes* with the glasses. Soon there was a fight at the table and we were thrown out of the library for the day.

Getting home from the town centre was always hard as our house was way up the mountain. I had a habit of stopping on this sewage tank for a break, and that's exactly what I did that day. I fished out my *Lord of the Flies* and continued reading. I couldn't put that book down even when I sensed somebody sneaking up on me from behind. When they removed my glasses, I jumped to snatch them back but had to keep cool when I realised it was Polly, one of the hottest chicks in the neighbourhood. She was eighteen, looked like Sade in 'Smooth Operator', and had just finished studying at St Michaels Secondary School in Mangochi.

She put the glasses on and struck a pose for me but before I could say anything she looked straight through me, as if she had seen a ghost. I turned round and there was nothing there, only trees and the wild flowers.

'What's wrong?' I asked.

She didn't say anything.

She took the glasses off, handed them back to me, and ran home, leaving behind a faint smell of her perfume.

Women, who understood them? I shrugged my shoulders and carried on reading my book. A few minutes later, Polly was back at the sewage tank with a neatly folded piece of paper in her hand and said she wanted to read me something if I would let her use my glasses. I handed them over to her quickly as she sat next to me.

'*How to French-kiss,*' she began.

'Huh?' I said, looking over her shoulder.

'*How to French-kiss.* Do you want to learn?'

I nodded my head slowly.

She handed me the paper instead and sat there looking at me with curiosity. I read the instructions in silence trying to follow her spidery but very neat handwriting.

1. Brush your teeth and get a good bath. Be nicely groomed, clean and fresh before meeting the other person. There's nothing worse than kissing the rear end of a garbage truck. 2. Get into a comfortable position – you can't kiss if your back feels like it's gonna break. Suggestion – sit side by side on a comfy sofa. 3. Hold your lover, firmly but gently – don't cause pain. Suggestion would be to hold the shoulders, the neck or gently on the side of the face, one side or both sides.

'You need the glasses?' she interrupted me with her hand on my thigh.

'No, thanks,' I said without looking up. 'They look better on you.'

4. Move your faces closer. Don't bump noses. Suggestion would be the guy angles his face slightly so you don't bump noses. 5. Kiss gently, normal closed-lips kissing, and close your eyes. Closing your eyes increases the sensations you feel, and also sets the mood. 6. Continue kissing gently. Get comfortable with simple closed-lips, lip-to-lip kissing before going anywhere else. 7. If fine till here, tentatively, slowly and lightly draw your tongue across the other person's lips. 8. Chances are from here, the other person may lightly part their lips. If so, slowly explore the other person's tongue in a light licking motion. 9. The tongue has a very sensitive surface, which is why tongue to tongue is the essence of French-kissing. 10. After you've tried lightly licking the other person's tongue, you can try sucking on it, wrestling with it (see

if you can hold it to the floor of their mouth) and other things like that. 11. Explore the other areas of the mouth. Especially the roof of the mouth. Lightly lick or tickle the area with your tongue. 12. Don't bite. Whatever you do, don't bite.

Polly was now laughing at how seriously I was taking the whole thing. I wondered what was so funny, and read on. When I looked up and saw her twinkling eyes I found myself showing her my teeth, like a monkey, ready for action. Step number 1 was a walkover for me: since Claire from Scotland had sent me the big box full of toothbrushes for Christmas, I had brushed my teeth incessantly. I did not know what to do with so many toothbrushes so I used four at a time, two in each hand. My little brother and sisters did the same. I sent Claire a drawing of an effervescing elephant and asked her for some toothpaste but she never replied. Anyway, my teeth were clean and I wanted to French-kiss now, so I grabbed Polly's neck with my hands and kissed her, one eye keeping track of the rest of the instructions on the sewage tank. I wasn't going to be a square again with another girl.

13. Don't swing your tongue round and round like a windmill. Explore lightly, don't drill your way through. 14. Breathe through your nose. Breathe through your nose. I say again, breathe through your nose. 15. Follow so far? You can lightly use your hands too, lightly rubbing the other person. Suggestions, along the waist, along the back, the arms, especially the inside of the arm, the neck, maybe running your fingers through their hair. Again, don't cause pain. 16. Continue kissing.

When I finished kissing and opened my eyes, Polly

breathed out like she had been under water for an eternity. My grip had been a little bit tight but I had done all right she said, catching her breath. I couldn't believe my luck. I was only thirteen years old sitting on a sewage tank, nibbling the neck of a stunning eighteen-year-old girl, who looked like Sade in 'Smooth Operator'.

I was shining.

10

But a couple of weeks later Polly took me to her ex-boyfriend's house at Likhubula Tea Estate to pay for all the kissing I did to her. His name was Julio and his dad was general manager of the estate. Polly told me he was as big a fan of Sun Ra as I was of Michael Jackson. He was a bibliophile too and believed life should be lived like a work of art. His favourite book, *The Picture of Dorian Gray* by Oscar Wilde. Like Polly, he had just finished his secondary school education.

Outside Julio's big house were a couple of kids fighting to blow up a balloon. It looked like the condom which I had wanted to use on Polly a few days before. I had been ready to have sex with her that day. I had shown her my swollen nipple and the gathering pubic hair on my crotch but she just laughed and took my condom, suggesting she kept hold of it for me until I was really grown. I told her she would get hysteria not having sex, maybe even epilepsy, but she did not believe me. She asked me, wasn't I afraid of *penis captivus*? I shouldn't have told her about *penis captivus* but following my excavations in Dad's medical drawers, I knew everything about sex now.

A small boy with a running nose began to cry, saying

he wanted to have a go at blowing up the balloon. Julio's mother came out to put down the fracas. She was shocked when she realised that what the kids were fighting over was in fact a condom. She snatched it away from them and shoved it in her bosom at lightning speed. She then greeted us with a very big smile and led us to the living room.

Julio was dressed like he was about to go out: Jheri curl wet look, pink headband with matching Converse shoes, reflective sunglasses, snow-white baggy shirt, tight blue Levi's jeans, a gold chain and crucifix around his neck. I felt like a native sitting there, looking at my reflection in his glasses. You could understand why Polly was still not over him. Polly talked to him while playing with my hand, trying to make him jealous I thought, but it was me that Julio chose when I unleashed Holyballism on him. He took me to his bedroom, leaving Polly all alone on the sofa, to show me some philosophical writing he had done.

The room was full of posters of girls in luminous bikinis and fancy perms and the bed had a pink bedcover decorated with a green peacock. The shelf was full of glossy magazines and two books, one battered paperback copy of *The Picture of Dorian Gray* and the other one a hardback entitled *Greek Loves*. Beside the bookshelf, a record player and his rare Sun Ra Collection with the apparently handmade record sleeves. There was no other music there, which I found strange for a guy who looked like a disco queen.

'I am an Aesthete: art for art's sake,' he explained, closing the door to reveal a poster of Sun Ra himself, dressed like the Egyptian sun god Ra. *Space is the Place*, the poster said.

'That's a very psychedelic message,' I interjected, pointing at the poster.

'What?'

'Sun Ra's emphasis of space over volume – insightful but ultimately unsustainable. A spacehead can only go so far. The trip eventually leads him to the truth and he has two options then: life or death. The thing is to defy the void and not give in to it. Anyway, as you were saying?'

'I believe that life is the highest form of artistic expression too,' he continued as he hurriedly flicked through his record collection. 'I want to live life with an intensity like that of a blue flame.'

'That's Walter Pater!'

'Yeah, Walter Pater . . .'

There was something fishy about his urgency.

After his patchy yet impassioned introduction to his philosophy, I told him that our philosophies about life were similar, but I did not concur with him that art should not serve any moral purpose. I told him that life was the absolute morality because it is life which has enabled us to be here and discuss these things. But I didn't think he was listening as he put on the record of Sun Ra's *Space is the Place* starting it in the middle.

Sitting next to me on the bed, he suggested we have sex while listening to it. He said it was funky and showed me the pages in the *Greek Loves* book – vases painted with old Greek men performing sexual intercourse on the thighs of young boys: '*Intercrural intercourse* it is called,' he explained. 'David and Jonathan did it too, also Michelangelo, Shakespeare, Arthur Rimbaud, Oscar Wilde, David Bowie and Boy George. *The love that dare not speak its name* is the highest form of love.' I refused his offer because I didn't feel like it and suggested we just sit there and listen to the surrealism of life in the Sun Ra music instead.

'In that case let's listen to *Heliocentric Worlds* instead,' he said and abruptly took off *Space is the Place*.

'So, why are you wearing women's glasses then? A flower in your hair? But I guess that's a stupid question after listening to all the sonic entropy in the Sun Ra. Anything is possible . . .'

'Oh, they ran out of men's glasses at the hospital, and the flower represents the other Holyballist slogan: *No further than the sun*. The way the petals curve in and out of the centre.'

Julio laughed, shaking his head.

'How many of these slogans have you got?'

'Too many perhaps. But I am just trying things out first. There is *Exercise and exorcise*, then *Let us play*, *The Sun is God*, *Set the controls for the heart of the sun*, *Da!*, *Become who you are*, *Choose Life*, *Be here now*, *Follow the Yellow Dwarf*, *Freak out*, *Style is a crystallisation*.'

'Isn't that from Wham!? Choose Life? You know, the T-shirts.'

'Could be. Holyballism is all over the place.'

'You know what, Samson? I am not gay either. I am also just trying things out. I just want to freak out like you – live my life as an experiment like Sun Ra plays his jazz, like Coltrane blows his horn, man. Come on, I thought you said your controls are really set for the heart of the sun.'

'Yeah, but I want to get there with style. I am no kamikaze.'

We found Polly fuming, fiddling with a doily; that was the last time I saw her that summer. She went away to do a secretarial course in Blantyre and then I never heard from her again. Julio went to South Africa to study and settled, recreating himself as a very rich young businessman known by the nickname Dodi. Many years later, in the euphoria of multiparty politics in the aftermath of the Cold War, he came back to Malawi for a while with a pretty Zulu girl. He was fond of riding about in a sky-blue Mercedes with her and waving his pistol around in the bars when drunk. They were shot dead by the police outside the Legends club in Blantyre.

Sleeping in the same bed as my brother was not the

same after the encounter with Julio. I found myself sleeping with two pairs of shorts. When, at the end of the summer holiday, I heard that he had been selected to go to Robert Blake Secondary, the same national boarding school in Dowa where Dad was expelled, I was very relieved. I could finally have the bed all to myself and stop having weird dreams about Greek men.

KAMUZU ACADEMY

1

*I am told that Kamuzu Academy is called the Eton of Africa.
When I return to Britain I shall call Eton the Kamuzu
Academy of England.*
                    Eric Anderson, Headmaster, Eton College, 1984

It was tough to get into Kamuzu Academy: one had to
compete with thousands of students from across the country
for about fifty places that were offered every year. My brother
and sisters, who were all above average pupils, had failed to
get in on two or three attempts. Emily had gone to St Mary's
Secondary School, where she had contracted the TB that
gave her an overheightened sense of her own mortality and
landed her in all kinds of trouble. Lucy was at Lilongwe
Girls' Secondary School, but she hated it there, being a bit
of a tomboy, and preferred to hang out with boys. Joyce was
at Stella Maris Secondary School in Blantyre, which she said
was a creepy place because of the watchman they had for
the girls' dormitories: the old man was able to escort several
girls to different toilets on the outside, all at the same time.
When they reported this to the matron, she had the
watchman called into her house one evening, and still during
that time another exact version of him was back in the hostel

escorting the girls to the lavatories. As for Elson, he warned me not to listen to the hype: he told me that I didn't want to study at Robert Blake Secondary School although it was famed to be one of the best boys' boarding schools in Malawi: the food and the first-year initiations were terrifying. It was a diet of *mgaiwa* and weevil-infested kidney beans every day of the week. The beans were laced with paraffin to stop the boys from wanting girls. Plus, in the first few days of his arrival there, he had slept on the cold floor because somebody kept shitting in his bed and he did not know what to do. I was determined not to go to a school like that. Kamuzu Academy was the place to be.

From 1978 to 1981 Banda had spent £30 million building the school in Mtunthama, Kasungu, on the very spot where he was introduced to reading and writing by the Scottish missionaries. It was to become the first grammar school of its kind in Malawi, modelled on the best of British public schools, his basic rationale being that you are not educated until you have studied Latin and Greek. He had since spent millions more every year to run the school: about one-third of the national education budget. It was Kamuzu Academy's policy under orders from Banda to employ European teachers only, preferably Anglo-Saxons trained at Cambridge or Oxford. 'No natives may teach here!' he had declared when he opened the gates of the school for the first time. The school's objective was to breed future leaders of the country. Everybody went there solely on merit and on full scholarship, no matter what background they were from.

In 1989, it was my turn to have a go at getting into the Academy. I made a drawing of the school, a red-brick Romanesque building, proudly perched on a glassy ornamental lake, like Narcissus, and wrote 'I SHALL SUCCEED' under it. I then resolved to work incredibly hard preparing for the examinations. My favourite study spot during the day was the tall blue gum tree at Mulanje Golf Course, where the rich tea plantation owners played. Every golf ball that zoomed over my head threatening to crack my skull spurred me on to work harder. I never left the golf course until sunset, when it was too hard to read. Then I would go home and study until midnight and in the early hours of the morning.

During that time I made friends with another boy, a Bush Liner who called himself Joe Bugner after the world heavyweight boxing champion. Joe, whose father was well connected in the MCP, boasted of having every paper in the history of Malawian primary school examinations, including those that were still to come. For this reason, he never studied much, but instead spent most of his free time lifting weights and eating *gondolosi*, a wild root that he said increased the size of your penis to bigger than average and made the girl think you were fucking her with your knee. When Joe let me look at some of his Kamuzu Academy past papers, I discovered that somebody must have been playing a joke on Banda: after several years you realised the numeracy and literacy questions were simply recycled or shuffled, so if you studied all the Kamuzu Academy exams ever issued, you had a chance of getting 100 per cent on both exams and looking like you were Einstein . . . But still, you had to be in the top twenty of the most capable pupils in your school to be allowed to sit the examinations at all. And in the year when I sat mine, Kamuzu Academy decided to issue entrance examinations in addition to the normal ones. This would include oral interviews and age verification by birth certificate; too many dubious fish were slipping through the net.

I was chewing *gondolosi* with Joe Bugner when I heard on the radio that I had been selected to go for interviews at Kamuzu Academy. Joe Bugner was so confident that I was going to pass them that he shook my hand and made a congratulatory prediction for me: 'You are the man. In future all that is wrong with the world you will only see on TV,' which was a pretty poignant remark considering that there was no TV in Malawi at the time.

When I got home a party had already started and Dad had bought me new clothes for my interview. They were dark blue Crown flares, a sky-blue checked short-sleeve shirt, and a pair of Bata trainers. I didn't mind the shirt but hated the trousers. When Dad bought you something, it was always according to his taste, which was stuck somewhere between the sixties and the seventies. But the shoes were great; they were called North Star, and they were the hottest Bata trainers on the streets.

I took the Crown trousers to Kachembwe the tailor, who changed them into baggy turn-ups – 1950s gangster-style according to his description. At the market, Mike the barber gave me a Bobby Brown haircut as seen on the cover of his album, *Don't Be Cruel*. I borrowed a necklace from Mum's dressing table to crown it all and I was ready to go.

I was whisked away in an ambulance carrying an epileptic to Queen Elizabeth Hospital in Blantyre and dropped at Wenela bus stop. From there I took the Chimphonda Bus Service to Kasungu. The conductor who came to meet me halfway down the road told me the old banger was faster than the more sleek-looking Stagecoach's Speedlink, which, being a 'government' bus, stopped at every bus stop.

The bus driver's visor was a crude board picture, hung with wire, depicting the most popular theme in Malawian painting: this shows a man, who has just escaped a lion on the ground, perched up a tree which he had been chopping down. He faces an erect black mamba, which is coiled at the end of the branch he is hanging on. The tree is leaning precariously over a river in which a crocodile with the most outrageous teeth awaits him patiently. The look on the man's face, however, is blank – like some wooden mask rather than apprehensive. The caption at the bottom of the painting says DEATH HAS NO ESCAPE. This particular painting, though, had the familiar wrong spelling; it said DEARTH HAS NO ESCAPE, which, thinking about it now, I guess amounted to the same thing.

The Chimphonda left Zalewa Road looking like Noah's ark. We were packed in there with almost every conceivable domesticated animal known to man: a chicken here, a goat there, a basket full of pigeons under the seat, a puppy and a guinea pig, a pig . . . Whenever the bus stopped, everybody looked out of the window, including the heavily breasted woman with the sweaty armpits who kept leaning over me. When I asked her what was happening she said she was keeping an eye on her bag of maize on the roof. 'Half the passengers in here are thieves.'

I held on tightly to my bag.

At one point the bus started going crazy, bouncing all over the place, but nobody looked bothered even though it couldn't have been the potholes. I shouted for help but the people around remained stoic and expressionless. Those who reacted merely looked at me like I was mad. It didn't feel like Noah's ark any more – more like a ship of fools. The painting ahead reminded me, DEARTH HAS NO ESCAPE.

Summoning up some courage I edged over to the driver and told him that I was going to Kamuzu Academy and did not want to die before I got there. But it wasn't the driver at all: it turned out that the driver was teaching the conductor how to drive.

When the conductor heard 'Kamuzu' he jumped with fright, stalling the bus as he tried to brake without changing down the gear. The driver took over from his student while the bus was still moving, without arguing, like he was taking orders from the Life President himself.

When we finally reached Kasungu, the pregnant woman at the back of the bus had given birth to a baby boy. That's how the conductor explained the scuffling passengers anyway.

I was so excited about getting into the KA minibus that I forgot my bag on the Chimphonda. I was left behind at the bus depot to wait for the bus to return the following day. I sat there in the cold, visualising my bag coming back to me intact that very same evening. I also found myself praying to God every now and then, just in case He existed. I needed that bag; all my interview stuff was in it. I needed the new outfit for my confidence, especially the North Stars – they added an extra spring to everything I did. Plus the hospital document obtained from the Paediatric Unit, a dubious graph paper that indicated that I was born on 23 November 1975, which Dad said would do in place of the birth certificate I did not have. What's more I needed to get to KA that very same night, for a good night's sleep before my interviews.

I was just dozing off when I saw what looked like the Chimphonda Bus Service coming back to the depot. I wiped the sleep from my eyes and indeed it was the same bus. There had been an accident halfway to Chamama. The bus mechanic, a giant of a man with his two front teeth missing, had cut off his own thumb while trying to change a flat tyre. The whole bus had come down on it when the jack gave way. Hard luck to him and good luck to me – I took my bag and hopped on the last KA minibus.

The road to Mtunthama was dusty and snaked through the heart of darkness – one mud village after another – for what seemed like for ever before suddenly switching to the smoothest tarmac and the brightest lights I had ever seen. Then we were at a huge arched iron gate manned by armed guards in army fatigues. The gate had the words *Honor Deo et Patriae* emblazoned across it in bronze. It felt like we had reached Neverland.

For the first time in my life, I slept in bed sheets and I felt like a prince. My roommate, who was from a remote village in Chikwawa, took the sheets off and heaped them up on the floor, complaining that they made him feel cold. He preferred the plain blanket which he skilfully wrapped around himself leaving only a tiny hole for his nose. I took his sheets and made my bed even more comfortable. In the middle of the night I woke up to find my roommate standing over me, pillow in hand, looking like a psychotic murderer. He had been trying to put his pillow under my head. He said he couldn't use it any more – it was making him have evil dreams. He slept with his head rested on his arm instead.

The Head Boy who showed us around the dormitories had introduced the bathrooms as *tepidaria* and you soon found out why: they were pure luxury. The water never ran cold in the showers: you would hang in there and sing a whole song, add a 'freakout' at the end and still the hot water kept on coming.

Breakfast was self-service to start with: lots of fruit, milk, rice and corn cereals, croissants, but that was only the Continental breakfast. Their speciality was the full English breakfast that followed, served by men in white uniforms, under the watchful eye of Mrs Saunders, an English chef who stood erect like a porcelain doll beside the high table.

2 Cumberland sausages
2 rashers of smoked bacon
2 eggs
4 mushrooms
1 tomato
Baked beans

2 rounds of bread
Black pudding
2 hash browns
Glass of orange juice
Cup of tea

When I told my roommate from the remote village in Chikwawa, a Seventh-Day Adventist, that the sizzling red meat, called smoked bacon, was actually pig, the abominable beast of Genesareth, into which Jesus Christ our Lord and Saviour had driven a legion of demons somewhere in Mark's Gospel, he pretended to be deaf until he was finished with it. But I did not judge him. We were now in paradise, and folk did not point fingers at each other in paradise.

The Housemaster, Mr Bernard, and the Head Boy, Kizito, who had the cheek to smoke when the teacher was not looking, showed us around the rest of the school. I couldn't figure out how old Kizito was, with a shaven rough chin like that, but he sure was not nineteen. For all I knew he could have been almost as old as Dad. No wonder the school was now demanding birth certificates.

The whole campus was surrounded by sports fields: hockey, football, basketball, tennis, golf, squash, chuckball (nobody has ever heard of it but it was there), an Olympic-size swimming pool, a gymnasium, an amphitheatre, a pavilion . . . you would have thought you were at the Olympics. Kamuzu Academy followed the Roman dictum *mens sana in corpore sano* to the last word.

The library, which was modelled on Washington DC's Library of Congress, had thousands of books spread over several floors in a spiral that ended in a dome decorated with Greek motifs. The centrepiece of the library was a large dictionary on the ground floor, a gift from one Ronald Wilson Reagan, the President of the United States of America.

Beyond the school premises were the staff houses – the Headmaster's looked more like an imperial villa – and the botanical and vegetable gardens under the care of the Chinese botanist, Mr Zheng. The whole 380-acre campus was incessantly irrigated and maintained by support staff in khaki uniforms who crept in and out of the woodwork like the Vietcong seven days a week so that the whole place remained green and pleasant against the scorching African sun all the year round. It is perhaps because of such contrast that Kamuzu Academy has remained the most beautiful place I have ever been on earth.

The written entrance examinations, maths and English comprehension, were a walkover. What was more intriguing was the lunch which had been blessed by the Head Girl in a familiar Latin prayer: roast beef and Yorkshire pudding with gravy, roast potatoes, green beans and carrots, followed by fruit crumble with custard for dessert. My roommate from Chikwawa still did not know how to use the cutlery despite the lesson I had given him during breakfast. He called the knife and fork 'weapons'. The spoon, he called a 'winder'. He stabbed the food and sucked his weapons at every opportunity. He wiped his whole face with the napkin, including his ears. He even blew his nose with it. And he could not stand the dessert; it was too sweet for him, which seemed strange for a guy who had put five sugars in his cup of tea that morning. He tried to mash the dessert up with his winder, but still did not like it, so he just held on to it until the waiter wrestled it away from him.

Come afternoon it was the oral interviews. The three teachers who interviewed me, one of them French, asked me, among other things, what I wanted to be in the future. I replied, a doctor.

'What kind of doctor?' the fat one with teeth like a rabbit asked.

'A real doctor,' I said.

There was laughter across the table and it worked: a few days later I heard on the radio again that I had passed my interviews, the first pupil ever to do so from Njedza Full Primary School. I was shining.

2

We arrived back at KA thinking we owned the place, but it did not take long before we realised that we were only *yaro*, the wretched of the school. First, on the day of our arrival, as our minibus approached the porte cochère of the administration building, there was a boy with a devilish grin on his face standing on the edge of the ornamental lake, who flashed us a piece of A4 paper that said *Arbeit Macht Frei*. Then, after registration, a group of us *yaros* carrying our heavy luggage were walking towards the hostels on the concrete pavement when a tall boy holding a red book on his head steered towards us from the opposite direction and crashed his way through us like a wayward bull whispering, 'Make way for Cardinal Richelieu, you bastards! Make way for the Cardinal!' We reeled, trying to stay on our feet and get back on the pavement as we had been told not to walk on the grass. That's when I braced myself for the teasing and bullying that all first-formers were subjected to at any other boarding school, even here at KA.

KA had six houses named after important people and places in Banda's autobiography: Kapeni, Gomani, Mbelwa, Chilanga, Mtunthama and Chilowa. I was in Mbelwa, which was named after a Ngoni paramount warrior chief from the Northern Region who gave Banda's tribe, the Chewa, a torrid time when they came to the country from South Africa back in the middle of the nineteenth century. Each one of us was given a second-form *avunculus* from the same house who would help us settle into the life of the school. They taught us basic things like how to make our beds and keep the rooms tidy, how to do a tie, polish shoes and so forth. Now I was really worried by the fact that Edmund Salamba, a former classmate of my brother's from back in Thyolo District, had chosen to be my *avunculus*, as the two did not get on very well.

I was right to be worried; the boy had some scores to settle. When I had dropped my bags, Edmund took me to his room and sat me on his bed, telling me to wait there while he looked for his roommate, so he could introduce us.

As soon as he left, two boys wearing sunglasses walked in and closed the curtains. The short one introduced himself as Romulus, the tall one as Remus. I automatically stood up and extended my hand to them saying, 'I am Attila the Hun.' I was ready.

They did not think it was funny and refused to shake my hand. I found myself laughing to calm my nerves.

'What's so funny?' Romulus asked, but he did not wait to hear my reply. When I opened my mouth to speak he slapped me across the face with the back of his hand.

'Fuck!' I said, my head still turned in the direction of the slap, my vision blurred by gathering tears. Still, I managed to see the stars.

Remus unleashed a long hollow laugh on me as Romulus checked that the corridor was clear of teachers. 'Hush, little baby . . . Hush,' he said at the abrupt end of it, pinching my cheek in an affectionate manner, and that's what actually made me cry out loud like a girl.

As soon as Romulus and Remus left the room, a thickset boy holding two fingers to his upper lip goose-stepped in from the corridor door. I wasn't sure whether he was supposed to be impersonating Charlie Chaplin or Adolf Hitler. I soon found out.

'What is your name, kid?' the boy asked me, extending his hand towards me.

'Über,' I replied, wiping my tears with the backs of my hands.

'Über who?'

'Mensch.'

'As in Superman?'

'Yeah.'

'How come?'

'Anybody who survives Malawi deserves to be called Superman.'

'What makes you think you have survived this country?'

'I would like to be a surgeon. You know, carve people up like Leonardo da Vinci, Christiaan Barnard.'

I wasn't pulling his leg. There were a lot of scholarships offered to Kamuzu Academy students from prestigious universities all around the world. If you got top A-level grades at KA, you would find yourself going on to study at Oxford, Cambridge, Harvard, Yale, West Point, Edinburgh and places like that. This was especially true if you wished to study medicine or surgery, for there was no school of medicine or surgery in Malawi at the time, and it was well known that most students who went abroad never returned unless they were crazy or wanted to become politicians. I had indeed made up my mind to be a surgeon and leave the evil little country they called 'Flames'.

'You are speaking too soon, Mengele,' the boy said, placing his hand on my shoulder. 'They weed here, you know that?'

I returned the arm to the boy, eliciting a sarcastic snort from him.

What he said was a fact, though. At Kamuzu Academy you lived in constant fear of being weeded if you were not good enough. If too many Cs, Ds and Es kept popping up in your end-of-term examination results, the next minute they would be sending you to an ordinary secondary school, where you lived on rotten kidney beans laced with paraffin to stop you from wanting girls. But I was not afraid of being weeded, so I just stared at his invisible moustache, wondering what I had got myself into.

'What are you looking at?' the boy asked me.

Without waiting for my answer, he gave me a stinging slap across my face. There was a salty taste in my mouth – my gums were bleeding. When I swallowed the blood my ears popped clear and I heard a chorus of slaps coming from the other rooms. I wondered if that was all they did to *yaros* here – the bastards!

'You like that, huh? *Yaro*,' the boy said, a wry smile on his face, his teeth looking like that of the dog Goofy in the Disney cartoon.

'Say, *Heil Hitler!*'

'*Futue te ipsum!*' I told him, in the only Latin swear expression I knew. It meant 'Go and fuck yourself', according to the Diptych anyway.

'This kid already thinks he's Cicero and he hasn't even conjugated yet.'

With that, the boy dived on me and dragged me from the bed to the floor, WWF fashion. He then stood up and stamped on me with his shiny Bata shoes as if he was mixing mud, hitting my head with nasty little fists that felt like iron hammers. Although I felt an overwhelming urge to spring on my feet and knock those two Goofy teeth out for him, I did not fight back because I did not want to get into any trouble and mess up my dreams like Dad had done at Robert Blake.

When I started crying, the boy told me to shut up and ran out of the room through the garden door.

'The Führer! The Füüührer!' somebody shouted after him from outside.

A moment later Edmund walked in, looking like he had set me up.

'You cannot report this, you know that? A rat is the worst thing you can be around here. Your time will come,' he said, opening the curtains and checking the corridor for teachers.

3

When I went to submit urine and excrement samples as part of a medical check-up, the lab technician was busy doing something else, so he asked me to put my stuff on the table where the rest of the specimens were. It was quite an overwhelming sight, the shit section, and I started to wonder if it was a good idea to study surgery. You could tell everybody dumped their stuff there in a hurry. But the gleaming urine section looked neat. I was intrigued by the girls' piss, particularly a sample by one Caroline Meya, which was as clear as water. It made the rest of the stuff look like bilharzias. I made up my mind to find out about the girl who pissed that kind of stuff. Was she as pretty too?

Then it was off to the tailoring shop for my school uniform. The Dame, Miss Tyler, a tall, skeletal, middle-aged woman with half-moon glasses dug into the bridge of her nose, simply looked me up and down and handed me my outfit: three cream shirts, two pairs of grey trousers, one gold-striped green necktie, a green V-neck jumper and a pair of black saddle shoes for classes; one gold shirt, a green blazer with the KA emblem consisting of the Kachere tree and the words *Honor Deo et Patriae*, green trousers, a pair of black dress shoes and a boater with a green-and-gold band for Sunday church services and other special occasions.

Over one-third of the national education budget and it still looked more like Harrow than Eton. Where were the black tailcoats, waistcoast, false collars, pinstriped trousers, white ties and bow ties that I had seen on the Diptych? Honestly, I didn't like the uniform much. All right, we couldn't be just like Eton, but I would have preferred the jacket to be round rather than have those slits at the back that made us look like pensioners. And how about a woollen waistcoat instead of that silly jumper? I would have liked the shirts to be button-downs on the collar. I needed a pin for the necktie. The boater felt like a piece of wood on top of my head – what happened to bowler hats? The shoes were OK, especially the dressers, but loafers with tassels would still have done a much better job.

When the Dame sent me to get my trousers hemmed, I asked the tailor if he could do me turn-ups instead, and whether he could create four tucks around the waist complemented by belt loops, two on each side of the fly, Chicago Depression gangster style. The tailor laughed, saying that the trousers were British fifties schoolboy style, and I would get used to them.

As for the girls, their class uniforms were grey gymslips that made them look like Catholic nuns. This place was set to make eunuchs of us all.

Then there were the PE uniforms. You could barely walk coming out of that tailoring shop with all those clothes weighing you down.

4

That evening, after the teacher on duty announced 'Lights out!' in the corridors, demons descended on the first-form dormitories. Some boy with a cracked voice announced in the corridors that Mary Leakey would be making a round in search of *Zinjanthropus boisei*, otherwise known as the Nutcracker Man. She had just come across his footprints on the toilet seat in the bathroom, so his sorry bones couldn't be far away. Mary Leakey, a grave-looking skinny boy wearing a khaki skirt and white blouse with thick plastic glasses, made her round excavating; you could hear her turning everything that was in her way upside down along the corridor. *Zinjanthropus boisei* turned out to be that roommate of mine, William Dennis, from Chikwawa. We were permanent *mesho* now. His shoes must have matched the stamp on the toilet seat, but my suspicion was that Mary Leakey just made the guess when she found out that William's surname was English. A lot of kids from the rural areas had Western surnames for some ironic reason. You got folk called Joseph Moffat, Jasmine Michael, Ruth Kennedy and they couldn't tell the difference between an 'r' and an 'l', let alone a toilet seat and a well.

While Mary Leakey had William Dennis carry her piggyback-style to the toilets where she was going to show him how to use the lavatory properly, someone wearing a top hat pulled over his eyes with a conductor's baton stick in his hand, walked in from the garden door and asked me my name. He seemed not to hear my reply. He kept asking me to speak louder, gesturing a fortissimo with his baton stick. I shouted, 'Samson Kambalu!' as loud as I could, he laid himself down to listen to the vibrations of the floor I was standing on but he still couldn't hear me until I woke up the senior students three blocks away, who piled into the room, slapped me across the face, telling me to shut up and go to bed, as if that was within my power.

Soon after William was returned from his business with Mary Leakey, a fat Nubian fellow, his ebony-black skin daubed in Vaseline, burst into our room. He was stark naked except for the red boxing gloves on his hands. The kid was hung like a donkey. He didn't tell us his name, but we soon guessed that he was His Excellency, President for Life, Field Marshal Idi Amin Dada, VC, DSO, MC, Conqueror of the British Empire (CBE) in Africa in General and Uganda in Particular. He chose to box my *mesho* and dragged him out of bed for a match because he was muscular with all the manual work he did back in the remote village in Chikwawa. He wanted me to referee them, which was no problem because I knew all the Jack Broughton rules of pugilism by heart from back in the days when Arthur taught me how to box to get my bouncing ball back. If Dingiswayo had agreed to fight according to the rules, I would surely have won that fight. I reminded the contestants of the rules, hoping that my *mesho* could have a fair fight:

1. No hitting below the belt.
2. No hitting an opponent who is down – on the knees is considered down.
3. Wrestling holds allowed only above the waist.
4. When a fighter has been knocked down, they have thirty seconds to pick themselves up and re-enter the fray. If they fail, or the fighter signals resignation, the fight is over.
5. To prevent disputes, every fighter should have a gentleman to act as umpire, and if the two cannot agree, they should choose a third as referee.

It didn't help. Idi Amin Dada broke every rule. The fight went on for ever, until the whole room reeked of foamy armpit sweat and I was too tired to referee and sneaked into my bed to sleep, leaving them to it.

I was just recovering from Idi Amin's left hook when a trumpet echoed in the corridors, followed by an announcement that the Twelve Caesars would now be making their rounds. The notorious Emperor Nero, a Greek-tragedy mask on his face, went about looking for the blood-sucking Christians, kicking their backsides while squeaking 'Twinkle Twinkle Little Star' on his fiddle. I was the only one who was spared in the whole block because I said I was a Holyballist, a follower of the Yellow Dwarf, the First Knight of the Order of the Yellow Diamond, and Nero kind of liked my religion, because he regarded himself as a work of art too, if I could remember his dying words: '*Qualis artifex pereo!*' But Caligula, perched high on his Incitatus, a miserable long-limbed *yaro* from Room 8 on all fours, did not care who I was. (He emphasised his point with a slap across my face.) I had to wrestle my *mesho* for what seemed like forever for his amusement.

At around 3 a.m., when all was quiet, we were startled awake once more by a procession of banging doors descending on our room from further up the corridor. When it was our turn, the door opened slowly, with a squeak, like in a horror movie. Then a boy with a messy Afro peered into the room, his eyes glinting in the dark. He drew at the huge joint between his fingers and exhaled an explosion of blue marijuana smoke over us. 'Partly cloudy but hazy!' he hissed, and shut the door with the loudest bang he could muster. The atmosphere dropped a notch or two in his wake. My *mesho* from the remote village coughed uncontrollably, fanning the air with a notebook.

I pulled the blanket over my head and rolled over to get some sleep but it was of no use; the drama continued in my dreams.

5

The first-year initiation torment went on intensively for a whole term and was resurrected sporadically throughout the year. There was a serious competition to see who could come up with the most notorious persona. With little space or time to make elaborate guises, what was needed was something minimal or abstract, but effective. Something you could dispose of quickly if a teacher suddenly turned up. But every now and then, depending on the teacher on duty, there were reckless nights like these, when assorted costumes and paraphernalia from the Drama Department, papier-mâché masks from the art studios, and even original *gule wamkulu* masks would appear, making the whole place feel like a Camoquine trip.

It was the presence of these *gule wamkulu* masks that made me suspect that this bizarre practice of initiating the first-formers had probably been brought into the school by members of the Nyau Secret Society from the remote villages. Partly Cloudy But Hazy was really a displaced *gule*, who was making his name known to all *yaro*. My suspicions were confirmed when I encountered other characters such as Keep Off the Grass, a chubby second year who made you walk on the grass when a teacher was round the corner, to land you in trouble. An eccentric name like that could only come from the *dambwe*.

During my six-year stay at Kamuzu Academy, I made a list of some of the intriguing characters that I had encountered

during the initiations in an exercise book that I took home
with me during the holidays to give my family a 'vision' of
the school. Some of the characters like Richelieu, Beethoven
or Keep Off the Grass consciously fashioned their own names
and attitudes, while others like Yahweh, Momus or Tea Bags
got their names from other students because of their obses-
sions and tendencies. I called the list, 'The Kamuzu Academy
First Year Initiation Carnival (1989–1995)':

Zinjanthropus

Aspirin

Diogenes

Crook

Leakey

Trad

You Are Not at a
   Holiday Resort

Venus

Any Questions

Still Life

DJ Zeus

Twisted

Tree

Gulo

Fish

Famine

Mosquito

Beyond the Pale

Void

Louis XIV (The Sun
   King)

Colleague

Untitled

Le Tigre

Warhol

The Lion, the Witch
   and the Wardrobe

Twelve Caesars

BBD

The Aborigine

Recumbent Figure

Momus

Yahweh

The Wright Brothers

St Expidus

Rain Man

Don Juan

Tetzel

Sisyphus

Don't Argue

Policeman

Dotted Line

The Vet

Zulu Nation

Heraclitus

Material Girl

Cow

Easy E

Red Biro

Daedalus

The Führer

Buddha

Churchill

Shakespeare

Pan

Don't Believe the Hype
  of Those People

King

PE

Ten Green Bottles

Mengele

Partly Cloudy But Hazy

Tyson

Walk About

Tuning Fork

The Ten
  Commandments

Roman Nose

Duck

Stephen

Teresa

Spoon

Mellow Yellow

Nimbostratus

Remus and Romulus

Rabbit 10

Rabbit 13

Reserve Bank

Caligula

Perspective Lessons

Peking Man

Mohammed

The Book of Revelation
  and the Monsters
    Therein

Rockefeller

Soldier

Private Property

Mr T

Goblins

The Jesuit

NWA

The Leap

The Moor

The Orange March

Paganini

Seneca

Moon

Salome

General

Thing One

Thing Two

Pliny

Evel Knievel

Dope Man

Near Death Experience

Natural Disasters

The Plains of Abraham

Locust

X

Electric Banana

The Irish Famine

Legwarmers

Electric Cable

The Land Surveyor

Litmus Paper

Picasso

Keep Off the Grass

John

Tea Bags
Tupac
Donne
Main Switch
Diggler
Cantona
Dr Dre
Dr Gonzo
Serial Killer
Firing Squad
Nesta
Mercury
Bean
Anonymous
Black Box
Schwarzenegger
Straight As
Keeping Traditions
Dracula
Idi Amin Dada
Paul Ince
Gazza
Orpheus
Volcano
Dada
Coltrane

Renaissance Man
Vasari (Lives of the
    Artists)
Black Jesus
Julian the Apostate
Spatial Concept
Magnot Line
Wrong Answer
Right Answer
Baboon
Goggle Head
Bokassa
Yellow Man
Rommel
Matchstick Man
Dionysus
Panzer
Remote Control
Richelieu
Bonaparte
MC Hammer
The Surrealists
Koresh
Bird
Nosedive

6

The school week began with an assembly in the auditorium
on Monday mornings at 7 a.m. We were welcomed by the

Senior Master, Mr Wedgewood, who the students called Boisveres. He was a very tall, grey-haired, bespectacled Englishman with an obscene shoe size, trained at Oxford and Makerere. He was married to a Ugandan and had lived in Africa for ever. His skin was turning brown and his face was a red mask.

When Boisveres asked the auditorium to stand up, the Head Girl and the Head Boy marched their way into the hall carrying Kamuzu Academy and Malawi flags. They were followed by a murder of crows; the Headmaster, Mr Oldbury, and his staff – all of them wearing graduation gowns complete with hoods and caps.

Mr Oldbury looked like a chihuahua. When all the teachers had taken their place on the stage behind him, he gave a little bark, and Mr Bridges the music teacher, sitting at the Steinway piano, introduced the first few notes of the school hymn, '*Honor Deo et Patriae*' and we joined in the singing. Mr Bridges with his greying beard resembled John Landis, the director of Michael Jackson's *Thriller*. The hymn had a Latin title but was sung in English and was pasted on the last page of our Anglican hymn books, which I thought was odd, but perhaps a perfect metaphor for the school.

Mr Oldbury's welcoming speech was all about the objectives of Kamuzu Academy and why the school placed emphasis on the classics: if anybody was to develop a sound understanding of the modern world, they would have to study the classics because to speak of culture in the modern world is to speak Greek.

> All the highest forms of artistic production self-consciously look to the classical world for their origin and authority. Modern theatre finds its ideals in the ancient theatre, and traces its defining history back through Roman comedy to Greek tragedy. Opera

began as the attempt to rediscover the power of those ancient theatrical performances. Novels, epics, poetry, all have their ancient parents. Art draws its models from the classical body, and constructs its museums like the classical temples. To be as beautiful as Venus, to enchant like a Siren, to strut like an Adonis, to be as strong as Hercules – these images ground our imagination and our language.

He also explained that democracy, the main feature of every civilised modern state, and 'politics' were Greek inventions. The classical spirit permeated our personal lives: the modern understanding of love, sexuality and even spirituality are all Greek.

He then told us first years that in order to remain at Kamuzu Academy we would have to maintain a certain level of academic excellence. To achieve that level, the first step was to learn not only to speak in English, but also to *think* in it. As Lev Vygotsky's tried and tested theories on the interrelationship of language development and thought had shown, *thinking* in English could only come to us through practice and for this reason the school had a policy that required us to drop our mother tongues and speak in English all the time. By doing that, we had nothing to lose and everything to gain because English was the lingua franca of the modern world due to the military, economic, scientific, political and cultural influence of the British Empire in the eighteenth and nineteenth centuries and that of the USA in the twentieth century. He gave us some statistics to illustrate the capital.

- 650 million people on earth speak English.
- By the end of the millennium over one billion people will speak English.

- Two-thirds of scientists use English.
- English is the language of computers: about 80 per cent of all information stored on computers is in English.
- English is the official language of the Olympics.
- English is transmitted to over 100 million people every day by the five largest broadcasting organisations in the world: the BBC, NBC, ABC, CBS, and CBC.

We finished the assembly with the Malawi national anthem:

> *O God bless our land of Malawi,*
> *Keep it a land of peace.*
> *Put down each and every enemy,*
> *Hunger, disease, envy.*
> *Join together all our hearts as one,*
> *That we be free from fear.*
> *Bless our leader, each and every one,*
> *And Mother Malawi.*

7

Art

G. Pogson, MA (Bath)

W.W. Crosby, BA (McMaster University), MFA (Glasgow School of Art)

J.D. Moggridge, BA (Newcastle), PGDip (Chelsea College of Art)

Art History

E.G. Hunter, BA (Courtauld Institute, London)

Biology

P.A. Kennedy, BA, MEd (Downing College, Cambridge)
P.M. Russell, BSc (Edinburgh), PhD (Queen's University Belfast)
M.T. Dale, BSc (Hull)
T.O. Harris, BSc (London), PhD (Glasgow)

Chemistry

R.C. Croft, MSc, PhD (Kent)
G.A. Tarbet, BSc, CChem, MRSC (Dunelm)
H.P. White, BSc (Imperial College, London)
T.G. Wade, BSc (Leeds)

Classics

J.D. Mackenny, MA (Lady Margaret Hall, Oxford), PhD (University College London)
R.D. Wedgewood, BA (Durham), MA (Makerere University)
T.M. Russell, MA (Corpus Christi College, Cambridge)
M.T. Clatworthy, MA (King's College London)
G.H. Benard, MA (Magdalen College, Oxford)
W.W. Smith, MA (Somerville College, Oxford)
G.U. Owen, BA, MA (Durham)
J.M. Baum, BA (Cambridge), PhD (Durham)

Design

E.J. Fox, BA (Brunel)
T.K. Noble, BSc (Leeds)

Drama

D.B. Bradley, BA (Goldsmiths College, London)

Economics

M.E. Willet, MA (Queens' College, Cambridge)
P.O. Smith, BA (Durham)
H.G. Cooke, MA (Hull)
T.A. Riley, BSc (Reading)

English

D.A. Gently, BA (Durham), MA (Oxford)

J.D. Thomson, BA (Sydney), MEd (New England), PhD (Cambridge)

W.T. Fairweather, BA (Bristol), MEd (Cambridge)

S.S. Sprawnson, BA (Cambridge)

J.A. Williams, BA (Reading), MA (Brunel)

K.D. Holiday, MA (Oxford)

P.E. Hutton, BA (Wales), MA (Canterbury Christ Church University College)

L.N. Mackay, MA (Oxford)

Geography

D.R. Willet, BEd (Loughborough), MA (Jesus College, Cambridge)

A.S. Jenner, MA, FRGS (Aberdeen)

M. Mackay, BSc (St Andrews)

P.J. Thorpe, MA (Peterhouse, Cambridge)

History

H.E. Thorpe, BA (Kent)

D.A.M. Hill, MA, PhD (St Andrews)

T.E. Newling, BA, MSc (University College London)

H.O. Butcher, MA (Merton College, Oxford), MPhil (Pembroke College, Cambridge)

M.L. Simpson, MSc (Univeristy College London)

Home Economics

J. Allen, BSc (Reading)

ICT

F.W. Rice, MA (Pembroke College, Oxford)

Mathematics

R.D. Walker, MA (Canterbury)

B.B. Smith, BEd (London), MEd (Leeds)

T.G. Corfe, BSc, MSc, PhD (Aberystwyth)

I.D. Evans, BBE, BEd (Queensland)

S.E. Barney, BSc (Bristol), PhD (Leeds)

R.S. Tomlinson, BA (Keble College, Oxford)

Modern Languages

H.D. Poulin, MA (Lady Margaret Hall, Oxford)

M.O. Danivet, MA (St Andrews)

D.H. Hutton, MA (Alberta)

T.D. Fournier, BA, MLitt (Université de Paris IV – Sorbonne)

S.I. Facer, MA (Christ Church, Oxford)

A.J. Pelletier, MA (Balliol College, Oxford)

Music

A.D. Bailey, GRSM, FRCO, LRAM, ARCM (Royal College of Music)

J.C. Bridges, BA, BMus (East Anglia)

D.A. Henwood, MA (Trinity College, Cambridge)

Physical Education

G.M. Dale, BEd (Exeter)

T.U. Gently, BSc (Edinburgh)

S.O. Taylor, BEd (Greenwich)

W.J. Harwood, BEd (Sydney)

Physics

J.S. Croft, BSc, PhD (York)

S.A. Spencer, BSc, PhD (University College London)

E.M. Radcliffe, BSc (Warwick)

H.E. Edgar, BSc (Manchester)

Religious Education

Rev. D.G. Oakes, MA (Selwyn College, Cambridge), MA (St Hugh's College, Oxford)

Most of these teachers were raving eccentrics but I guess you had to be out of your mind to teach in Malawi: Dr S.E. Barney was the tall, pencil-thin maths teacher who always wore polka-dot bow ties. His cheeks resembled a pair of fresh milk scones when he came in from Eton College but by the time he was finished with Kamuzu Academy they looked like hot cross buns. Behind his desk he had a poster of a man holding a lever with a caption that said, *Give me a place to stand and I will move the earth. – Archimedes*, which distracted me a lot as I tried to add up my figures. Dr Barney twitched a lot, giving off an air of great intelligence, but maybe he was just stressed. Many of the teachers voiced their inability to come to terms with the surreality of Kamuzu Academy. Mr Walker had a papier-mâché god in his house, a boy with four arms (one of them broken during transportation from England) and an elephant's head. As a Hindu (he looked more like a hippy to me), he believed that God was everywhere; you just had to make a vessel and summon Him to come to lie in it. He gave my classmate, Lameck, a detention when he asked him why he hadn't chosen Pamela Anderson as that divine container instead. After his sojourn at Kamuzu Academy, Mr Walker went to teach and practise his religion in peace in India. He died there, clubbed to death by thugs – or was it *thugees* – which we thought was not surprising; his shiny bald head had looked inviting. A former British Army officer, Mr Clatworthy, the Greek teacher, had the whitest shirts and the shiniest shoes in the school to go with his well-pressed suits, narrow pinned ties and cotton bush hat. He liked to put aside at least five minutes of his lesson to tell Irish jokes: 'Have you heard about the Irishman who tried to blow up a car? He burnt his mouth on the exhaust pipe!' Mr Pogson had the ugliest wife among the teaching staff. So ugly, it rendered her beautiful. She made an excellent model for his Gothic landscapes, which he painted while high on the local cannabis supply. He was said to like hanging around in houses of ill repute on student trips.

The art teacher that followed him, Mr J.D. Moggridge, looked like the mad Nietzsche. He was intriguing company. As he watched you paint he would put some of his outrageous moustache in his mouth and chew on it, thinking of the next comment or tip. He had a Greek wife and made oil paintings of sunlit Greek doors obsessively. When Mr Moggridge was around we wouldn't starve. The young rosy-cheeked brunette, Miss Allen, from the Home Economics Department kept popping into the art room with her cakes, cookies and lemonade. We thought she fancied him, which was very lucky for Mr Moggridge because most young male teachers complained of a lack of females on campus. Miss Allen's vulnerable look (she was too pale to tan) made her attractive but her stunning figure was let down by bland sandals and the oversized cotton dresses that her grandmother had made her for tropical weather. Her legs would have looked fantastic in high heels and fishnets.

Miss Mackay was the flat-chested, anorexic-looking, heavily bespectacled middle-aged woman obsessed with dates as if she was On Kawara. If you forgot to date your work and underline it in red, she would give you a smiling zero with the biggest ears. Green was for the title, purple for the answers, brown for mountains and the contour lines, blue for oceans, rivers and lakes I think, but you couldn't always predict them. There were too many colours to remember from the chart she gave us during the first lesson with her that I had since lost. You spent half the geography period fumbling through your crayon set, your hands shaking, asking around for the right colour. Mr Ngwira, her classroom technician, who was as emaciated as his boss (in his case because of hunger as Kamuzu Academy support staff were paid on Malawian scale), said she needed a boyfriend. I thought geography was the most boring subject in the world. Especially when you had to study Japan.

Dr R.C. Croft, a retired Scottish chemist, shook and rattled a lot; his Parkinson's was far gone. He never came anywhere near the test tubes but his wife made physics fun. There was a wicked sense of humour behind her calm and almost expressionless demeanour. For example, making a bunch of African kids with almost no hair on their heads experiment on the Van de Graaff machine. Mr H.E. Thorpe taught the Second World War with passion – perhaps the reason why there were so many *Führer*s and *Il Duce*s around the school during the first-year initiation carnivals. He was from Manchester, wore double-breasted suits with heavy shoulder pads, looked more like Alex Ferguson than He-Man and coached the Kamuzu Academy First XI, the only team with football boots in Mtunthama. I liked him because while my tutor was busy calling me an idiot, he called me an independent thinker. It was a strange compliment, I thought, to come from the most Machiavellian teacher on campus. Maybe not.

Mr Thorpe was very close to President Banda and was suspected of being his spy among the expats. While other teachers were busy distancing themselves from the hand that fed them, calling the school elitist, exposing the students to seditious literature and subversive political thinking, Mr Thorpe was happy to rub shoulders with Banda's board of governors for the school, advising on future policy. At the end of school terms he would act as the school grand inquisitor, leading a team of teaching staff searching students' bags before leaving campus because lots of school property was going missing; T-shirts, trainers, cutlery . . . I wondered if they had tried to search the starving support staff first, themselves even. This was KA after all. Maybe they did in our absence. Mr Thorpe went on to become the Headmaster of Kamuzu Academy when it was privatised, and received an MBE from the Queen.

The music teacher, Miss Bailey, claimed we could not hear minor notes because Malawian music came only in whole tones and put emphasis on rhythm rather than melody. She had an especially hard time teaching me how to play the piano because I was too jumpy. At first she thought it was because of all the tribal African rhythms imprinted on my psyche, but later on she changed her mind saying I suffered from attention deficit hyperactivity disorder and needed to be put on medication. I took that as a compliment on my ability, so I jumped more. Miss Bailey was an excellent musician. She produced musicals for the school: *Just So Stories*, *The Pirates of Penzance*, *Joseph and the Amazing Technicolor Dreamcoat* . . . I never took part in them, even for laughs, because I thought musicals were too square. But I did enjoy the scenery painting.

Whereas the British teachers were often plump and only cared about their suits and left their hair and shoes boring, the French were trimmer and took care of everything. They looked as if they had just stepped out of an Impressionist painting. Monsieur Poulin wore a boater, multicoloured striped shirts and linen suits and taught in a state-of-the-art French laboratory. He tried hard to hustle the French language and I loved his lessons. We got to listen to music and watch slides of Paris. He would always play Alpha Blondy's song 'I Love Paris' at the end of the lesson, or some intriguing Manu Di Bango. On Wednesdays after school he showed French movies, which everybody loved because they were really sexy. We watched Jean-Paul Belmondo, Alain Delon, Brigitte Bardot, René Adorée, Marcel Marceau and the like, paroxysmic legs under the lecture-theatre tables. But in the end M. Poulin left KA heartbroken. The attaché from the French Embassy who delivered the film reels took his wife away from him. And I did not go on to study French at GCSE level partly because the Beatles did not sing in French. Mr Poulin's replacement, the tall Monsieur Fournier had the tubercular-chic of Chopin. His after-school activity was the Philosophy Club in the VIP lounge outside the Headmaster's office, where he analysed passages from Deleuze and Guattari with forensic rigour. When he first arrived at the school he had introduced himself to us as a descendant of Napoleon Bonaparte, which some of the boys in the class did not buy. The 'not tonight Josephine' did not have a child with Josephine, or did he? But M. Fournier did spark off an air of privilege: he was a graduate of both the École Normale Supérieure and the Sorbonne. Like a true Frenchman, he was a snappy dresser and liked to come to the disco with his English fiancée. He danced well for a white man until you realised that he was a one-trick Don Juan. He had a single dance routine, which he inflicted on his partner over and over again, twisting her this way and that way until the time she collapsed to the floor with exhaustion and they broke up.

Mr A.J. Pelletier was a French-Canadian midget from Quebec, but I suspect when he came to Africa in 1953 as a Catholic priest he found it did not matter. He renounced moribund monkery and popery, ordered himself a pair of suede shoes and a box of cigars from back home, married a Malawian nun and settled. One afternoon while watching his latest tape of ice hockey he confided in me that white women did nothing for him, he preferred black women, which was convenient. He bought a lot of my student artwork and gave me commissions to design posters for his classroom; a great patron of the arts. In all his time at KA Mr Pelletier never gave out a detention and yet all pupils were on their best behaviour in his class. His knowledge of pupil psychology was demonic. His maxim for learning, '*What is wrong must not be written*', I thought a bit harsh.

My favourite teacher was Mrs D.A. Gently. She looked like Princess Diana: nice long legs in short skirts slit at the back to just the right height for the imagination to run wild; buttoned-up blouses, which revealed the outlines of her bra (I think she was 34D, like Princess Di); bouncy golden hair over big blue eyes; speech that vacillated between genius and bubblehead but always red hot. I fell in love with her the first time she walked into the classroom and started writing her love letters, which she was able to read but not follow through. The way I did this was simple: the first thing she had us do at the start of every English lesson was to write in our diaries, which she kept 'secured' for us in her storeroom. She was not supposed to read them but I wondered if Her Royal Highness could resist the temptation of knowing the innermost secrets of an African child. I addressed my diary to her (*Dear Dionne* it said, for that was her first name) and played out all my teenage fantasies on her. Every lesson, I would watch the Princess to see if she had been reading my diary. Mrs Gently always taught while looking in my direction, so I thought she did. Or was my lecherous drool freaking her out? I doubted it. There was definitely something special going on between her and me and I knew it would remain so as long as it remained below the surface. One time, on returning from holidays, I had red nail varnish on my nails. The Princess took me to the storeroom and cleaned it off for me, telling me not to do it again. It was sexy. The incident fire powered my dreams for days. Every holiday, I made sure I came back with nail varnish so she could clean it off for me, and she did so without complaining, our fingers touching. When, after two years, I did badly in my English paper because I could not be bothered to punctuate, she recommended me for the top set anyway before returning to England at the end of her contract. I chose to believe that was a coded message to say she loved me back and that she would miss me too.

8

The owner of the crystalline urine sample turned out to be the pretty daughter of Captain Meya of Air Malawi. One evening after supper, I followed her to the Appian Way, a long pavement that connected the administration building's porte cochère to the dining hall; in between were the classrooms. The Appian Way was the heart of KA after-school social life. Boyfriends and girlfriends would meet in the alleys, holding hands, and whispering stuff into each other's ears. The Appian Way was also partly en route to the girls' hostels and so it was here that hopeful boys hung around to radar and ogle the girls passing by for those few precious minutes before prep time. The lucky ones who managed to get a date would disappear into the shadows with their catch. The frustrated ones, like the boy they called Yellow Man, would perch on top of the arches and sing down to the passing girls, *'I'm a girl watcher, I'm a girl watcher . . . Watchin' girls go by, hey, my my my,'* until the teacher on duty ordered him to climb down from there – *Hoii!* First-form boys were not allowed to watch though, so when the second-formers saw me taking a chance they blocked my way and told me to go back to Subura. The Subura Way was a dark back passage to the boys' hostels, named after a shanty town in Rome where Julius Caesar had languished when he was still a menial.

One Saturday afternoon I managed to get a date with Caroline at the exedra near the Music Department, but I messed up after giving away my intentions too soon. When we sat down, I immediately put my arm over her shoulders and let my arm dangle conveniently over her breast. When she didn't protest I squeezed it. That's when she took a deep breath, removed my hand from her shoulders, placed it back on my lap and stormed off. I couldn't run after her to apologise because I had a big hard-on in my trousers, and for some stupid reason I was wearing my boxer shorts instead of my tightest Y-fronts. But I had other plans to catch Caroline: I would show her what she was missing.

That evening, in the auditorium, there was a school debate entitled 'West is Best' organised by the Head of Classics, Dr Mackenny. I, like the rest of the *yaro*, was reluctantly seated somewhere among the first three rows of the auditorium feeling like a country bumpkin. I had tried to sit at the back when the lights were turned down but the senior students recognised my Bobby Brown haircut and evicted me from the area. Alvin, a cocky guy from Tanzania who moved the motion, wasted no time in showing the house where it was at: he pointed out that to have a debate called 'West is Best' in Africa was laughable because to be born in Africa is to be born a loser, not because of the continent's dire economic and political conditions (these are merely symptoms) but because Africa is the hardest place on earth for humans to thrive.

'Booooooooooh! That's nonsense! Africa is the cradle of mankind!'

'Precisely, ladies and gentlemen, precisely!' Alvin said, taking a piece of paper out of his pocket.

'Booooooooooh! Booooooooooh!'

'Let me finish, ladies and gentlemen. I won't be long. This is a knockout. Since Africa is the cradle of mankind, people living here are also constrained by virulent diseases and debility caused by organisms and parasites that evolved in parallel with the human species.'

'Booooooooooooooh!'

'You guessed right, ladies and gentlemen, everything is much harder to do in Africa and that's why the tyrannical pharaohs were able to rule for so long (bilharzia was rife along the River Nile), why some Africans offered themselves up to the slave traders, why nobody thought of the wheel in this part of the world for thousands of years, why in this day and age the continent has lagged behind in most things that constitute modern civilisation.'

'Boooooooooooh! Boooooooooooh!

When the motion was passed to the floor, I put my hand up right away and the Chairman pointed at me. The auditorium went silent like a ghost was drifting by as I stood up. You could hear the drunken Keep Off the Grass snore in the corner, risking being found out by the teacher on duty.

'Mr Chairman, I would like to ask the house,' I cleared my throat dramatically and turned round to face the audience from my menial seat, 'when you look at Mr Shaka Zulu right there,' I pointed at the guy onstage opposing the motion, who was wearing synthetic leopard skins, 'and compare him to me,' I pulled at my viscose shirt front, and tidied up my collar, 'who is more pleasing to the eye?' With that I struck a pose, raised an eyebrow and sat down. The whole house was in chaos as if I had just declared myself the Messiah: I had become the first *yaro* ever to stand up and ask a question during a debate before the whole school. And I wasn't even asking a question, was I?

That night I got slapped on the way to the hostels and found dog shit in my room, with a note on my desk saying, *Welcome to the West*, signed by the new *gule* on the block: Dog Shit in the Park and Sidewalks, Dog Shit Everywhere. But I did not mind. I was satisfied that Caroline was impressed by my bravery because as Nietzsche said, a woman loves a warrior.

9

The following weekend I approached Caroline again, at the *gigi,* wearing my Michael Jackson leathers. I felt a little bit out of place in there though, because it seemed like everybody else had moved on. It was the second Summer of Love. Acid house, retro psychedelic T-shirts, denim cut-offs, ankle boots and body-popping were all the craze now. Never mind. Some things were timeless and Michael Jackson was still doing his thing with *Bad.* I thought *Bad* was even hotter than *Thriller.* You just had to watch 'The Way You Make Me Feel' and 'Smooth Criminal'.

The house was jumping to Technotronic:

> *Pump up the jam*
> *Pump it up*
> *While your feet are stompin'*
> *And the jam is pumpin'*
> *Look ahead the crowd is jumpin'*
>
> *Pump it up a little more*
> *Get the party going on the dance floor*
> *See cuz that's where the party's at*
> *And you'll find out if you do that*

I was busy gliding across the dance floor this way and that way, pissing off the acid revellers who liked to dance on one spot and leave all the tripping to their minds, when I conveniently bumped into Caroline. She introduced me to her petite friend who looked like Sade in the 'Sweetest Taboo' video and wore the prettiest yellow dress I had ever seen. The Summer of Love was on all right and I must have been bowled over by Sade; all the girls I fancied now looked like her. This one's name was Salama and she was the daughter of the President of Tanzania, Ali Hassan Mwinyi. When I asked Salama to dance that was it. She enjoyed dancing with me the old-fashioned way so much that she never left. Caroline slipped away into the acid ravers, never to talk to me again.

It was going to be like that with any other girl at KA. I would ask them out but they would dump me quickly because each weekend I dissed them to dance with Salama. I not only liked her sophisticated moves, her cinnamon skin and her big brown eyes, but also the glamour of dancing with a president's daughter. In the hostel, I bullshitted the guys that Salama was my girlfriend. The boys were like, 'Nice one, hang in there, you know African politicians, that girl must be loaded with millions.' The truth is that it took a long time for me to fall in love with Salama enough to ask her out. My heart was with Mrs Gently. Besides, I wasn't going to risk it if I didn't mean it. I could not bear to lose her as my dance partner and all the make-believe that came with it.

10

Every Monday afternoon after school was Etiquette with the Dame in the dining-hall gardens. She said you were closer to God in the garden. We would sit there under the shade eating cucumber sandwiches, drinking tea, sweating away while she taught us how to conduct ourselves like true English ladies and gentlemen. She said that the best way to start conversation was to comment on the weather: 'Hot, isn't it?' came the question, and the reply was invariably:

'Indeed it is.' You had always to express agreement. Any contradicting response would be considered rude, which was easy enough in Malawi, because, except for June and July, it was always hot, the sky forever blue.

'The riff-raff call every meal dinner or tea; this is a mistake. In the course of a day you have breakfast (sometimes brunch), lunch, afternoon tea, and supper in the evening. When in a restaurant, what is described as an entrée on the menu is the main course. Do not put your elbows on the table in formal company or during the early part of the meal. Do not start eating until the host has invited you to do so. The napkin is to be laid flat on your lap, not tucked at your neck. With the cutlery always start from the outside in. When there is a selection of knives, the smallest one is the butter knife. Put it on the side plate to your left after use. Hold your cutlery with elegance, like you are pointing at your food. When you eat peas do not scoop them with the fork but flatten and pierce them. Do not speak with food in your mouth. Do not interrupt people when they are trying to speak. Say please and thank you . . .'

One afternoon, I was dragging myself to Etiquette when I heard a familiar hesitant electric guitar riff and a lousy foot drum emanating from the BPR (band practice room). This time I decided to risk a detention by missing Etiquette to find out what the noise was all about.

It was four second-formers who called themselves the Crazy Cops, and they were crazy all right. On vocals and keyboards was Edwin, whom I knew as Maginot Line, or Orpheus. On bass, Simeon (Caligula). The guitarist was Remus – real name, Happy – who, along with his friend Romulus, had given me a good beating in Edmund's room and inflicted further torment under the names Void and Momus. On drums was Peter (Moon, Roman Nose). All of them were learning to play their instruments on the job. I found them struggling through a song called 'Hush Little Baby':

'A major, A, A, oh! E, E major . . . Let's start again A, A, F sharp . . . Damn! Peter, go soft on the drums, I can't hear myself.'

'You are kidding me?'

'Oh, F off. What are the fuckin' lyrics again?'

'*Hush, little baby, don't say a word, Mama's gonna buy you a mockin' bird, If that mockin' bird don't sing, Mama's gonna buy you a diamond ring . . .*'

'OK, OK, let's go.'

'Shit. Wait. I got a blister on my finger.'

These guys thought they were the Beatles or something – I wanted to hook up with them right away. I couldn't play a lick on the guitar but, what the heck, I was home here. Besides, the Diptych said that Keith Richards learnt to play guitar on the job too. He took lessons from Brian Jones and was soon developing the distinctive five-string open-G tuning style that led to 'Honky Tonk Women' and 'Brown Sugar'. And when Keith Moon joined the Who, he had not played drums before, and they had to lock him out of the studio when recording the vocals, because he was very bad at singing. On one recording Pete Townshend can be heard shouting at him, 'I've seen ya!' as he tried to sneak back into the studio to sing. I had also heard that Prince's 'When Doves Cry' had only one chord and I knew at least one chord on the guitar. (Later, when I learnt to play the guitar properly, I realised this was all poetic bullshit, probably cooked up by some overzealous tone-deaf fan. Prince used three chords for that song: A major, G major and E minor.) Then there was the Corsican guitarist, Henry Padovani, who had joined the Police simply because he looked good in sunglasses and leather pants.

When Happy laid down the gleaming Fender Telecaster

to rest his fingers I asked him if I could have a go. I knew he could not refuse me. He regretted bullying me as Remus and Momus. He had always preferred himself as the dreadful but gentle Void anyway.

I laid down an anonymous bar chord on the second fret of the Telecaster. There was a piercing feedback in my amp and Edwin put his hands to his ears, but I did not panic. Feedback was cool. Jimi Hendrix used it as part of his improvisations, like when he did the 'Star-Spangled Banner' at Woodstock while most of the people were leaving. The Edge had just done the same on 'Bullet the Blue Sky'.

I swerved round to face the drummer, killing the feedback along the way, and began to strum a manic, funky rhythm like George Michael's 'Faith'. Then I stepped right up to the microphone like the man in the last verse of Dire Straits' 'Sultans of Swing' and spat, 'I gotta have faith!' into it. The drummer felt the vibe, rolled his tom-toms, cymbals and all and we were jamming, foot drum and hi-hat trying their best to keep up.

I was sweating a deluge when I finished, Edwin still fumbling across his keyboard looking for the chord I had just played. I wiped my sweaty brow and waited for the verdict, clutching the Fender close to my heart like Jeff Beck.

'That was cool, man,' Happy said finally, taking the guitar back.

They let me join the band. They had been looking for a rhythm guitarist anyway. Happy said he could only play single notes like B.B. King. I excused myself when they asked me to help them with 'Hush, Little Baby' telling them I would start next week. (*I had to go and learn how to play the guitar first.*) What kind of music was 'Hush, Little Baby' anyway? Wasn't that a nursery rhyme?

I went into the library and borrowed *The Guitar Handbook* by Ralph Denyer and anything else I could find on rock'n' roll. I wanted to be a guitar hero right away, so, the following nights, instead of conjugating my Greek and updating my Latin vocabulary, I spent my prep time drawing posters of chord shapes, scales, modes, guitar models and guitar heroes for my bedside corkboard. Robert Johnson, who'd sold his soul to the Devil for killer blues on the crossroads of Highway 61. The duck-walking Chuck Berry, who travelled with nothing but his Gibson guitar, confident that any serious rock'n'roll musician knew his music. He was so stingy, he demanded to be paid upfront in cash and always set his concerts to an alarm clock. John Lennon, who the Jive Talker thought gave an artistic edge to the Lennon/McCartney songwriting partnership: Paul was but the Beatles' session musician although he thought 'Penny Lane' and 'Eleanor Rigby' were exceptional and 'Yesterday' . . . I wondered if he would have said the same about Paul if I told him Paul liked to compose his songs in the lavatory. John Lennon had quipped, 'If you want to give rock'n'roll another name you might call it Chuck Berry.' Chuck was rock'n'roll all right, in the original sense of the word. He ended up in big trouble for installing cameras in the ladies' toilets of his club. The hip-thrusting Elvis Presley, who did not strum that guitar, only used it as a prop. Elvis was not the first one to perform 'Hound Dog' though – Willie Mae 'Big Mama' Thornton did it first but because she was black the song never got anywhere beyond the R & B charts. Bob Dylan, who took his name from Dylan Thomas, penned the line *There must be some way out of here, said the joker to the thief* and sang 'Lay Lady Lay'. Jimi Hendrix, who played his Strat upside down and with his teeth when he was on fire. A month before he died from a Vesperax overdose, he mused:

I've turned full circle. I'm right back where I started. I've given this era of music everything but I still sound the same. My music's the same and I can't think of anything to add to it in its present state. When the last American tour finished I just wanted to go away and forget everything. I just wanted to record and see if I could write something. Then I started thinking. Thinking about the future. Thinking that this era of music, sparked off by the Beatles, had come to an end. Something new has to come and Jimi Hendrix will be there.

The main thing that used to bug me was that people wanted too many visual things of me. When I didn't do it, people thought I was being moody, but I can only freak when I feel like doing so. I wanted the music to get across so that the people could just sit back and close their eyes, and know exactly what was going on, without caring a damn what we were doing onstage.

I think I am a better guitarist than I was. I have learnt a lot.

Then there was Pete Townshend, who interrupted concerts with long intros, swung his right arm over his Rickenbacker windmill-style, and always destroyed the set when he was finished with it. He had to play loud because he'd had hearing problems since the time Keith Moon had loaded his drum kit with explosives and set them off behind him on the *Smothers Brothers Comedy Hour*. And he was into this Indian guru who said my name, 'Don't Worry Be Happy'. I thought if I was that guru, I would be worried. Mark Knopfler, who was left-handed but played with his right hand, finger-picking on his Pensa instead of using a plectrum because he was a classically trained guitarist. He was so humble when the band played the pub circuit he would ask the manager to turn the volume down, so that the people chatting in the audience could hear each other. Brian May, an Imperial College dropout, who walked around with pockets full of sixpenny coins that he would use as plectrums. Eric Clapton is God. The Edge and his infinite guitar, and once again John Lennon, who sang 'Come Together' with a lyric that uncannily resembled a line from Chuck Berry's 'You Can't Catch Me' and was sued for it, not by Chuck Berry but some white guy who owned the publishing rights. And Bo Diddley, also known as the Originator because he came up with all that revolutionary rock'n'roll stuff that came in the sixties, even rap – you just had to listen to *Who Do You Love*. When he became the first black person to be invited on *The Ed Sullivan Show* he played the funky 'Bo Diddley' instead of Ernest Jennings Ford's square mining song, 'Sixteen Tons'. Sullivan permanently banned him from the show. But Bo Diddley got screwed too like the rest of them. Everybody was playing his music while he languished in the ghetto, because he hadn't read the small print in his contract. Anyway, I now just wanted to be like the old flattop in 'Come Together'. Free:

> *Here come old flattop he come grooving up slowly*
> *He got joo-joo eyeball he one holy roller*
> *He got hair down to his knee*
> *Got to be a joker he just do what he please*
>
> *He wear no shoeshine he got toe-jam football*
> *He got monkey finger he shoot coca-cola*
> *He say 'I know you, you know me'*
> *One thing I can tell you is you got to be free*
> *Come together right now over me*
>
> *He bag production he got walrus gumboot*
> *He got Ono sideboard he one spinal cracker*

He got feet down below his knee
Hold you in his armchair you can feel his disease
Come together right now over me

He roller-coaster he got early warning
He got muddy water he one mojo filter
He say 'One and one and one is three'
Got to be good-looking 'cause he's so hard to see
Come together right now over me

My dreams of becoming a surgeon went out the window. I was rubbish at maths anyway. I decided I must be dyslexic or something: I always knew how to work out a problem but frequently I would come up with the wrong answer because I wrote down 5 when I meant 2. And the sciences were boring unless you were Einstein; the experiments never worked. It was as if you needed to work in a vacuum to get the right answer and there were hardly any vacuums around. One and one and one is three and that's all I need to know.

But I had to learn how to play the guitar fast, so that Thursday I attended a guitar workshop with the music technician, Mr Lemani, who taught me D and E in addition to the A major I already knew (that anonymous chord I had unleashed on the Crazy Cops). I jammed the chorus of the Rolling Stones' 'Satisfaction' right away.

I can't get no . . . !
I can't get no . . . !
I just can't get no . . . !
I can't get no . . . !

It was hard to do that riff and sing as the same time. But my rhythm sense was good; Mr Lemani couldn't believe I had never played guitar before. He said that I sounded like Syd Barrett on *The Madcap Laughs*. I told him I wanted to sound like Johnny B. Goode to start with.

And, sure enough, by the following Monday I had learnt enough chords to bullshit my way through the Crazy Cops practice session. The first thing I did when they handed me the gleaming Stratocaster was to ask them to forget about 'Hush Little Baby', and go for Bo Diddley's 'Bo Diddley'. In my intensive research I had discovered that 'Bo Diddley' was basically the same song as the traditional British lullaby 'Hush, Little Baby', only funkier. And the most important thing was that the song, like a typical Bo Diddley composition, had only one chord: E major. The emphasis was on rhythm rather than melody. That would surely make everybody's life easier. But Edwin the band-leader was not too sure about my suggestion, saying that we were the Crazy Cops not the Bo Diddleys. I told him that Bo Diddley was Southern Negro slang for 'nothing at all' and that what mattered was the groove, but he didn't buy that and went on to inflict the square 'Hush, Little Baby' on us. Luckily enough everybody was crap – the keyboardist played loudly as if we were the Pet Shop Boys – so that when I was out of key nobody noticed. I was busy trying out all these solos and tritones and nobody heard a lick. All I had to do was take my shirt off, stand there with my gleaming Stratocaster, thumb my bogus chord shapes, and chew gum like I was Sid Vicious.

What I really wanted to play was hot guitar hero stuff, like Jimi Hendrix's 'Hey Joe' and funky numbers by Prince and the New Power Generation, 'Raspberry Beret' and stuff, but you soon realised that they were damn hard – that some chords like C7–5, G9 and G11 you just can't fake. And I should have learnt how to do the splits as a baby in order to do it like Prince. So I settled for Edwin's bizarre compositions and the reggae tunes by Bob Marley, Black Uhuru, the African Bush Doctor and Mutabaruka because they were easier to play somehow, and they made our blistered bassist, Edwin's best friend, happy. He said he was a Rastaman and all you needed to play Rasta songs were three chords – major, dominant and subdominant, a bit of beef with Babylon and you were away chasing those crazy bald heads out of town – preferably while the Greek teacher was passing. 'Redemption Song' was hard to play though and the break in 'I Shot the Sheriff' . . .

But it was not due to lack of talent that I could not get the Crazy Cops to play rock'n'roll and funk like I played their junk. There was hardly enough time to practise and turn those riffs, bends, hammer-ons, pull-offs, power chords, frettappings, bends, vibratos, trills and slides that you knew in your head into music. The KA timetable and curriculum were anti-guitar hero: school was from 7.30 to 15.30; games or activities such as rugby, cricket and etiquette were from 15.30 to 17.00, supper 17.30–18.10, prep 18.30–20.30, lights out was at 21.00 for juniors and 22.00 for seniors, and that was it. Band practice time was thus one and a half hours long, over thirty minutes of which was for setting up the fancy Music Department instruments and tuning up (or more accurately breaking up the strings). There was hardly any time for guitar 'freakouts', to really learn the soul of the instrument: the keyboardist and bandleader Edwin had started the band so he played most of the extended solos.

I was often found in the tepidariums practising after lights out by the first-year initiates or by the overzealous teachers on duty such as Mr Benard, who liked to hang around in the dark, listening, to see if the boys were having sex. I ended up with lots of detentions and was always exhausted. If there was any time to practise at all, it was over the weekends, but this was only if you were willing to make a mess of the never-ending assignments and risk being weeded out from the school. I made myself a dummy guitar in the shape of Django Reinhardt's 1932 Selmer Maccaferri at Craft Design and Technology to practise quietly during prep time, but this drove my *mesho* from the remote village mad: he said he did not give a damn about rock'n'roll, you hear?

There he was crossing the Alps with Hannibal, while I was crossing Abbey Road barefoot with the Beatles. Then I was off to Stockholm, trashing hotel rooms with Jimi Hendrix, getting arrested by the police and thrown into jail. He listened to Cicero making speeches against Cataline in the Capitol, and I supported Bob Dylan on guitar during his first attempt at performing with an electric band at Newport Folk Festival. As the crowd hurled missiles at the stage, accusing Dylan of selling out, he told us to stay put. But waiting in the wings was Pete Seeger brandishing an axe, threatening to chop up the electric cables if we didn't get offstage quick. As my roommate watched the Messenger collapse after delivering news of the victory at Marathon, I was exchanging licks in double-four time with Django Reinhardt in the Bal-Musette, eyeing Frenchwomen getting all hot in the audience. Then I would make a quick exit to Club UFO for a session with the Pink Floyd Sound. Our different worlds would cross and clash, even blows were exchanged, and as we fought, I had a big grin on my face because I pictured myself fighting alongside the Beatles in some dodgy Hamburg club. Keeping your chops together was very hard in that *chambre.*

When I came back to school after holidays, where there were no Fender Stratocasters or DG-10 Acoustics, I had to start all over again, because my hardened fingertips had grown a new layer of skin, not to mention a wrist too stiff for the riffs, solo runs and bar chords.

I skipped Etiquette to practise with the Crazy Cops on Mondays, got detention every week, and spent the precious two hours of Saturday-evening entertainment copying passages from Juvenal and the *Oxford English Dictionary*.

Concert pianists from Germany, ballet dancers from London, jazz dancers from New York, orchestras, Hollywood movies: all came to KA. Then there was the Saturday *gigi*, where the beautiful Salama waited to dance with me. I missed out on most of them but didn't mind. I was always out of detention in time to see the end anyway. I now just wanted to be a guitar hero, so I could one day play guitar at Wembley Stadium – even more so since watching a recording of Live Aid . . . Freddie Mercury, Mark Knopfler, Sting and David Bowie strutting their stuff to the kind of adulation that God could only dream of. I also wanted to sing 'The Man Who Sold the World' and 'Ziggy Stardust'.

I was in detention so often that the Senior Master decided not to mention my name at the Saturday assembly, suspecting I was wallowing in the notoriety. He warned me that if I received another Fatigue (punishment after three detentions), I would be heading home on suspension. That's when I decided no more Crazy Cops and went back to Etiquette.

I took GCSE music in the hope that I would have more time to practise, but it was not to be. Popular music made up only a fraction of the syllabus and I had underestimated how difficult classical music was. Most of my time was spent learning how to play the piano, or transcribing passages from Bach, Beethoven, Mozart, Tchaikovsky, Brahms, Chopin et al. It was like starting to learn to read and write all over again. At the end of it all I only managed a C in my music and a lousy pop demo for my coursework. My overall grades were affected, especially in the sciences where I wasn't a natural, but they were good enough to avoid getting weeded out:

Art	A
English Literature	A
Greek	A
History	A
Latin	A
CDT	B
English	B
Mathematics	C
Music	C
Physics	C

SISERO

The philosopher creates, he does not reflect.
Gilles Deleuze

1

Since moving to Mulanje Dad had been steadily getting rich. I followed the changes each time I returned home during the holidays.

First he got rid of the hospital beds and installed new ones, complete with mosquito nets that had no holes in them. Mum had always smoked the bedrooms with cow-dung coils before we went to bed, but now she used Doom. On top of that, we played outside with mosquito repellent on our skin and, every three months, we each took a dosage of three tablets of Fansidar. Malaria completely disappeared from our house.

Then he bought a new seventies-style sofa set with green-and-yellow-striped upholstery. A dining table, cooker, fridge, microwave oven and a toaster followed. Mum, who had studied home economics in the convent, was now able to put her skills into practice. She bought some new cookery books and made excellent vegetable soups, pizzas, casseroles, lasagnes, curries, fruit salads, fudge cakes, and all kinds of desserts. We went from eating maize porridge for breakfast to Nestlé cereals in semi-skimmed milk from the Malawi Dairy Industries instead of the EEC skimmed-milk powder. Our bread spread was Stork margarine; the smelly EEC butter was banished from the house. Mum now fried her fish and doughnuts in Covo instead of USAID refined vegetable cooking oil. And as a special treat we had Universal Choice Assorted Biscuits for our afternoon tea.

The fruits on the trees around the house – pawpaws, mangos, bananas and date palms – were allowed to ripen because we left them undisturbed. The birds were happy; they were all over the place because the well-fed dogs and cats left them alone.

We had a gardener; the flowers and the lawn thrived. Our house looked like a picture postcard, or, as one friend of mine put it, a picture from a Jehovah's Witnesses tract.

To crown it all, Dad bought a three-in-one Kenwood stereo, which pounded like an earthquake and shattered your ears at full volume. I played all sorts of records on it and danced to the music whenever I could. I choreographed disco routines which I performed at KA variety shows to mesmerised audiences.

Dad's favourite LP at that time was by one Minnie Ripperton, called *Perfect Angel: Adventures in Paradise*. On it was a song called 'Loving You', which he asked me to play for him again and again, as if I were his personal DJ. The lyrics were very unlike his puritan character and they embarrassed everyone, but he did not seem to care.

> *Lovin' you*
> *Is easy cause you're beautiful . . .*
> *Makin' love with you*
> *Is all I want to do . . .*
> *Lovin' you*

Is more than just a dream come true . . .
And everything that I do
Is out of lovin' you . . .

When Mum caught the lyrics and asked why he had turned
into Mr Giovanni Casanova all of a sudden, his reply was a
startled 'Ha? I am a multimillionaire' and a quick walk away
from the stereo like he was hiding something. Where was
Dad getting his money? Everybody knew civil servants got
paid starvation wages. From experience, I knew there were
two possible explanations: either there was a shortage of
medicine or a record number of people were getting sick.
It turned out to be the latter.

2

By the time I was in third form, Emily had found a boyfriend
at the clubs whom she intended to marry. Dad organised a
lavish wedding ceremony for her, which I had problems with.
I had never liked weddings. They were too embarrassing. A
boy and a girl holding hands and all these grown-ups clapping hands and ululating at them, thinking they were going
to have sex. I planned to avoid my own wedding day when
I grew up. I dreamt of just waking up in a hotel room with
my wife, somewhere far away from the parents, on honeymoon, the bedside table strewn with wedding photos. In the
pictures my bride would be all in white, holding an armful
of roses, and I would be wearing a top hat, holding the Holy
Ball under my arm, and that would be us done. I therefore
spent most of my sister's wedding party hidden away in my

bedroom reading *The Catcher in the Rye* and watching Dad through the keyhole as he met all these mysterious people in the living room one by one, as if he were the Godfather. They turned out to be wealthy businessmen, top politicians and civil servants looking for back-door remedies for various maladies they had. Dad administered medicine to them in return for the generous gifts they had made to his daughter on her wedding.

A cough syrup for the General Manager of Chimbiya Tea Estate. Big white tablets for the District Education Officer's diarrhoea. Yellow and red capsules for the District Commissioner, who had just suffered from a stroke. His mouth was twisted into a slanted O, and he was no longer able to move his left arm.

Mr Ndalema, of Khama Langa Transport, walked in with a slight limp. He had just recovered from shingles. There were white patches of skin running from his cheek all the way down to his back. But he now had swollen lymph glands in his groin, armpits and behind his ears. Dad gave him blue jelly tablets for that, one jelly a day for the next two weeks and those glands would shrivel and disappear without a trace.

There was a white coating and a lump on the tongue of the Right Honourable Lembani, the Malawi Congress Party MP for Mulanje Central, and he had a speech to make on Monday.

Mrs Dama, the widowed owner of Oriental Express Minibuses, was worried because her baby daughter did not cry any more.

I had a slight headache and needed some aspirins.

Why was everybody sick all of a sudden?

The woman of the mountain, Mama wa Chifufu, was still picking her flowers, but she was now skeletal-thin, had a terrible skin rash on her chest, and coughed like she had consumption. Her rendition of 'Ring a Ring o' Roses' was barely a whisper. Still, we kept seeing dodgy-looking men lurking near her glade.

Manyumba, the grocer, closed his retail shop and opened a coffin workshop instead. He said there was more money in coffins.

Kachembwe, the tailor, had moved on; nobody knew where. Some said to Mozambique, which was a shame, because I had all this new fabric and I wanted him to design a costume for my new variety-show performance at school.

When Emily's groom finally turned up, he was wearing dark glasses like a gangster. He said he had trachoma; his eyes itched and were red from all the scratching, so the minister excused him.

When Dad had walked the last guest to the door, and turned round to declare himself a 'multimillionaire', I cringed because nobody in the house was laughing at that affirmation any more.

3

After taking my GCSEs in the summer of 1993, I went home to find Dad had bought a brand-new VW Golf. He decided to teach Mum how to drive and she was a natural, but something weird happened as soon as she learnt how to control the car on her own: she headed straight towards an acacia tree and smashed the car. Dad thought she had done it deliberately and he was furious. The following day, while phoning around for a panel beater, he had a swollen upper lip as if he was the one who'd had been in the accident. It was a food allergy, something he had never had before. Little did we know that his days in paradise were coming to an end.

My love of playing music totally extinguished by the unyielding ledger lines, lack of practice time and regular access to a guitar (there was no music shop in Malawi), I turned to art where I got an A for my GCSE without even trying. I now wanted to be an artist when I was finished with my studies. I kept thinking of the drawing Jimi Hendrix made of Elvis Presley after watching him live in concert. I realised that most of my guitar heroes were former art students anyway: John Lennon came from Liverpool Art College; Keith Richards dropped out of Sidcup Art College before meeting Mick Jagger from the London School of Economics to form the Rolling Stones. Pete Townshend studied at Ealing Art College where he met John Entwistle to form a skiffle band that led to The Who. In fact, his guitar-smashing performances were inspired by his former art teacher, Gustav Metzger, whose auto-destructive art was based on the concept that every idea had an agent within itself which caused it to self-destruct. David Gilmour and Syd Barrett met at Cambridgeshire College of Arts and Technology. Clapton studied stained-glass-window designs at Kingston Art School. Kurt Cobain . . . Art was just the other side of the same coin. Besides, artists were now also becoming big stars while they lived: Andy Warhol, Julian Schnabel, Jean-Michel Basquiat, David Hockney, Peter Blake, Jeff Koons . . .

In my art class there was a boy who signed all his work, 'Fredson the Young Artist'. He kept getting the art prize. His work improved faster than the rest of us although he did not seem to work harder. I thought he had natural talent but discovered his secret after I made friends with him to improve my painting and drawing skills. Fredson was a secret bohemian and his god was the French midget artist Henri de Toulouse-Lautrec because he had a big penis and slept with the most beautiful women in Paris. He had a picture of 'the prick on paws' on his corkboard. Fredson's girlfriend was a flat-chested nymphomaniac from outside the campus, the daughter of a policeman. She had short hair and dressed like a boy, playing it so cool people thought she was a KA student. Fredson, of course, called her Le Melinite (The Explosive), after the working name of Lautrec's fling, Jane Avril, who worked as a cancan dancer at the Moulin Rouge. After lights out, he would sneak her in over the school walls to have sex with him. On Sundays, when the school timetable slackened, you could find them in bed together all day, talking and laughing, the room, which he called Le Rat Mort (The Dead Rat), smelling of sex. Fredson made numerous nude drawings of her for his own private use. Thus while the rest of us were busy going through *The Story of Art* by E.H. Gombrich, hopping from one style to another, being jacks of all trades but masters of none, Fredson's single obsession with Jane Avril's wafer-thin figure unwittingly advanced his technique.

Fredson proved what I had suspected all along from looking at art books: you could never become a great artist without studying the nude, the female nude in particular. Ingres did it, Picasso did it, Degas did it, Dali did it, now I was going to do it – and get the art prize at the next Speech Day. I had been trying hard for years to get the music prize, but it had always eluded me because there was a boy in our class called Luke who kept beating me to it. Luke did not care much for music, said he wanted to be a computer scientist, but God had blessed him with perfect pitch anyway. He could transcribe the hardest concertos (including those of Niccolò Paganini) perfectly, and he had been studying music for just three years. His choice of instrument was the flute, which he said he had learnt to play just so he could initiate the first-formers as Pan, the Greek god of hunting and rustic music.

I was determined to get the prize right from the beginning with my A-level art, but I was not going to be sneaking in dusky maidens from the support staff villages to model for me like Fredson the Young Artist. That was just too risky. You could get expelled from school for that. I had a better plan to see naked girls without compromising myself.

Fredson told me that the best part of being initiated into the Gule Wamkulu was that when you wore the mask you were allowed to watch the women bathe at the river. It was blasphemous for them to cover themselves up when an ancestral spirit only wanted to watch for a little bit. Dad's home village of Misi in Dowa had a strong masking tradition, and I figured that if I allowed myself to be initiated like Fredson, I could spend a couple of weeks drawing the women at their toilet by the river, like Degas. And so, in the middle of that awkward summer holiday brought about by the smashed VW Golf, I left home early for Dowa where I hoped to study the nude.

4

Gule Wamkulu, which literally means the 'Great Dance', is a Chewa masquerading tradition employed by those who have 'bought the Path' into the Nyau brotherhood, an ancient secret society for males. The brotherhood was possibly formed to address the imbalance of power between men and women when the Chewa was still a matrilineal society.

When a Nyau initiate puts on the *gule* or 'mask' he becomes the law and ultimately the meaning of life itself – the 'Great Dance'. Whatever he does in that state is infallible, whether good or bad. It is beyond good and evil. Gule Wamkulu thus offered a breather to the Chewa men who were marginalised in everyday life by their in-laws, as well as a sense of solidarity with one another.

However, since the Chewa converted to Christianity, the men turned into anachronistic Victorian 'gentlemen of leisure' and the women, to something resembling slaves, Gule Wamkulu has become confused as the men have held on to it for various reasons, some of them akin to my desire to study the nude. It would make more sense if the women took over what has survived of the tradition, since they are now in most cases the marginalised group. As I reached Misi Village and my relatives for the first time in several years, the women got out of my way, kneeling and greeting me from the bushes, because I was a man. Furthermore, it was the women tilling in the hard maize fields in the scorching sun, gathering the firewood in the forest with babies on their backs, doing the laundry at the river and drawing water at the wells . . . Where were the men? They were seated under the trees, philosophising, drinking beer, discussing the current affairs of the village. They were polishing their Bibles and their shoes getting ready for church. They were busy terrorising the neighbourhood with *gule*.

Nearing my destination, I was stopped by three stocky boys wearing worn-out hot pants and soiled Bermudas. They wanted to know if I had bought the Path. It was a hard life living in a Chewa village if you hadn't bought the Path and this is one reason it had taken me this long to visit Misi Village again. But now I was ready.

'Where do the animals come from?' one of the young men asked me.

I had no idea where the animals came from in this village, but I decided to take a chance, and answered, 'From the river.'

It was the wrong answer. The boys looked at each other, laughing, shaking their heads. Another one tried again.

'Where do the animals rest?'

The bag on my shoulders was killing me. I just looked at him grinning and waited to see what would happen next.

The boy put his fingers on his lips, blowing a whistle.

'Guleyo! Guleyo! Khwiyo, Guleyo!' he called. A crippled gule with a long red face and outrageous sideburns, wearing a suit made of sacks complete with a white shirt and red tie, limped on to the road from the nearby bushes. I recognised the gule right away: its name was Simoni, after Simon Peter, and it was based on the Victorian Presbyterian Gentleman. Everybody knew Simoni well because it was one of the many masks popular in MCP propaganda. Simoni marked the arrival of the missionaries in Malawi and represented the Christian Church. The MCP used it to scare people out of the houses to go to political meetings and to sing praises about Life President Dr Hastings Kamuzu Banda. Now, if the Church and an Englishman praised you, you had to be a really good man.

Simoni rushed at me with his flywhisk while the boys cheered him on. 'Guleyo, khwiyo, Guleyo!' I spun round and ran for my life down the road, the gule limping close behind me.

When he grabbed hold of me, I told him between breaths that I had come a long way to visit my uncle Bizieli. The gule suddenly let go, the yellow eyes in the mask's mouth lighting up. He gestured to his entourage to come over and they in turn spoke to me:

'What is your name?'

'Kondwani, Kondwani Kambalu.'

Not able to contain himself any more the mask spoke to me directly, possibly breaking hundreds of years of tradition.

A *gule* was not supposed to have direct conversations with human beings.

'Are you the Kambalu at Kamuzu Academy?'

When I said yes, the *gule* screamed '*Aii!*', took off its mask, sackcloths and all, and dropped them to the ground to expose my long-time-no-see cousin, Gilbert, in denim hot pants. I should have guessed from the beginning that he was the wearer of the mask with that limp; as a child he had suffered from polio which left his right leg slightly shorter.

Gilbert, now a sweaty, muscular young man who made me think of Okwonkwo in Achebe's *Things Fall Apart*, put me on his shoulders, lifted my bag with his right hand, and limped with me towards the village with his crew like I was a returning wrestling hero. He left his mask lying right there on the road.

'You have left your things behind,' I told him.

'What things?'

'The animal.'

'Oh. Don't worry about it. It's nothing.'

I supposed so. Of what use was a mask to a cripple?

My grandparents were long dead; the family showed me their unmarked graves. My uncle Bizieli and my aunts, who had never made it to the city, were still there looking like crude wooden representations of my father. They killed a couple of chickens for my dinner and, later that evening, we sat around the fire to talk but they didn't say much in my presence, only introduced me to the neighbours who came into the house one by one, stared at me in awe through the smoke before walking out again.

I slept in my father's unfinished fired-brick house: the only one of its kind in the neighbourhood. He had been struggling to finish the house for years. It had a tin roof, which sang like a banshee when the wind blew. The windows and doors were made of grass.

The following morning at breakfast I asked Gilbert if I could buy the Path.

'What would you need *gule* for? You are the chief of the village now, greater than the Path.'

'Oh, cut the bullshit. I don't even have A levels yet.'

'A levels?'

'Don't worry. I want to know something about women.'

'I see. So you want a girl. None of the girls here are of your standard. Shouldn't you be going out with white women by now?'

'I wouldn't know what to do with them.'

'You're kidding me.'

'I am not kidding you.'

'You wouldn't know what to do with a woman?'

'No.'

'Don't they teach you about that at the Academy?'

'They do but only in diagrams.'

I took out the little Leonardo da Vinci textbook from my bag and showed him some reproduction drawings. He regarded them this way and that way, then fell on his back in a fit of laughter, hands on his six-pack, feet in the air, like a giant cockroach. When he sat up again, his shorter leg spilt the maize porridge.

'That is not a woman,' he said. 'You really do need to buy the Path then.'

5

The *dambwe* was a collection of grass shelters in the middle of the graveyard where they had buried my grandparents.

In the afternoon, Gilbert, who was going to be my *phungu*, took me there blindfolded. We were welcomed into the fold of the fresh initiates with thunderous drumming and a bunch of toothless elders singing:

> *Mwana alirayo abwere adzaone, yeee!*
> *Mwana alirayo adzaone chinyama, yeee!*

We were stripped naked, bathed in ash and mud, then we sat up listening to *gule wamkulu* jive. I was too hungry to take anything in. For bed, we were packed in a grass shelter like sardines. We had to shift sleeping positions simultaneously under the command of some *phungu* who shouted, '*Titembenuke!*' when it was time to do so. At dawn, a mortar drum announced the arrival of Gutende, a sadistic *gule* who was going to teach us *mdulo*, all we needed to know about life. He wore a big, black wooden face that had two long antelope horns on top. He destroyed our shelter with his horns.

'*Who wants my horns? Who wants my horns?*' he sang in a Barry Gibb falsetto as he woke us up with a crack of his leather whip.

'*Nobody, keep them for yourself!*' the *phungus*, watching from a distance, sang back at him.

Gutende whipped us into a procession and took us down to the river for a bath. The water was ice-cold. Our penises and scrotums shrunk to nothing. Gutende mocked us, recommending *fulang'onga* right away: one of his assistants, a toothless old man, took a sisal string and skilfully connected our scrotums with it making a circle. Gutende, standing in the middle of the circle, then whipped us into opposite directions to demonic drum beating, shrieking and ecstastic singing from the *phungus*:

Gayile zimbe! Gayile zimbe!
Ayi ạyi nchimbowa!

If Fredson the Young Artist had told me about *fulang'onga*
I wouldn't have gone there to buy the Path. But there was
nothing I could do now except cry and hope for the best; I
pulled the string towards me to ease the pain, hurting the
two boys next to me, and the same pattern was repeated
around the circle until everything turned into comedy for a
brief moment. Then one boy cried out like an animal and
was loose from the circle. His balls and penis fell on the big
rock. They carried him away, drowning the horror with more
drums and singing. The lump of human testicles on the rock
fired everybody into a frenzy and, in no time, we were *animals*.

Gutende's sex education was downright weird. He taught
it in riddles:

Do not eat grasshopper, meat without taste.
Do not take your father's penis and put it on the top
shelf.
Children, I am going to the funeral, don't play with
each other.
There is a dead body in the house . . .

I never bothered to ask my *phungu* to translate because whenever he talked straight, I was convinced that it was all bullshit:

Do not sleep with your wife when your daughter is
having her first menstruation.
A menstruating woman should not be allowed to put
salt in the food she is cooking for her family.
Don't sleep with a woman when she has gone to the
moon.

His ideas for foreplay were equally bizarre:

Pull the woman's labia before you sleep with her.
Let her pull your balls before she sleeps with you.
Sleep in a woman's vagina whenever you can after
making love at night. It keeps the children strong.

Anyway, after it all Gutende took off his mask and
revealed himself to be the village headman. Then he showed
us how to make our own masks and choreograph around
them. He told me that a mask is not only the thing you
cover your face with, but the whole outfit, including the
paraphernalia and the music that goes with it. And that the
mask is not a *representation* of a spirit, it *is* the spirit. That
cheered me up a bit; I wondered if I should have paid more
attention to all his jive. This guy's refusal of metaphysical
distancing sounded as if he had spent the night before with
the Jive Talker. I felt revitalised and approached my chosen
mask with outrageous enthusiasm.

When the masks were ready, and the Gule Wamkulu
steps mastered, we were taken to the *bwalo* for our debut
performances. The village headman sat on a stool under a
mango tree flanked by a rosy-cheeked anthropologist with
an Apple laptop on his lap. I wondered if it was he who had
been influencing the village headman's jive after all. As we
appeared in the arena one by one, the village headman spoke
to him and he typed frantic notes into his computer. Every
now and then he would also take a picture, which really
excited the new *gule* and sent the accompanying singers and
drummers wild.

The first to dance was Maliya (Mary). He wore a blue
dress, a white scarf around his head and red beads around
his waist and neck, which he showed off while dancing. The
body of Mbiyazodooka (Broken Pots) was covered in mud.

He wore nothing but a makeshift black balaclava and rags around his waist. On his head, supported by one hand, was a fragment of a broken earthenware pot. Mbiyazodooka was a zombie on his way to the spirit world and he needed help to get there. So when he took to the floor he pitifully begged in his song, *'Give me a goat, beer, a chicken, and do the great dance for me.'* The onlookers threw coins into his pot and sang back to him, *'Go back to your home at the grave.'* Kabvizanza (Tramp) wore a raffia Charlie Chaplin suit with sisal frills around his waist and danced with a live snake in his hands, which freaked out the whole *dambwe*. Demu (Dame) was a very camp *gule*. He wore a round, black wooden mask and sang women's songs shaking his bottom to the beat. As he finished, the village headman recommended that he be given a new *chitenje* to calm him down. And then it was my turn.

I was Sisero, the towering *gule* leaning against the tree, prodding about impatiently as I waited for my go, because those fancy wooden stilts were killing my feet. I based my mask on the Roman orator Cicero and the mad Nietzsche. I was the spirit of a progressive native who had read too many books and had gone slightly berserk. On top of the awkward wooden stilts, which were covered by a nineteenth-century-style double-breasted tail suit made of sackcloth, I had a pink wooden head, which had tiny ears and bulging eyes like a hippo. An outrageous moustache covered the mouth completely, which sometimes made it difficult to see where I was going. I carried with me a red copy of Herodotus' *The Histories* in my left hand and a little wooden hammer in the right for destroying idols. Perhaps the mask could have done without the inconvenient stilts but I was afraid of catching jiggers again. Everyone had to dance barefoot.

I gently grooved to the rhythm on to the *bwalo*, spitting about obscene Latin expressions at the onlookers in a

Prince-like falsetto: to the village headman, *'Quin futuis uxorem tuam foedam?'*; to the audience, *'Mande merdam et morere! Mande merdam et morere!'*; and to the anthropologist, *'Suge meum aquaeduct.'* I noticed at the other end of the arena a man in a polyester suit reading from a shiny black Bible, denouncing the Gule Wamkulu performance as the work of the Devil. He had a phoney American accent and, though he looked Malawian to me, he spoke through a translator. He also had with him a choir of singers who tried to drown out the Gule Wamkulu music with choruses. I tried to scare him off the arena with my hammer and height, squealing *'Te rogo ut futuas te ipsum! Te rogo ut futuas te ipsum!'* His entourage fled, but he didn't budge. Only when I came right up to him did I realise he was blind. I left him alone and slowly grooved back to the centre of the *bwalo* to finish my routine.

I did all sorts of mad things with Sisero and nobody could touch me because I was, by definition, beyond good and evil. Like any *gule* I had a crew of strong young men who accompanied me everywhere just in case somebody out there questioned my infallibility and tried to knock me off my stilts. I plodded around with my crayons writing graffiti on mud huts, most of it in Greek. I hurled some more insults in Latin at the people, especially the elders of the village, and I disrupted their meetings, *'Merae fabulae sunt, et eas esse tales scis! Merae fabulae sunt!'* I sneaked up to the mud huts and whispered to the unsuspecting natives sleeping in there, *'The horror! The horror!'* like Kurtz in *Apocalypse Now.* I played drums with my little hammer, smashing them up like Keith Moon. I kicked over beer drums from the fireplace. I drove witch doctors from the market, tipping over their medicine gourds. My crew infiltrated a local church service once and stole the pulpit while the minister was preaching from it. We exchanged blows with members of the congregation before we managed to get away. The crew had to carry me off because it was difficult to run away in those stilts.

Most of my time, though, was spent at the river, doing what I had really bought the Path for, studying the nude. I would sit quietly for hours on the rock where the boy had lost his testicles (his bloodstains were still there) like a cubist sculpture, making pastel sketches of the voluptuous dusky maidens washing below. The girls did not seem to mind. In fact they loved it: a new ancestral river spirit called Sisero was watching over them.

But it was not long before I began to suspect this was not the case. The truth is that they probably just felt safe enough to play striptease with the ancestral spirit because of my awkward wooden stilts. They knew I couldn't catch a duck in them. Whenever the other *gule* with human legs tried to join me on the rock to watch, the maidens dressed up quickly and scuttled away politely.

Before leaving the *dambwe*, the village headman revealed to us one more secret as we were having our heads shaved: that the lump of human testicles on the rock was just a trick to fire us up. He said that they were actually a goat's testicles.

I started my A levels as a master draughtsman.

6

Banda's fall began when Pope John Paul II visited Malawi in April 1989 and denounced his human rights record before the Catholic bishops. They in turn wrote an anti-MCP pastoral letter, which was read in churches in March 1992. Then the West called Banda a dictator, and ordered him to introduce democracy immediately. When he protested, they cut aid to the country. Strikes followed as workers across the land demanded better pay and working conditions. Within the same year, Banda reluctantly announced a referendum for multiparty democracy and in the following year he lost it. The Decency in Dress Act of 1971 was revoked: women were allowed to wear trousers and minidresses, and second-hand clothes flooded in from overseas putting the local textile industry out of business. Dreadlocked Rastafarians were allowed into the country to see the Emperor's View in Zomba. The South African lesbian singer P.J. Powers gave a concert in Blantyre. The market was liberalised; chicken eggs were imported from South Africa, street vendors swarmed the streets, shanty towns mushroomed around the cities.

Amid the chaos of political change, Banda came to Kamuzu Academy for his last official Founder's Day celebration. By this time I had kicked Fredson the Young Artist off the top spot in art and I was asked to man the school art exhibition in the administration building.

That's how I met Dr Hastings Kamuzu Banda.

Something strange happened the night before his visit. The concrete ceiling around the reception area came down on the exhibits and the maintenance department had to work in total panic through the night to fix it. But what really fascinated me about the president's visit was his bodyguards. They walked in wearing dark suits and tinted glasses and did a clean, systematic security sweep of the area, adjusting their earpieces, talking into their sleeves and then vacating the room again, all within seconds. Before I worked out what was happening, Banda and his 'official hostess', Mama Kadzamira, were shaking my hand, and I was telling the two about the artwork.

While I was sitting my A levels, Banda had lost Malawi's

first multiparty election to Bakili Muluzi of the United Democratic Front (UDF). Normal funding for the school was cut and half the school was sent home to ordinary secondary schools where they would eat rotten kidney beans laced with paraffin. A third of the staff were made redundant and those who stayed took a 20 per cent pay cut. GCSE pupils were going to be allowed to go to university straight away without A levels but, unlike those of us who were doing A levels, they would start as first years. We would start as second years. We had a new headmaster now: Mr Hill. The previous one, Mr Baker, had fled the country under pressure from his French wife.

My dreams of studying art abroad, at the Royal College of Art or the Chicago Institute of the Arts, were crushed as KA's monopoly on international scholarships was revoked. What was I going to do? Study at the University of Malawi? They hated us there, because Banda had said that none of the Malawian lecturers had been fit enough to teach at KA. And now they *were* fit to teach us all of a sudden? I wouldn't be able to look them in the eye. Chancellor College had a fine-art course, but the studios had no paints or brushes, so they focused almost exclusively on clay and soapstone sculptures. Malawi was perhaps the only country in the world without an art shop. I wanted to do some contemporary multimedia work, you know, like a urinal signed R. Mutt 1914, a bottle dryer, a leap into the void, a line of bricks on the floor, a can of the artist's shit on a plinth, a blue canvas, a red canvas, a white canvas, a black square on a canvas, a spiral jetty, a neon light that said *Run from fear, Fun from rear*, a grainy video . . . but I was not going to be able to study any of that at Chancellor College. All the lecturers there – and I knew their work – were bent on Zimbabwean soapstone cubism and did not seem to be aware of the new art.

Emily and Lucy had not managed to get into the University of Malawi, but they were now qualified secretaries and were working for a law firm in Blantyre. Joyce and Elson were at the University of Malawi's Polytechnic (also in Blantyre), studying Accountancy and Business Administration respectively. They would soon get good jobs with tobacco companies or aid agencies. But, as for me, even if I qualified to be an artist, where would I show my work? There was not a single fine-art gallery in Malawi, let alone a museum. And most of the artworks sold on the streets or at the occasional Wildlife Society fund-raising events were curios and airport art bought by pretentious Africa adventurers and tourists who had never been to an art gallery back home: soulless African masks, mock fetishes and crude batiks that in most cases were a front for marijuana dealers. And who would need my qualification? Apart from the Fine Art Department at Chancellor College, which had no paint or brushes, there was not a single art school in Malawi where I could scrape a living as an art teacher or lecturer. It was not surprising that when the careers officer gave us mock interviews and I said I would like to be inter-viewed for a possible career as an artist, everybody in the room laughed including Salama, which totally destroyed me because I had just realised that I was now in love with her.

7

I was no longer showing off when I held her tight on the dance floor. When I asked her out, she didn't know what to say, and when I tried to French-kiss her, she refused, although she would let me kiss her boobs and do all kinds of stuff to her. But I wanted her to love me, so I pressed her to say that she loved me back. She finally said that there was no point in us going out. It was just too late because soon we would be parting. She would head back to Tanzania, and then to the UK to study, and that would be that. I told her love would find a way, but she said she didn't love me, which took me by surprise. All the time we'd been together. We'd met when we were both thirteen and we had grown alongside each other. All those dances and Sunday-afternoon walks around the golf course. Still, she couldn't bring herself to love me back. She added that she was a Muslim and that her family would disown her if she married a Christian. I said I was not a Christian but she just laughed. Then, during one of our walks, she went on to say she could not really love me back because I was queer. It totally crushed me because I thought she was the last person on earth who would presume that about me. She went on to explain how she had arrived at that conclusion.

'Look at your hair, Samson. Why the perm? You look like a scarecrow.'

'I am an artist.'

'"I am an artist." You speak like a girl.'

'Michael Jackson does too and he's not queer.'

'Are you sure?'

'You can never be sure about anything but death. That's what makes life interesting.'

'What are these tight jeans all about? How did you get into them?'

'I used soap. I love them. They make me feel like I could spring out of any situation faster than a grasshopper.'

'Aren't these women's shoes?'

'Could be. I got them second-hand at the market, but I love them. They give me height, you know, like Prince.'

'The girls were talking about your nail varnish the other day.'

'Oh, that was my sisters. They liked to practise their make-up techniques on me during the holidays. And I used to keep the nail varnish on because Mrs Gently would take it off for me. It was very sexy. I haven't done it since she left though.'

'They don't love you, you know.'

'Who?'

'Your sisters.'

'Of course they do. It was only play, Salama.'

'How about the face cream? You look like a mask.'

'I don't like spots. Do you? Anyway, I like the androgynous look. You know, like Mick Jagger, Prince, Michael Jackson, David Bowie . . .'

'You wore your earring in your right ear at the disco.'

'Oh, that? It's like George Michael . . .'

'It means you're queer. Don't you know wearing an earring in your right ear means you're queer?'

'It couldn't. George Michael isn't queer! You're kidding me.'

When she finished her evaluation of my six years of experimental fashion at KA I was shattered. But it had been a long time coming. My English teacher, Mr Fairweather, a failed opera singer, had gone to greater lengths than Salama to prove that I was gay and he had probably influenced her opinion because we'd been in the same class and she hardly ever had an opinion of her own. I wondered how she had been able to put up with me for all those years.

8

I had a friend named Watson who used to come to my room to discuss girls and stuff after lights out. We sometimes did this until late into the night. On one of those nights, Mr Benard, the Greek teacher who liked to eavesdrop, heard us laughing at some lewd point and walked in. He put the light on and saw us lying on the bed, side by side in our boxer shorts – it was hot – my roommate fast asleep on the other bed. He put us in detention. I gathered later that he thought he'd witnessed a bundling scene and spread various rumours among the staff and prefects saying that I was queer. Eventually the whole school believed it.

And that's when Mr Fairweather began to destroy my self-confidence and my love of English literature, which I'd been studying for my A levels together with art and history. In every lesson he found something gay about me. He would run his finger along my face and show me what he had gathered. 'Look at all this lead on your face. You are queer.'

Once when I said I did not like my father that much but loved my mother to bits, he said that was a typical homosexual trait. But I hated Dad at the time because I suspected he had Aids and was going to take my mother with him when he died. The last half-term I'd been home, he was having night sweats, so he preferred going out drinking until dawn to staying home. He would drive home so drunk he slept within seconds of shoving the car into the garage and switching the engine off. We had to pull him out and put him in bed. It's a miracle he never had an accident; only the usual swollen upper lip, but that was an allergy. Maybe he wanted to kill himself in a car crash because he had seen what was further down the road for him. My sisters whispered among themselves that he'd had an affair with a coloured patient of his from Luchenza. She'd just died of consumption.

When Mr Fairweather asked me to read from Maxine Hong Kingston's *The Woman Warrior*, he said I was perfect for it because I read like a girl, and when I laughed at the hypocrisy and extravagances of Polonius' speeches in *Hamlet* he called it a giggle. It went on and on until I started to think maybe there was something I didn't know about myself.

Then one day when I was doing my prep and my roommate was in the bathroom, Mr Fairweather, who was on duty, walked in to take the register. When he realised that I was alone, he came over to my desk, put his arm around my shoulders, kissed me on the mouth and asked me, 'How do you feel?' as I choked. When I reported the incident to the Senior Master, he played it down, saying that Mr Fairweather was probably joking, and that I should now concentrate on finishing my A levels. That was the most important thing for me.

But I could not get the incident out of my mind. So, to get my sanity back, I joined a couple of guys who had been making night trips to see their girlfriends at the girls' hostels on the other side of campus. I went to see Jackie, who I thought had fancied me for years. She and Salama did not get on very well. Jackie was happy to see me when I tapped on her window and we got romping in her bed right away, kissing and rubbing each other down. No sex, although I am sure we would have done it if we had had a condom. When it was time for me to go she asked me not to tell anyone about it, adding that if I did tell anybody she would kill herself. I didn't think she was serious, but it seemed an odd thing to say.

So when Salama said that I was queer, I was crushed because she was the one person on earth who should have known that I was a follower of the Yellow Dwarf and that self-expression was my religion. I had made the Holy Ball and taken Christianity back to where it had come from: the sun. Standing there on the hockey field watching Salama's dress dance in the wind a few yards away, Jackie's expression came back to me and I used it. I told Salama that if she did not love me back I would kill myself.

Salama was scared although she did not express it at the time. She went back and told the teachers and prefects that I was going to kill myself. The Senior Master called me to his office and told me that I could break any rule I liked if I felt down but that, for God's sake, I shouldn't kill myself or anybody else. After that, I think I was secretly put on suicide watch. For the final few weeks left to me at KA there was always someone keeping an eye on me. By this time the school electricity had been cut by the new democratically elected UDF government, which condemned the school as elitist. We studied by candlelight. I destroyed my diaries of six years, which were full of Salama, Mrs Gently, and dreams of playing an electric guitar at Wembley Stadium and Madison Square Garden, and retreated into the obscurity of the Art Department.

9

My time at KA ended with a letter from Chikondi telling me that Dad had been promoted to Senior Clinical Superintendent. He was going to be transferred to the Ministry of Health Headquarters in Lilongwe to oversee the running of all the hospitals in Malawi; the Jive Talker's ultimate dream had come true. That lifted my spirits and I hurriedly left for home after my last examination paper. When I got there, however, I was greeted by a scene straight from Alfred Hitchcock's *The Birds*. I thought I was dreaming: our house was surrounded by an army of terrible scarecrows, which did not seem to be scaring anybody away; there were hundreds of screaming black crows perched in all the trees and there was somebody in the backyard trying to shoot them down. Most of the windowpanes had been smashed and replaced with cardboard; there were bits of broken glass all over the place.

What was happening here?

When Dad had gone to collect the keys to his new office in Lilongwe, he'd collapsed at the door and had been confined to his bed ever since. They couldn't find out what was wrong with him. Alongside that, there was something weird happening: the crows perched in the trees were attacking our house every evening, soon after sunset and again before dawn. The house was gradually losing light as the windowpanes were being replaced with cardboard.

Grandad had been called from Ntcheu to help, and he had erected the scarecrows around the house to try to fend the birds off, but we were not sure whether getting rid of the crows was a good idea: with every crow that we shot down or scared away, Dad seemed to be getting weaker and weaker. When he went to the hospital they still couldn't find anything wrong with him.

My mother tried to persuade Dad to see a witch doctor for an answer but he kept refusing, saying it was mere superstition. Then one day when Mum said that she had found a witch doctor from abroad he accepted.

Dr J.J. Solomon was brought to our house at night to avoid gossip. He was a light-skinned, emaciated man, who claimed to be an Ethiopian refugee, which was believable because he looked like Emperor Haile Selassie. He wore a threadbare military uniform complete with medals, and had a soft, green toy snake, which looked like the Loch Ness Monster, wrapped around his neck. (One could get all sorts of weird things from the refugee aid agencies.) He was barefoot like a *gule*; Ethiopia was a far-off country, and all that walking seemed to have left the soles of his feet as hard and cracked as dry clay. He looked as if he had never worn a shoe in his life.

Dr J.J. Solomon saluted Dad and started his procedure by chewing and spitting stuff all over the place and reading a selection of verses from his little Gideon Bible. He then threw a series of burning sticks at the crows in the trees, but they did not budge. Next, he reached into his tattered Adidas rucksack, which he said stood for Addis Ababa, and produced a stethoscope. That's when I recognised him as the man from Bruce's village. It was the very stethoscope which had once belonged to Dad and which I'd sold to him. Now he'd graduated from witch doctor to Ethiopian refugee witch doctor, speaking broken English. I put on a cap so he wouldn't recognise me and sat back to enjoy the show.

I had read a good deal about quack doctors on the Diptych during my stint as Dr Lionel Lockyer and they had always fascinated me. A good quack doctor would heal you as long as he turned his bullshit to a fine art. Dr J.J. Solomon, however, was not sophisticated enough for us; a light-skinned complexion did not make one a direct descendant of King Solomon and his diagnostic skills could only work on the natives. As he used the stethoscope to listen to Dad's heart, joints and head, we were all trying hard not to laugh, including Dad. Then he produced a medicine gourd, which he claimed contained the Balm of Gilead, an elixir whose ingredients grew only in the fertile regions of Judaea. Carrying a blond flywhisk in one hand and the gourd in the other, he spoke in tongues and danced around the house like a madman. When he came out of the trance, he dipped the whisk in his medicine and sprinkled its contents all over the house, then suddenly collapsed to the floor like a wounded animal, panting and sweating profusely. His foul smell choked the atmosphere, and most of us put our hands to our noses.

After a few minutes, he got up and took a piece of tattered blue carbon paper from his Adidas bag and rubbed it across a piece of cardboard several times, calling upon a long list of his ancestral spirits – among them the Queen of Sheba – for help. Then he suddenly stopped the chant and lifted the carbon paper to reveal smudged writing on the piece of cardboard paper. When he had read what was written on it he shook with terror screaming, '*Ayi! Ayi! Ayi!*' He then showed us what his ancestral spirits had just revealed to him, and we all burst out laughing when we saw what it was.

The handwriting was bad but confident, like that of a child. It simply said 'POOPSYA' (DANGER), like the word written on the electricity poles outside, a sign which even the illiterate natives knew implied death. 'You are in danger, Chief!' Dr J.J. Solomon said, pointing a trembling finger at Dad. (He needed to cut his fingernails.) 'Somebody wants your job.'

Dr J.J. Solomon asked for his money upfront, before he could carry out the last phase of his treatment. Stuffing the money underneath his balls in his trousers, he took an old, rusty Nacet safety razor blade from his Adidas rucksack and asked Dad to come forward for several small incisions all over his body into which he would rub *khini*. As he whetted the blade on a piece of stone, Dad looked more curious than shocked at the whole thing.

'Can you please use my own razor blade instead?' he asked Dr Solomon.

'The medicine will not work,' the witch doctor said, spitting on the floor.

'OK, then. Can you at least boil the razor?'

When the razor was ready, Dr J.J. Solomon was not happy because it was warped. Mum had overboiled it. Nevertheless, he made several small cuts on Dad's skin and rubbed the black powder from a gourd in the wounds. He then asked us if we could get in line, ready to be cut with the same bloodstained razor. We all screamed NOOOOOOOO! and ran out of the room in hysterics.

By this time, Grandad had already walked out of the room unimpressed, to carry on shooting down the birds.

Surprisingly, the anonymous *khini* and the Balm of Gilead gave Dad some energy, and the following day he rose from his bed and went to work. A few days later, a real doctor, a visiting German orthopaedic, diagnosed him with gout. We chose to believe it was gout and not opportunistic gout, but I think we all suspected it was Aids. Real gout did not give you swollen upper lips, night sweats, persistent diarrhoea, lesions all over your face, depression and a general lack of energy.

Grandad appeared happy for Dad: 'Gout is the disease of kings,' he said, shaking his hand. The following day he packed away his gun and went back to Ntcheu.

A couple of weeks after they found the skeletal Mama wa Chifufu dead, we moved to Lilongwe so Dad could take up his new post. They buried Mama wa Chifufu right there in her glade, surrounded by wild flowers and the muscular wood-bearing men from the mountains whom she loved and who would soon be joining her in the earth.

LILONGWE

1

Coming to Lilongwe was a bad idea. Dad was the boss indeed, chauffeur-driven and all, but now he worked solely in administration and thus had no access to drugs, so once again he was back on the starvation wages of a Malawian civil servant. And still he had five kids to feed. Emily, Lucy and Joyce were all now married and faced their own struggles in Blantyre.

We went back to maize porridge for breakfast, and the bitter smoked fish *utaka* for lunch and supper. We rarely had sugar for our tea. The diet was not good for Dad, who was sick and needed special meals for the gout. No more red meat, which was just as well because we could only have afforded it around payday in any case.

Dad got as thin as a skeleton, his eyes black and swollen like a chameleon. In fact he resembled a *gule wamkulu* mask. His bedroom looked like a makeshift pharmacy: drugs in bottles and boxes neatly displayed in the cabinet, on windowsills, on top of and under the dressing table. He rarely went to work. He would sleep all day and then in the late afternoon he would put on his London suit and tie and go for a walk until his gout-riddled feet could take him no further.

What he liked to do in the evenings was to sit down

with the *Independent* and read it to Mum, who he demanded be by his side all the time. He liked the passages that rejoiced in the fall of Banda and supported the UDF, the new party in government. It had just been announced that the ex-president at over a hundred years old would be put in a wheelchair and pushed to the High Court where he would be tried for the murder of the three cabinet ministers in Mwanza District back in 1983.

I hated Dad for that because I was MCP and Banda was my hero. Here was an ungrateful man. Banda had sent his son to a school dubbed the Eton of Africa for free, and he had the cheek to say bad things about him. The president hadn't even sent his own relatives or the children of his cronies to the school. Even now, Kamuzu Academy was being resurrected into a private school for rich kids, mostly those of Asian businessmen and children of the new breed of corrupt politicians. The subsidised tuition was £5,500 a year and rising, which was money a multimillionaire civil servant could only dream about! It seemed like Dad did not appreciate what I had achieved. In fact, I felt that he was probably jealous of my education. My ten GCSEs alone turned his E in O-level English into an eternal joke. And I'd just received my A-level results: A in art, B in the general paper, C in English and D in history. Maybe he was not too impressed but I was suffering from a broken heart when I sat for the exams and my grades were more than enough to get me into the University of Malawi for goodness' sake.

I told Dad not to judge Banda. If you're looking for a saint don't look in politics. Had he not read Machiavelli's *The Prince* on the Diptych? Camus said the road to freedom was long and hard; democracy is not something that comes overnight. In Athens, only free men were allowed to take part in democracy: no slaves, women or non-citizens. And even in the West, democracy did not come overnight; it came with education and the slow birth of a strong middle class. The Magna Carta was not written for the riff-raff; you couldn't practise democracy without a well-educated section of society. We had a long way to go in Malawi, with an impoverished middle class of only 10 per cent and just over half of the population literate. And even if Banda had wanted democracy, the West, who wanted to contain the spread of communism by propping up dictators all over the place, wouldn't have allowed it. Just look at what happened to Comrade Julius Nyerere and Kenneth Kaunda, how they took out Patrice Lumumba. It wasn't Banda's fault. He had worked with what was available to him and did a pretty good job; he was no child-eating Emperor Bokassa or Idi Amin. Rant over.

Dad said he understood my argument, but those who lived by expediency must die by expediency surely? So it was right that Banda should at least be thrown in prison for all the people he had fed to the crocodiles in the Shire River . . .

'OK! OK!' I said and stormed out of the room, slamming the door behind me hard so he would die of a heart attack. A few seconds later I reopened the door and was back in the room armed with a response to counter his argument.

'You know what I think about the whole thing, Dad. I think they shouldn't throw Banda in jail. The fact that he is Malawi's first president is enough to spare him all the humiliation he is going through. George Washington owned slaves but Americans still have a monument for him. Think of all the evil things Oliver Cromwell did – he still has a statue in front of Westminster Parliament. Napoleon Bonaparte . . . The British royal family sent so many people to the executioner but they are still reigning supreme, exempt from tax, wearing chunky diamonds and riding gold chariots. All these hypocrites advocating democracy forget that people like stability and will always need their gods and Africans are no different. But we can learn from history. What Africa needs is not dictators but rather 'super-dictators' – SDs – modelled on the British Crown. They should make Banda an SD instead – let him have all the benefits of power: dignity, respect, security and wealth without the power and leave all that political squabbling to the commoners . . .' But I had to stop because the old man had fallen asleep.

2

Dad was forced to take early retirement because of ill health. We were going to be kicked out of the house after a grace period, but we had nowhere to go. The only house we had was Dad's unfinished shack in Dowa and nobody was going back there with him. It was too remote. We were too urbanised for that; we wouldn't cope. Everybody was moving into the cities anyway.

Trying to sort out our situation, we discovered that if Dad died, the death gratuity we would get would be enough to buy a modest house in Area 49. Secretly, I planned not to let anybody use my share of the gratuity for a fucking house. I was going to use that money to buy a one-way ticket to South Africa and that would be that. I planned to get there, buy a fake ID, work and pay for a fine-art degree somewhere. Witswaterand maybe. There was a bit of an art audience in the new South Africa. And who knew where a successful career there would take me?

I could travel the world like Picasso, meeting beautiful women.

And so, when Dad got a lump sum after leaving work, we bought him a video set and silently hoped he would die within the grace period. He was finished anyway. He was but a living skeleton now, with all the HIV in him.

3

Dad, too, realised it was the end: his favourite film at that time was *Scarface*, the story of Tony Montana, a Cuban refugee who becomes a millionaire in the USA through drug dealing. Dad liked to see the last scene, where Tony, fired up with cocaine, shoots all these Colombians with an M16 rifle fitted with an M203 grenade launcher. He holds the gun down around his crotch shouting in a weird accent, '*You wanna play rough? OK, say hello to my little friend! You like that? You whores! Cowards. Go ahead. Come!*' He wipes his nose and takes bullets from his adversaries and he's still standing, shouting, '*I am still standing, ha?*' until somebody shoots him from the back and he falls dead into a pool overlooked by a golden orb that says 'The World Is Yours'. When the credits started rolling, Dad would let loose hollow, mocking laughter that sounded like the Devil.

As for my mother, her favourite movie was *The Mighty Quinn*, with Denzel Washington, especially the part where Ubu Pearl, the crippled witch in the wheelchair, is locked in a house, which is set on fire. She is stoic in her death; un-repentant for all the people she's killed with the poisonous snakes out of her basket. Mum liked to watch that scene again and again, her eyes glowing red from the fire on the brand-new video screen.

The end was definitely on its way. There was a creepy atmosphere in the living room: a perfectly healthy woman sitting on the sofa cuddled up to a laughing skeleton, like some medieval painting on the Diptych.

I never joined the strange couple to watch these movies though, just in case mosquitoes slipped into the living room. I was not yet convinced that mosquitoes could not spread HIV; all the blood that was on your palm when you killed the mosquito! I knew what Sod's Law was. *Anything that can go wrong, will.*

I also put aside my own cutlery and wore slippers in the bathroom.

4

Then the end came for Dad. It started with thieves breaking into our house and stealing everything except what was in the bedroom where we'd been sleeping. Everything Mum and Dad had worked for over thirty years, from the chairs, the Diptych and the painting of St Paul's Cathedral in London that said 'I SHALL SUCSEED' on the mantelpiece, to the cooker and the fridge . . . That finished Dad, but I was happy he was being punished for his sins in this life. There was no hell waiting for him down there. He must have caught the grin on my face because he suspected it was me who had arranged the robbery. My reaction to that was as ambiguous as possible to make him suffer more. I truly hated him, now. Murderer!

He could not take it any more. Soon after the burglary, his temperature rose dramatically and he took to his bed. He moaned about his bones all night, which made me hate him all the more because he had stopped moaning in English, switching to a type of Chichewa which I'd last heard when I was at his home village of Misi in Dowa, buying the Path. Whereas before he would say, 'Oh my God', 'Damn it!', 'Jesus!', 'Oh!', 'Shit', 'Fuck' and 'Bloody hell', when the gout stung him now he said, *'Mayi koto ine!'*, *'oMama!'*, *'oDada mayo ine!'* He had betrayed the silent pact we had made with the Diptych. But I guessed he was free to do what he liked now with the Diptych gone. The way he had held himself and spoken English over the years you would have thought he was done with the primitive way, but opportunistic, HIV-induced gout had cut him down to size and now he was moaning like a native instead of a gentleman.

Dad was not to be the only progressive native who had his past catch up with him. In 1997 I was disappointed to hear that Banda, that number-one progressive African who spoke the Queen's English all the time, had regressed into his native tongue too after a brain operation at Garden City in South Africa. On his deathbed, he cried, *'Moto!'* (Fire!) *'Mayo koto ine, mayo koto!'* (untranslatable) and when white friends visited him at his retirement house at Mudi, he stood to attention as if for an inspection by a colonial officer. The natives were happy to hear that the pretentious bastard had died like that; especially more so when they heard that the poor old man's dying word was *'Moto!'* They said he was heading for hell, but I did not think so. He was returning to the sun where he'd come from; everything good and bad returned to it.

I made up my mind that when it was my turn to die, I would make sure that I groaned and gasped in English, not in Chichewa, and that would be a measure of how successful my life had been.

5

Law and order was getting out of hand in Malawi as the nation struggled with the new realities of democracy and human rights. The natives were wondering why, when a thief was caught, two days later he would be back in the village. That was because of bail, or the fact that if no charges were brought against the person within forty-eight hours, suspects were supposed to be released. Since the police could not afford to dwell on petty crimes, many of the thieves were released, and so the natives began to take the law into their own hands. Who the hell is Amnesty International anyway? This is time for freedom and not taking orders, you hear? It was a hard time for thieves because, once they were caught by the mob, most were burnt to death on the spot. That was the method of execution approved by the natives and that's how my cousin, Chosadziwa, who lived in Biwi township, met his fate.

They poured petrol all over his body and set him on fire. The gases inside him expanded while he was still alive. He exploded and died splattering the onlookers with his entrails. When Mum went to the funeral with my other brothers and sisters, I was told to stay home and take care of Dad.

I was sitting on the veranda working on some Van Gogh-style pastel drawings of sunflowers Mum had planted in the front yard to cheer me up, when I heard unsteady footsteps inside the house. I looked through the window and it was skeletal Dad in the middle of the empty living room, wearing nothing but a red tie around his neck and his brown, worn-out London shoes from the seventies. He had now totally lost his mind and was obviously trying to go out on one of his evening walks. I rushed to the door and held it in so he could not leave, not in a state like that. When he realised that the door was locked, he fell to the floor and screamed, '*Ayo!*' (untranslatable). Muttering under my breath I was like, 'Yeah, stay in there and die, mother-fucker!'

Then I watched him trying to crawl back to his bedroom, but his limbs failed him. His Aids-induced gout was far-gone; his knees were swollen. Nevertheless, he suddenly stood up in defiance of all the pain and began to dance about the room. It was like the Dance of Death: his steps were all over the place but they eventually formed a pattern. It was the unmistakable *champweteka nchimanga* rhythm of *gule wamkulu*. He must have bought the Path too when he was back there, in his remote native village in Dowa. The bastard! Was this really where the Jive Talker had come from, the blooming *dambwe*? I found myself humming Camille Saint-Saëns' *Danse macabre*, which was in an alien 3/4 time to undermine his efforts: '*Pompoo! Pompoo! Pompoo! Pompoo! Pompoo! Pompoo! Pompoo! Pompoo! Pompoo! Pompoo!* . . .'

He soon fell to the floor, giving in to the stinging gout in his bones.

I made some sketches of him, trying to crawl back to the bedroom: Dad on all fours, looking like Bobo the mangy dog. Dad on his back with limbs held up like a dead insect. Dad on his hands, trying to get up like a wounded soldier in a Vietnam movie. Dad folded up in two like a foetus, with his hairy balls appearing at the back of his thighs. Dad on his back, moving his limbs out like a snow angel as he weed on himself, laughing like the Devil . . .

Mum found me busy mouthing *Danse macabre* at *vivacissimo*, conducting an invisible orchestra with a pencil, sunflowers and nude drawings of Dad scattered around the place: '*Pompoo!!! Pompoo!!! Pompoo!!! Pompoo!!! Pompoo!!! Pompoo!!! Pompoo!!! Pompoo!!! Pompoo!!! . . .*'

She was shocked, but what could I do? Everybody was going insane. In her hands was Dad's crude painting of St Paul's during the Blitz. 'I SHALL SUCSEED.' They had found it in Chosadziwa's house, the only object he'd stolen from us that he had failed to sell on the streets.

We'd thought it had to be a close relative. You should have seen their eyes exploring the contents of the house when they'd come round to visit us.

Mum returned the painting to the mantelpiece.

For my part, I was shocked by Mum's support for Dad. Why? This man had brought home a disease that was going to kill her and leave us orphans and she still thought he was the most beautiful man in the world. It made me confused. Could it have been Mum who had brought the HIV virus home? But I dared not confront her with my feelings because I just could not face the grim reality anyway. On the surface, I decided to pretend that what Dad was suffering from was nothing but an acute case of gout. To suggest that it was Aids that had turned him into a skeleton would be to admit that Mum was going to die too, and I would surely never get over that.

The following morning, Dad was taken to Lilongwe Central Hospital, where they placed him under the hospital bed of a native suffering from a neglected case of gonorrhoea. All the beds were full and placing newly admitted patients under other people's hospital beds was normal. The nurses had told my mum that there were no exceptions to the rule in the new democracy of equal rights. When I heard that from my tearful sisters, I hurriedly went to the hospital to give the nurses a piece of my mind but I did not find Dad under the bed. As I stood there wondering what had happened, Dad's bed sheets in my hands, like St Peter in the empty tomb of the risen Christ, the decomposing skeleton reclining on the bed tapped my shoulder and pointed a weak finger at the window. The big black letters on the building outside read MORTUARY.

6

I was at least relieved to hear that Dad's last words were a triumphant, 'I am a multimillionaire.' The autopsy said it was meningitis that killed him, but as they put his body in the ambulance bound for home, I heard the nurses gossiping that it was the gorilla disease called Slim that came down the Kinshasa Highway.

He was laid in a pauper's coffin for viewing; he would have preferred a casket. He had died with his mouth wide open (presumably as a result of his last effort to pronounce the 'air' part in 'I am a multimillionaire'), so they put some crude bandaging work around his head to make him look decent. Instead he looked like a mummy that had just been excavated from the pyramids at Giza. They should have stitched him together, embalmed him or something, but they didn't. Maybe they were afraid of all the HIV in him. Maybe the undertaker had been off sick that day. And instead of his three-piece London suit they'd wrapped him up in colourful African prints, in keeping with tradition. Those natives! Dad would have hated those freaky Indonesian holland wax textiles.

My whole family and the coffin were loaded on the back of a lorry bound for his burial in Dowa. There was hardly any room, our dusty feet rested on the coffin. I looked around; my sisters, Mum and some relatives were crying. My brothers, Bond and Elson, like me, were not, and perhaps that's the way things should have been. The whole family was happy for Dad, for he had suffered a long time from the illness and death was a gift to him.

Going through his personal files looking for a CCAP membership card, my mother could not find anything except letters of his correspondence with one L. Ron Hubbard from the USA. In one letter Hubbard told Dad that he was the only Scientologist in East Africa. Looking at the letters the native minister wondered what the hell the Church of Scientology was. He finally concluded that he was a Christian because there was a cross in the Scientology logo and agreed to conduct a Christian funeral for him. Then they buried him alongside the unmarked graves of his ancestors. They put heavy stones over his grave which seemed stifling to me. Looking at the whole thing, I made up my mind to let people know that I was not bound to that piece of land in Misi Village in Dowa, and I was not a Christian. I'd gone beyond that (call me a super-Christian if you like) and found the meaning of life in the sun. I would not be resurrecting on the last day for some God to judge me, and so I would like my body to be cremated to Frank Sinatra's live version of 'Where or When', my ashes (or the yellow diamonds should I die a rich man) scattered at sea. Then folk would have to exercise and exorcise with the Holy Ball on the beach because I would return on the next wave to do it all again.

7

After Dad's passing Mum was not the same. Soon after the funeral she had looked relieved and happy. She had spent years nursing her husband and that had been wearing her out, you could tell. But now she was free to do whatever she wanted. Instead of Aids she chose to believe that her husband had died of gout, the disease of kings, caused by all the jive he had subjected his body to, and she looked to the future optimistically. She planned to enter the new multi-party politics and stand as MP for her home village in Ntcheu. She planned to start a business, open a nursery for infants, a retail shop or something. She was all-hopeful and I give her credit for her attitude because it made us relax even if it was just for a while.

She cut her hair and rejoined the Catholic Church after years in Presbyterian exile. But sadly on her confirmation day a strange boil appeared on her face and she could not look us in the eye. Thereafter, she became short-tempered with everybody in the house. 'Why are you still sleeping? Why is the meat not well cooked? Do you want to die of gout like your father? Why is there no salt in this?'

Then her conversations took a fatalistic turn. She suspected she was having a heart attack, high blood pressure, a stroke when she looked fine to me. After all, there was no history of diabetes in her family. Her daughter back in the village in Ntcheu, whom she had left with the missionaries before leaving for the city back in the sixties, had died of a tumour in her stomach a couple of years before and left a little girl that Mum brought home to take care of. Mum suspected the little girl was bewitching her (presumably because she had neglected her mother while she lived) and shouted at her for no apparent reason. She sounded as if she wished she could die from any of these things; I guess anything was better than an undignified death from Aids.

When she received Dad's death gratuity, she started buying a new dress for herself every week instead of a house. If only one could buy a new body. She would wear her pretty dresses and drink jive with Bond, who was only sixteen, there in the sitting room while listening to the radio. It was weird seeing the two. Bond had quickly grown tall and looked uncannily like Dad. Anyway, it was like the old man had come back and Mum was happy once more.

We were lucky that when the grace period had elapsed in our government house in Area 47, we were given another house (albeit much smaller in Area 18) as Mum supposedly looked for a house to buy.

I fought hard and secured my share of the death gratuity before Mum could spend it all on new dresses and jive and left home for South Africa armed with a music demo from my GCSE coursework, killer drawing and painting skills, and my GCSE and A-level certificates. I also carried the dubious South African address of Lucy's ex-boyfriend to show at the border. I heard they hassled you a lot at the borders if you did not have a destination address.

I had to pass through Blantyre to organise my passport. It took for ever to come through and my funds were running low. I queued at Blantyre passport office for two weeks. The Asians, Nigerians, white people and some fat-looking Malawians never queued, so I went to the back to find out why: corruption was rife, of course. Had I forgotten I was in the Fourth World?

There was a well-fed official there, receiving Manila envelopes stuffed with money in return for the passports. That was for the Asians and Nigerians and the fat Malawians.

As for the whites, it was considered rude to let a white man queue or wait for anything in Malawi.

I walked into the fat man's office, gave him my name, date and place of birth and put a quarter of my death gratuity on his table along with my name.

'You don't have to do this, you know,' he said, not looking up from his paper.

'Yes, I know. But I need to go to South Africa urgently to get some medicines. My mother is dying.'

The fat man shrugged his shoulders, and went back to reading his paper.

When I returned in the afternoon, the fat man was still reading his paper but the money was gone and my passport was ready.

There was a spelling mistake in my name though. It said SAMSON KONI KAMBALU, instead of SAMSON KONDWANI KAMBALU. When I pointed this out to the passport officer, he told me that he had shortened the name Kondwani to Koni because Koni was better.

'This is my gift to you, my good friend,' he said, turning a page of his newspaper.

JOHANNESBURG

1

It was an early morning in September 1995 when I took my seat on the Mecca Tours Bus headed for Harare. While I was waiting for the bus to fill up, a red-eyed Rastaman walked on, saying he was selling South African rands. I already had some rands on me, but I had extra kwacha that needed changing so I offered to buy R200 from him. He got my money but as soon as he handed me the two hundred-rand notes, they felt wrong. On closer inspection they were not even counterfeits but turned out to be colour Xeroxes. I shoved them back at him, asking for my money. He glared at me with the fieriest eyes I had ever seen.

'I don't want no games, you hear, mon? I have just given you proper money and now you want to play me with that trash, mon.'

Clever bastard he was, mon. With moneychangers all over the place how could I have proven it was him who had played me? And he knew that buying money on the street was illegal; the police would only put me in jail if I complained. I let it pass as a valuable lesson.

As I stared blankly into space, not believing what had happened, somebody sat down on the seat next to me. I jerked away from them, quickly reaching for my wallet to make sure it was still there.

'Hey, easy, Samson. Are you OK?' It was Jester Namale, a former student from Kamuzu Academy who had graduated a couple of years ahead of me but never went to university.

'I'm OK, man. How are you doing? Where are you going?'

'Harare. I've been saving up for two years for this moment. I'm fed up with this country; it's a peasant. If this is the warm heart of Africa, the continent doesn't have long to live.'

'She is also called the Cinderella of Africa.'

'Hahahaha! That's rather too optimistic, isn't it? Why is that?'

His hyena laugh cheered me up.

'Originally the country was created as a labour pool for the British Empire in Southern Africa; she is not supposed to function as a country per se . . .'

'Well, I think Cinderella has done her bit and deserves a break now, don't you think?'

'Yeah, it's about time she put on her glass shoes and went to the ball. So, what are you going to do in Zimbabwe?'

'I don't know but any place is better than this. I'm going to stay with my uncle and look around. See what happens. Maybe I could do some advertising work, copywriting. How about you? Where are you heading?'

'Joburg. Work. Study art. Travel the world.'

'Paradise City. You must be loaded then?'

'I was ten minutes ago.'

'Joburg is the place to be, man, but my money wouldn't take me that far. We will see when I get my stuff together in Harare.'

It was late in the afternoon when we reached the Nyamapanda border post between Mozambique and Zimbabwe. There was nobody at the Mozambican immigration office except a boy with one leg selling roasted birds and a sweaty chubby man who walked on to the bus and collected our passports together with a fee of K50 each. When he was finished with them, we headed to Zimbabwe, where we were greeted by a black-and-white portrait of Robert Mugabe and a notice that read, *If you are not happy with us, wait until you get to Heathrow.*

We reached Harare late in the night. I was impressed that everybody wore shoes in Harare, even the beggars. Jester and I decided to book into the Monomotapa Hotel for the night, and we shared a room to save money. It was hard to sleep because there was a dance club below our room that shook all night long to a song called 'Dindindi Full Time' by some blind singer named Dr Love. The following morning, back from breakfast, Jester complained that he could not find his wallet underneath the mattress where he'd hidden it. I told him to hold on while I went to the reception to phone the police and that was that. I was not up for games any more. I suspected Jester just wanted me to share my father's death gratuity with him. I left him at the hotel, took the 'Moonraker' and headed for the South African border – which I then realised was stupid because I had behaved like a thief. It took me a couple of days to shake off the feeling that I was being tracked down by the police.

2

When I got to Joburg, I checked into the Tivoli Hotel, on Kerk Street. On the way to my room I passed an open door, from which a white skinhead with Chinese dragons tattooed on his arms greeted me in what I presumed was Afrikaans.

I had barely put down my bags when I heard a knock on the door.

'Hi, my name is Botha, where are you from?'

'Samson. I'm from Malawi.'

'Oh, Banda. I like Banda. Malawians, nice people.'

'Yeah. They say that Malawi is the only place in the world where the pedestrians will apologise to you if you run them over.'

'Why is that?'

'Anger takes too many calories. You wouldn't survive the day if you got angry.'

'What does Malawi mean?'

'Flames, Land of flames.'

'Bloody hell! Is it that bad?'

'It's the arsehole of the world, man.'

'Hahahaha!'

'The spot where Lucifer fell when he was chucked out of the Heavens . . .'

'Do you like girls?' He made two breast motions on his singlet with his hairy hands. I noticed he had a sun tattoo on his shoulders.

'Yeah, man, you got some?'

'I got some here. Give me a sec.'

He disappeared back to his room.

I had played it cool there but my heart was beating fast. He came back with a brown envelope filled with five pornographic magazines.

'All these. Take for twenty-five rand.'

'I got twelve fifty,' I said. I was getting wise to the streets each growing day. Jester had told me to always cut the price on the street in half to get a good bargain.

'Twenty-three.'

'Fifteen.'

'Twenty. That is a very good price, my friend.'

'OK.'

'Do you need an ID?' he asked me, as I put away my fat wallet.

'How did you know?'

'Lots of Malawians stop here. I give them IDs to find work. I got a brother who works in the Home Office.'

'How much?'

'Five hundred rand. You just sign. I will do the rest for you.'

He brought me the document and the briefcase from which he had taken it.

All I had to do was fill in my name, sign on the dotted line, and give him R500, which was a fortune, but well worth it to become a citizen of South African gold and diamonds. It sounded too good to be true, but with money anything was possible, so I decided to give it a shot.

He took the money and sealed it together with the document in an envelope, saying he'd be back with my ID the following day. To guarantee his return, he gave me the keys to his room as insurance and we parted in the streets.

3

I wasn't too sure what to start with, skyscraper-gazing, window-shopping, sampling exotic food on the streets or the women in the brown envelope. I headed for the fruit stalls in the market.

You could tell this was Paradise City, indeed, because the beggars not only wore shoes, but some were even white.

Now I had heard of 'powhitetrash' in Maya Angelou's *I Know Why the Caged Bird Sings*, but white beggars, now that was very interesting. Whenever I saw a white beggar, I stopped to give them money, just to make sure I was not dreaming. I felt like a multimillionaire. It must have been so much harder for the white beggars, surrounded by so many rich white people, because although Prester John had handed the government to Mandela, he still owned all the economy; blacks were still being stuffed into scary taxis and headed towards the shanty towns while any serious white person had a car and headed towards the leafy suburbs of Rosebank.

I bought fish and chips and a bagful of grapes. I had never seen fresh grapes before – the fruit of the vine that the Bible kept harping on about. At Kamuzu Academy we only got raisins. I went to the bottom of the blue-glass skyscraper in central Johannesburg and looked up in parallel to it to see if I would fall. I laughed with excitement, swaying to and fro like a reed in the wind. I popped the grapes one by one, their sweet juice spraying down the back of my mouth. Tears ran down my cheeks.

Back at the hotel in the evening, I propped myself up with a pillow and drooled over the porn magazines. Naked women of all colours, shapes and sizes: black, Asian, white, thin, fat, buxom . . . they were all in there. This sure was Paradise City. You would never find anything like that in Malawi. I thought that was probably why a lot of people were dying of Aids. The only time you got to experience a woman, it was the real thing. Here was a solution to the African Aids crisis: give the native some porn for goodness' sake.

I was busy perusing when I suddenly felt like vomiting. I headed to the bathroom and heaved up tons of grapes.

4

I spent the following day in bed, waiting for my ID, while trying out the new art materials I'd bought in the first art shop I had ever seen. I drew naked women from the porn magazines, simple slow ink drawings that looked like David Hockneys to kill as much time as possible, but Botha was still nowhere to be seen and I soon ran out of drawing paper. To pass more time, I censored the drawings out with pages from the Gideon Bible I'd found on the bedside table. I pulled out a page at a time, and then used a coin to mark a round patch of the page, which I cut out with a pair of scissors. I then used the patch to censor out the private parts, like Eve's fig leaf. Next I stuck the page from which the patch had been made next to the figure, so the holed page reflected the censored figure. Phone numbers of the models were written at the bottom of each drawing and used as titles. I called the drawings, *The Women of Joburg*. Then when I became doubtful about Botha ever showing up again I changed the title of the series to *Facts and Figures*: I cancelled out the phone numbers and wrote over them all the facts and figures on the economic condition of Africa that I knew from my A-level history, one fact per figure:

- Every child that is born in Africa has a loan amount of $380 that must be paid.
- Many hunger experts believe that ultimately the best way to reduce poverty in Africa is through education. Educated people are best able to break out of the cycle of poverty that causes hunger.

- African unemployment rates are at crisis levels, with over 65% of college graduates out of jobs.
- 33 out of 41 countries identified as Highly Indebted Poor Countries (HIPC) are in Africa.
- One in five Africans is affected by conflict.
- Life expectancy in sub-Saharan Africa is 46 years.
- Africa is the only major region in the world to see investment and savings per capita decline after 1970.
- It may take sub-Saharan Africa two generations to reach the average living standard it enjoyed in the middle of the 1970s.
- About half of the people in sub-Saharan Africa live on less than $1 a day, and the average income per capita is lower today than in the late 1960s.
- The majority of African countries are marginalised in world economic relations. Their share of world exports is only 1.8%.
- The First World nations allot just $47.6 billion a year in foreign aid to Africa, while extracting $178 billion in debt payment.
- In sub-Saharan Africa 186 million people are under-nourished.
- In sub-Saharan Africa 70% of women above the age of 25 are illiterate.
- Women produce between 70% and 75% of all the food in sub-Saharan Africa.
- More than 40 million Africans work in the informal sector, which safeguards the livelihood of 200 million people.
- More than 100 million children in Africa have no access to primary school education.
- If the world's richest 225 people gave 4% of their wealth, they could wipe out world poverty altogether . . .

It was late in the night when somebody knocked on my door. I was taking a shower because those naked women had made me so horny, my balls hurt. I was twenty years old, but somehow I was still a virgin – my ambitions the only outlet for the 40 million sperm that a man produces a day.

Botha brought bad news as I had expected. The Home Office had been very busy that day. He gave me back my sealed envelope and told me that he would try again for the ID tomorrow. I was not complaining, but the following day, when I knocked on his door, he was gone. I opened my envelope for the money and found nothing in there; only folded sheets of newspaper with pictures of a smiling Nelson Mandela. The toothless old woman who was cleaning the room felt so sorry for me that she offered to buy the old pair of shoes, which I'd used to travel to South Africa, off me. When I asked her why, she told me that she was a *sangoma*, and she would use the shoes to make magic to punish the likes of Botha. I sold them to her for R10.

5

I needed to find work before the rest of my money ran out, but in the meantime I continued sampling the goodies of Joburg: video-game booths, fruit machines, cinema, Kentucky Fried Chicken, Nandos, fine wine (I loved that, now I had a glass every night), McDonald's, lobsters, shrimp, pizza, Burger King, Chinese, Mexican, biltong, Castle Lager . . . I bought a good stolen Canon camera off the street and went around taking pictures of it all, including banks and shopping malls. In Randburg the armed guard pointed a gun at me for taking pictures of the bank cashiers counting money using machines like in Al Pacino's *Scarface*.

'Put your hands on your head, sir.'

'Who? Me?'

'Yes, you, sir. Put your hands on your head, now.'

'What have I done, sir?'

I felt stupid like a native coming out of there, several hours later. They thought I had been planning an armed robbery and refused to let me go until the immigration department verified my identity.

That evening after a few glasses of wine in a steakhouse I lined up ten white beggars on the street to give them some dole like I was the Home Office. I told them nobody was getting anything until they queued properly – *People, where are your manners?* Then I gave them two rand each.

'Thank you, sir,' they said, bowing their heads, and I was like, 'No problem,' and went on to give them some humanitarian jive as I staggered away back to my hotel, hand on my wallet.

'Don't spend it all at once! I will be here again tomorrow, same time, OK? You heard her sing about Mr Big Spender – that was my cousin Tiny Rowland . . . ! I love you all! Black/white it don't matter to me . . . we are all the same inside . . . *Harambe! Harambe!* I will spend my money wit u! And you too. And you . . .'

When I looked for work, everybody wanted an ID. Some were turned off when they realised that I was Malawian because of Banda's friendship with apartheid South Africa. Whenever Mandela had called for a strike during his struggle against the apartheid regime, Malawians were simply flown in by TEBA (The Employment Bureau of Africa) to take the place of the striking South African workers, wrecking the whole thing for the ANC, sending them back to the drawing board in Caxito. And now that Mandela was out of prison and black South Africans were free, things were going to be tough for Malawians. Maybe I could have looked for an illegal job washing dishes or cleaning the toilets, but I couldn't do it because that surely would have raised the Jive Talker from the dead. And what if another Malawian bumped into me and told my mother back home that, after all that, Samson was scrubbing floors in Johannesburg? She would have died of a heart attack.

I fished out my GCSE music demo and decided to look for a record deal. I was sure they wouldn't ask me for an ID. I couldn't imagine a rock star with an ID or work permit. I couldn't imagine Kurt Cobain singing 'Smells Like Teen Spirit' with an ID in his back pocket.

I found the EMI House in Steeledale, walked up to the reception desk, and asked for the producer. One had to be confident about these things. The receptionist looked at me as if I was crazy. But then she took a deep breath and gave me two addresses: one to which I could send my demo; the other, a minor label back in Hillbrow that would be prepared to listen to my demo right away. Umunthu Records, it was called. 'Humanity Records' in English. It was a dingy place that doubled as a brothel and smelt of alcohol, tobacco and urine, but the dreadlocked producer there did listen to my demo. He thought I was musical, but asked me why the hell I wanted to sing like an American. I told him it was because I had *chosen* to. The Beatles had also chosen to, and the Rolling Stones, the Who, the Bee Gees, Cream, Eric Clapton, Dire Straits, David Bowie, U2, Abba, the Sex Pistols . . . Bo Diddley. They had all chosen to sing like Americans. Those who did not didn't get famous, people like Kasambwe Brothers Band, Nkhamenya Boys Quartet, Songani Swing Stars and the Chimvu River Brothers Band . . . *the truth must side with power or it will perish again and again* – Nietzsche. At various points the world had been condemned to mimic or parody the Egyptians, the Greeks, the Romans, the British; now it was the Americans. I was a perfect product for my time.

But he didn't buy my philosophy. He said that Mandela was out of prison and that this was the new South Africa. People were more interested in the music of their mother tongue than imperialist mimicry. He showed me LPs of top South African artists who previously sang in English but were now proudly singing in their native tongues after Mandela's release; Juluka, Steve Kekena, Brenda, Yvonne Chaka Chaka, Chico, Thandeka (the lesbian who'd come to Malawi under the name P.J. Powers!) . . .

Well, all I'd ever wanted to be was Michael Jackson, not Michael Yekha, so we parted company.

That night, at some club in Yeoville, I noticed a midget of a man perched on a stool at the bar sipping gin and tonic. He looked like the Bushman in *The Gods Must be Crazy*. He had a gold tooth and wore a purple three-piece suit. His delicate pinkie finger was adorned with a diamond-studded gold ring. It flashed when he lifted the glass to his mouth. He was ice cool. He had to be a talent scout, a musician, or something, so I drank down my Castle Lager and switched on my hottest dance moves when the Notorious BIG's 'Juicy' came on. Soon all eyes in the club were on me. The Bushman was toasting his drink to the scene moving his head to the beat. I had him in my pocket: I imagined that he worked for Virgin Records and that he would sign me for a recording contract right on the spot. He was going to put me in a flat in one of the leafy suburbs and then he would groom me for international superstardom.

I would be too hot for the South African *mbaganga* scene, and so he would ship me to America. He'd get me an

American speech therapist and voice trainer who would polish my *yeahs*, *gonnas*, *babys*, *luvs*, *yahs* and *oohs* until they sounded like Prince. A string of funky hit records, all written out for me by Prince, would follow, like he had done for Tevin Campbell. First album done, I was going to change my name from Samson Kambalu to something else – Samson? Samson Samson? Samson Samson Samson Samson Samson . . . ? The possibilities were endless, you know, like from Harry Webb to Cliff Richard; Robert Marley to Bob Marley; Steveland Judkins to Stevie Wonder; Roger Barrett to Syd Barrett . . . It was going to be something funky like that. And then I'd be a superstar . . . I would be shining, man, I would be shining!

Satisfied with my effort, I approached the bar to buy myself a beer so I could talk to the pygmy record executive. I was sweating like a motherfucker. The Bushman offered to pay for my drink and we discussed business:

'Man, you can really work the floor. Where did you learn that?'

'On the streets man, on the streets. I just watch and take it all in. I've been dancing since the age of eight.'

'I can tell. That was all very professional, man.'

'That's because I am professional. I can sing and play the guitar too and a bit of piano. I know all the minor and diminished chords as well, and chromatic scales.'

'OK. So what kind of stuff do you play?'

'Funk/rock, you know, Prince, Lenny Kravitz kind of stuff. I also like Pink Floyd; *Ummagumma*. I just love that album.'

'Why not some rapping, man? That's the in thing – rock'n'roll is dead, man, rock'n'roll is dead.'

'Rock'n'roll never dies, man.'

'They said the same about jazz. So, what do they call you?'

'Samson, Samson Samson.'

'Samson Samson? Like that?'

'Yeah, like that or Yellow Diamond . . . It would take more than one Delilah to stop me.'

'That's cool, man, but tonight I only got one. You wanna have a look?'

'Huh?'

And so the record executive from Virgin turned out to be a pimp who went by the name Manelo. I was disappointed, but charmed by it all, because this was the first real-life pimp I'd come across and Iceberg Slim's books, *Pimp, Trick Baby, Long White Con, The Naked Soul of Iceberg Slim, Airtight Willie and Me, Mama Black Widow, Death Wish* and *Doom Fox*, had always cracked me up. They were among the first books I had encountered after book censorship was relaxed, following the introduction of multiparty politics in Malawi.

Manelo introduced me to a voluptuous, red-lipped Hottentot Venus wearing a black leather skirt with side pleats that showed off her ripe, red thighs. She was no Mrs Robinson but when she started talking to me I knew it was the end of an era: her lips, hips, bum and nipples sticking out like that and I was a bit tipsy now, and really horny.

'*Sabuwona.*'

'Yeah.'

'*Uphilile na namhlanje?*'

'Yeah.'

'*Unyakwazi ukuthetha siNgezi?*'

'Yeah.'

'Where do you come from?'

'The warm heart of Africa . . . '

'I like Malawians. South Africa men no good.'

I noticed a red condom in her generous cleavage. I took

a long drink from my glass and asked the barman to put some gin in the Coke.

'You like this?'

'What?'

'This.'

She had discreetly lifted the hem of her leather skirt to show me what was there. She was wearing silky black underwear . . . It was like the movies. *Pretty Woman* or something.

'Yeah. I like.'

'Touch.'

I looked around the club. Everybody was busy getting on with it, so I touched just a little bit, on the wet patch. It was steaming hot.

'How much?' I asked.

I hailed a taxi and took her to my hotel room right away. I paid her in the elevator on the way up.

I made her keep her clothes on. I wanted her that way, on all fours, on the bed. I whipped it out, slipped on the condom, pulled her underwear to one side, saw her dark juicy rump and mounted her doggy-style like in the porn magazine under the bed.

'Fuck IDs,' I said.

'Yeah,' she agreed.

'Fuck IDs! I say . . . Fuck work.'

'Yeaah.'

'Fuck BFAs. Fuck conceptual art. And rock'n'roll? Rock'n'roll is dead, man. Rock'n'roll is dead . . . Fuck South Africa. Fuck fu . . . fu . . . fuck. Fuck Madiba! Fuck de Klerk!' I thrust deeper and deeper, then, suddenly, really deep. 'Yeah, fuck the world!'

'Yeeeeeeeeeeeeeeeeeees!'

'Ooooooooooooooooooooh!'

*   *   *

This is the end, my only friend the end. This is the end, my only friend the end. The end of our elaborate plans. The End of everything that stands . . .

'You are done, no?'

'I am done. Fuck it all.'

I wiped my brow and stood there looking at the broken condom on my penis. She put it away with a tissue saying she did not give a fuck either.

'I have got five kids to feed,' she said, showing me a clenched fist as she walked out of the door. 'Five.'

6

I went to bed and hoped never to wake up again but I did, with the rays of the sun on my face to yet another morning glory. I felt a great sense of my own mortality but it felt good. From now on I had my own cross to bear. It was the first time in weeks that I'd slept well without the nightmare of Dad's dead feet, the way they had protruded out of the hospital blanket in the corridor as those nurses took him away to the mortuary, gossiping. And now that I could no longer point fingers and knew what the honey pot tasted like, I forgave Dad or whoever had brought the HIV home. Sex was the stuff of life and was worth dying for. Sex had built and destroyed whole kingdoms and civilisations. Sex made the world go round. It made most things I had lived for up to that point seem trivial in comparison.

Thinking about it, maybe Dad had gotten the HIV virus on the operating table doing a Caesarean or something. Maybe he'd accidentally stabbed himself with an infected syringe, not being a real doctor. And who'd said it was him? It could have been Mum. Besides, he was not the first one to contract an STD in history: Flaubert, Columbus, Beethoven, Schumann, Schubert, Baudelaire, de Maupassant, Abraham Lincoln, Van Gogh, Nietzsche, Wilde, Hitler and Dinesen all had syphilis . . . It was as if the history of genius was but the history of STDs . . . Mum and Dad were just unlucky, and anyway, it wasn't so bad dying in their fifties. For ever young.

I decided to return to Malawi. Study soapstone, paint wildlife for the tourists, have sex and that would be it. So much for Conceptual Art. So much for travelling the world. I made up my mind not to leave South Africa without a couple of boxes of watercolours. I had about ten years to live if that hooker had given me the Aids virus. Bearing in mind that life expectancy in Malawi was thirty-four and I was twenty that was not too bad. Mum was going to die too anyway, and I didn't care to live long in a world without my mother. And the thought that one day I could become older than my parents freaked me out. All cool people died young and I was going to die young like Jean-Michel Basquiat, there among my soapstone sculptures and watercolour paintings. What better work of art can an artist create than himself anyway? I was pretty pleased with what I had become so far. To crown it all, I just hoped that when the end came I would be consumed by TB like Kafka, Keats, Byron, Paganini, Chekhov, Poe, Orwell, Emily Brontë . . . I'd play it cool to the end like Chopin in his Piano Sonata No. 2 in B flat Minor. As for the music ambitions, rock'n'roll was dead anyway . . . Kurt Cobain had committed suicide in time, he was no fool: MCs and technique-toting DJs were taking over. Tupac had done *Me Against the World*, the Notorious BIG had done *Ready to Die*, 'Juicy' was hot in the club. I should have spent time rapping instead of singing at Kamuzu Academy, but what did I expect from a British public school?

7

I telephoned Mum and asked her to wire me some of Dad's death gratuity if there was any left because I had used up my entire inheritance and I wanted to come home in a true prodigal son fashion. She said that sounded good and she wired me the money right away, but for some reason the bank in South Africa was going to take a week to release the cash.

When they kicked me out of the hotel, I headed to the central train station for the night, but nobody was allowed to sleep inside – vagrants were running the place down. I struggled all night trying to stay awake because it was very cold outside and there were these security guards in there who kept an eye on you to make sure you weren't sleeping. Then I changed my strategy. For the next few days, I slept in the park during the day, under the warm sun, and went to the station in the evening to stay awake all night thinking or reading. Up in Yeoville I'd come across a cheap, second-hand copy of *Down and Out in London and Paris*, and I followed Orwell, a Russian *plongeur* named Boris, a tramp named Paddy and a *screever* named Bozo as they looked for employment, food and a place to rest their feet. The book had cracked me up when I'd come across it on the Diptych and I read it again and again, laughing at *scathful harm, condition of poverte* like Dad had laughed at death. When I'd run out of all the small change I had left, I ate from the abandoned food stalls in the market and at the Universal Kingdom of God Church, where I pretended to be a Born Again. The minister was impressed by my tongues, which he thought sounded like jazz and my Pentecostal theology: I told him the only true religions were

Catholicism and Pentecostalism because they put emphasis on ritual and experience while the rest of Protestantism was really a guise for rationalism and its logical conclusion was atheism. The trouble with Catholicism, though, was that it was the seat of the Antichrist, as could be seen when you added up the Pope's official title, Vicarius Filii Dei. He gave me extra bread and jam for the last point.

8

As if to make sure that I would make it back home, Mum had sent me extra money on top of what I had asked for. At Park Station, as I boarded the 'Destroyer' bound for Malawi, a man in a business suit who said he was a salesman for the Witwatersrand Gold Mine approached me with briefcase full of gold necklaces stamped '24 carat'. He said the collection was part of Mandela's Equal Opportunities programme to ensure the fair distribution of gold among South Africans, which I thought was bullshit because I was wise to the streets now. I thought he was a thief who was selling genuine 24-carat jewellery stolen from the bank vaults of Randburg. I bought one gold necklace off him because it was such a bargain. I wanted to go back to Malawi with at least one decent present for Mum, who had been great to me.

By the time I reached the Malawian border, however, the 24-carat gold necklace had turned a rusty green, so when I got home I did not tell Mum about it. Instead I asked her for a little bit of money to develop the 'Paradise City' pictures from the Canon camera, so the whole family could see the exciting things I had witnessed in South Africa.

When the big envelope from the Fatchi Photographic Studio came through I called the whole family into the living room and opened it in front of them. There was nothing in there except hundreds of glossy black cards with a note asking if there was something wrong with my camera.

I fished the camera out and checked it: the flash was as blindingly bright as ever. I passed it round for verification and everybody thought it was all right until it landed in Bond's hands. After a brief examination he declared the camera was not a Canon.

'It says Camon!' he said.

'Really?'

'Really. Have a look. You've been had.'

Linda, holding the glossy blanks in her hands, couldn't believe I had been that stupid.

'It's one of those arty things, all this, isn't it?' she said sympathetically.

'Which arty things?' I asked, examining the lens.

'You know. Conceptual art.'

'Yeah. Malevich.'

My little nephew, Bryan, who was learning to speak, pointed a finger at the camera in my hands and spoke through his milk teeth: 'Camon,' he said.

ZOMBA

Remember when you were young, you shone like the sun.
Shine on you crazy diamond.

Pink Floyd

1

I had returned from South Africa in time to start the second year at the University of Malawi's Chancellor College in Zomba to study fine art and ethnomusicology. The students had been on strike for almost a year. The food was bad. The new democratically elected president, Dr Bakili Muluzi (not a real doctor), was a former market vendor, and he did not think much of tertiary education, so he had no problems making substantial cuts to university funding when he came under pressure from the World Bank and the donor countries.

When the window period had elapsed since my encounter with the South African prostitute I braved it out and travelled to Blantyre for an HIV test in Limbe.

The testing centre was a converted old shop with a sign that said 'The Future Family'. A short stocky man, wearing an orange T-shirt that said 'Ibiza' on the front, welcomed me. In his hands he carried a worn-out billiard cue and he led me into a waiting room full of men playing billiards on a huge red table in the middle. They were all waiting to get tested and I had no choice but to watch them play and listen to their lewd conversations as they sunk the billiard balls, one by one. It did not take long before I gathered that each one of the men loved sex and that the stocky man who had welcomed us had two girlfriends but did not know which one to marry. As the men took bets on the billiard game, I wondered about my odds.

The buxom nurse briefed me about living with HIV saying that it was just about eating a balanced diet, exercising well and making sure you did not get any more of the virus. She then took a blood sample from my finger and showed me a little device with a matchstick-sized white strip of paper in the middle, before explaining the HIV-testing procedure.

'In a moment you can return to the waiting room. I will call you back in thirty minutes for the results. If you see two red bands on this strip it means you are positive, no lines or any other number of lines, negative.'

'Is that the Western Blot test?' I asked.

'No. This is the HIV test,' she said.

'I know. I mean the method you are using.'

'Oh. This? It's called the Same Day Testing Method. It works and it's quick. You don't have to go through the agony of waiting for days.' The nurse straightened herself up, displaying her big bosom, which distracted me for a few seconds. I looked down to the floor.

'It's just that the Western Blot test can be confusing. The two-band reading changes from place to place. In Australia, for instance, the two bands means it's negative. So you have to know which method you are using.'

'It's a good method I am using,' the nurse said, opening the door for me.

An hour later when she called me back in (she had been having lunch – the lab smelt of fish and chips), she showed me only one sharp red band on the strip. I was ecstatic.

Back in college I pinned the black glossy photographs from the Camon camera on the corkboard beside my bed: all negative. Whenever I looked at them I felt as fresh as a newborn baby. An HIV-negative baby.

2

In the aftermath of the euphoria came a great need to thank somebody for my new life, but not only that: the cross I had laid down after gambling with Death in the South African hotel was laid on me once more now that I knew I would live. I needed somebody to help me carry the cross, so once again I took a leap of faith and enrolled in Chancellor College's catechumen class, in order to become a Catholic like Mum. On Confirmation Day, however, I had the wafer but refused to drink from the cup because of some dodgy-looking residue in it – I was afraid of catching the virus. There was a pencil-thin cate-chumen in the line before me, coughing and wheezing, and I was not going to sacrifice my new life for him or any of that lot. It was then that I realised that the whole Catholic thing was self-deception. Anyway, I was really horny now, I couldn't see myself going through the three years of studying ahead of me without sex, and I certainly wasn't going to have it without a condom and I wasn't going to have eight children like my mum and dad. I was no multimillionaire. Condoms were no absolute guarantee but sexual abstinence at twenty-one was obscene. I told myself to take it easy, next time.

Then there was all this anger welling up in my soul. I realised that restoring my faith in God again would make me an incredibly angry man. I would have to heap the blame for all the trouble I had seen on him and I could not stand for anything that would justify the killing of my mother. Instead, I took some of my book allowance, bought one of the cheap 'Made in China' Wembleys (they were now all over the place with the liberalisation of the market), made a Holy Ball, and went back to my expressionist religion. I picked up where I had left off and continued to *exercise and exorcise*. Yes, if there was going to be a god in my life it had to be the indifferent but life-giving sun. And what's more, it made me love my skin. I was truly blessed.

3

Free from original sin once more, I set out to look for a girl-friend to have sex with. It was harder than I imagined and took me a whole year because of my *mesho*. When he was not attending lectures, eating at the cafeteria, or speaking in tongues at the chapel (he was a part-time Born Again), all he did was lie in bed and read Charles Dickens over and over again. Thus he seldom left the room, day or night, so it was difficult to entertain prospective girlfriends in depth when they came over for a cup of tea.

I fell in love with a beautiful law student, an Asian girl, her name Ekta Mistry. When I invited her over for a cup of tea one night, my roommate stopped reading and watched

Ekta while playing with his balls under the blanket. I don't think that he was aware that he was being ridiculous. He had an unconscious habit of playing with his balls when he was reading. When I said something impressive to Ekta, the *mesho* interjected out of the blue:

'*Mesho!* Catch that bird. You are doing great.'

Ekta never came back to my room. When I complained to the *mesho,* he said that it was not his fault. Asian people in Malawi were racist, and would never let their daughter go out with a black boy anyway.

Well, I tried the black girls and it was the same thing. He watched them while playing with his balls too, butting in at my best moment:

'*Mesho!* Catch that bird. You are doing great.'

They all ran away. I did not know what to do with the *mesho* because, constitutionally, he had a right to do whatever he liked in his room, so eventually I gave up on the girls for the rest of that year and settled for the Saturday night blue movies in Lecture Theatre No. 1.

In third year, however, I got lucky. I got a new *mesho,* Sicily, and he was cool. Best of all, he was never in the room. Most nights he was to be found in a ditch, dead drunk, singing: *What shall we do with the drunken sailor? Early in the morning.* He was so shy with girls that he preferred sleeping in a ditch to being in the same room with me as I was trying to get a girl. In no time I had a girlfriend, a lapsed Born Again and physics major named Grace, with whom I had sex whenever we were not attending lectures. The demons must have come back to her sevenfold when she quit being a Born Again. You should have heard her curse in bed.

By the time I was in my fourth and final year, Grace had developed a bizarre technique to stop herself from cursing during sex. She counted the strokes.

1, 2, 3, 4, 5, 6, 7, 8, 9, 10, 11, 12, 13, 14, 15,
16, 17, 18, 19, 20,
21, 22, 23, 24, 25, 26, 27, 28, 29, 30, 31, 32, 33, 34, 35, 36, 37, 39, 40,
41, 42,
43, 44, 45, 46, 47, 48, 49, 50,
51,
52, 53, 54,
55, 56, 57, 58, 59, 60, 61, 62, 63, 64, 65, 66, 67, 68, 69, 70, 71, 72, 73,
74, 75, 76, 77, 78, 79, 80, 81, 82, 83, 84, 85, 86, 87, 88, 89, 90, 91, 92,
93, 94, 95, 96, 97, 98, 99, 100, 101, 103, 104 . . .

When I asked how she never missed a stroke with all the excitement, she said that she was a sex machine, which was all very interesting but it was difficult to prepare for my final exams with her counting going around in my head every other three seconds or so. She was literally fucking my wits out that girl and so, with a heavy heart, I ditched her. I was determined not to let another girl spoil my academic results again.

She went back to her Born Againism, clutching the Bible with the same zeal as the Kama Sutra handbook she had inflicted on me.

4

And, sure enough, at the end of my studies I graduated with distinction: a double-major BA in Fine Art and Ethnomusicology. Both the Music and the Fine Art Departments wanted to employ me as a Staff Associate.

I had always wanted to join the Music Department

although I didn't care about world music: I was deep into hip hop now – *gettin' jiggy wit it*. I had studied ethnomusicology for three years solely because Professor Gibson was in the department. He was an American ethnomusicologist who sent all his associates to the USA for further studies. I figured that if I joined him he would send me there, then I would switch to art and study for an MFA at the Chicago Institute of the Arts, like Jeff Koons, do some blow-up stainless-steel rabbits while listening to Common Sense. So when at the end of my studies the professor invited me to live with him as we waited for the vacancy to be finalised, I was ecstatic. Not for long though.

The professor's house turned out to be a harem of desperate native boys. They were all over the place. I would be sitting on a sofa, lift up a cushion and without fail find an original Oompa-Loompa underneath it, smiling at me.

When the professor was not teaching he liked to entertain his dusky harem in return for all the services rendered. I must admit that his cooking was incredible – much better than his piccolo playing. The meatballs, carbonnara and rhubarb crumble were memorable. He said his brothers were good at cooking too. They were all professional chefs in New York. The Oompa-Loompas, mouths full of custard cream, told him they couldn't wait to meet them too, right here in the Warm Heart of Africa.

After the meals the Professor would put on quality videos, although I would have enjoyed a break from the recurrent theme: *Philadelphia*, *Top Gun*, *Shawshank Redemption*, *Deliverance*, *Kentucky Moon*, *My Own Private Idaho* . . . No *Jungle Fever*, *Basic Instinct* or *Fatal Attraction* for the Oompa-Loompas.

Every night without fail, one of the professor's boys would creep up to my bed and ask if he could suck my penis for a little bit. I told each one of them that they were too ugly to do it to me, but they kept on coming and eyeing me like new meat from the shadows. I had to tuck myself in like a mummy as I slept.

In the end I applied for a job in the Fine Art Department, where scholarships to the USA were harder to come by, but at least I was going to have a house of my own and would be able to sleep easy.

5

The university gave me a nice flat on the green slopes of Zomba Plateau, complete with servants' quarters. I moved in with a puppy, a mongrel, I had bought to celebrate my new life. I named him Bono because he never let go of his bone.

I employed a cook, a watchman and a gardener and paid them generously because they had sizeable families. The cook had four kids and slept with them in the one room, together with his wife. The pay must have been very good indeed. The cook's wife came to my house one evening and asked me to cut her husband's pay by half because he had taken himself another wife and there was not enough room in the house.

But there was nothing I could do to help her, really, because when I spoke to the cook he told me to tell her that he knew his human rights in the new democracy, you hear? And I knew what he meant by that, so I let him get on with it. Legally, he had a right to fit as many wives as he liked in that room; there is no limit to how many wives you can have in Malawi.

I converted one of the rooms in my flat into a painting

studio. The rest of the house was used to exercise and exorcise with the Holy Ball, writing my thoughts on the walls while being watched by Bono, who said *'Woof! Woof!'*, and the bemused two-wife cook, who called me 'Professor' when handing me a cup of tea.

I managed to squeeze all my lectures in between Monday and Wednesday, which gave me the rest of the week to paint and sculpt 'wildlife' in the caveman style.

Among the speech-making lions, painting monkeys, singing hippos and marching elephants and antelope, was the watercolour *Moondancer*, a cosmic voluptuous woman dancing under the four phases of the moon in the most primitive manner. She danced in space, before a starry night, which looked like the face of an ancient rock in Mwana wa Chencherere. In fact she was inspired by a stripper I had seen in one club in Yeoville back in Johannesburg and the moon was actually the disco ball. Anyway, the moondancer was cool and she brought a lot of much needed expatriate patronage to my studio. And why not? If Michelangelo had his own way all the time, he wouldn't have painted the Sistine Chapel.

6

One hot afternoon, a curvy young Scottish brunette, who worked as a volunteer editor in the publication wing of the Department of Theology and Religious Studies, came to my house to see some wildlife paintings. When she reversed her Toyota to park in my drive, she flattened Bono who had been sleeping there in the sun and killed him on the spot.

I told Susan not to worry about Bono; he was only a dog, but she could not buy that, which I understood, because she was British. Her blue eyes tear-shot like diamonds, she paid for the dead puppy, bought two paintings from me, and also stayed for dinner to tell me her full name which was Susan Louise Reynolds and to show me how to cook; the trifle was a disaster because she had used an entire grapefruit, and grapefruits in Malawi are very bitter.

As we toyed around with the dessert, I discovered that, like me, she was a big fan of John Donne, especially his profane poems. I took a copy of the complete works of John Donne from the new Diptych and we discussed 'The Flea' for the rest of the evening.

> Mark but this flea, and mark in this,
> How little that which thou deny'st me is;
> It suck'd me first, and now sucks thee,
> And in this flea our two bloods mingled be;
> Thou know'st that this cannot be said
> A sin, nor shame, nor loss of maidenhead;
> Yet this enjoys before it woo,
> And pamper'd swells with one blood made of two;
> And this, alas! is more than we would do.
>
> O stay, three lives in one flea spare,
> Where we almost, yea, more than married are.
> This flea is you and I, and this
> Our marriage bed, and marriage temple is;
> Though parents grudge, and you, w'are met,
> And cloister'd in these living walls of jet.
> Though use make you apt to kill me,
> Let not to that self-murder added be,
> And sacrilege, three sins in killing three.

Cruel and sudden, hast thou since
Purpled thy nail in blood of innocence?
Wherein could this flea guilty be,
Except in that drop which it suck'd from thee?
Yet thou triumph'st, and say'st that thou
Find'st not thyself nor me the weaker now;
'Tis true; then learn how false fears be;
Just so much honour, when thou yield'st to me,
Will waste, as this flea's death took life from thee.

From that day until she left home for Scotland some months later we were inseparable.

7

By this time Mum had retired from teaching. She took what was left of the death gratuity and half of her pension and started to build herself a three-bedroom house in Phwetekere, somewhere between the mud-hut villages and the city. She struggled to finish it but moved in anyway when her time ran out at the house in Area 18. She still had to raise some money for the windows so in the meantime she improvised with cardboard shutters. It uncannily aped the house we had had in Mulanje when Dad's HIV had first reared its head.

But it was all too beautiful for tears.

At least her children were doing all right: Emily and Lucy were working as secretaries for a law firm in Blantyre, Joyce was a chartered accountant with a British accounting firm, Elson was working as a project manager for a German aid agency, and Chikondi was studying economics at Chancellor College where I was teaching fine art. Only Linda, who was studying to be a secretary, and Bond, who attended some private secondary school when not jiving with Mum, were still at home.

We all came to her rescue and supported her by whatever means we could.

With money earned from my wildlife pictures I installed windowpanes and electricity in her house. It's a shame that none of us could afford the Aids drugs that were said to be available on the black market somewhere. Mum never raised the issue, so everybody just kept quiet and hoped for the best. It sounds pathetic now but one could only do so much around the abyss called the Fourth World.

By the time I got my new job at Chancellor College I had been living under the shadow of my mother's imminent death for seven years. Every time I got a phone call or letter from home I had to sit down and take a deep breath. And every time I saw Mum, I couldn't look her in the eye because I was busy searching for the portentous spot on her face. I made more and more Holy Balls from what was left of my King James Bible and continued to exercise and exorcise, in order to stay above the water. There was power, wonderworking power in Contingency, in the eternal immanence.

When the Fine Art Department studios ran out of soapstone, and the Head of Department was up in the mountains of Ntcheu gathering a new supply, I took my Holy Ball exercises and exorcisms to the vacant studio – Studio 2 – and staged what possibly was the first conceptual art exhibition in Malawi.

The Holy Balls, twenty-four of them, were strewn across the empty studio floor and people were invited to 'exercise and exorcise' with them and write their thoughts in the big book entitled *Holy Ball Exercises and Exorcisms, Chancellor*

College, Zomba. There were no guidelines as to what to write and so most of the responses were off the cuff; exorcisms as varied as the visitors, ranging from those directly connected to the work to the entirely abstract.

This is the best I've seen ever in Malawian art.
You are an inspiration to upcoming artists that anything goes and art is more in the head than in the hands. At least we are coming to an age where we have to be open and free, not be bound by prescribed rules of society. We have to expose our inner selves. Keep it up.
MISONZI GUNDO EH/28/99 (ART STUDENT)

Sam,
This is more than critical thinking.
Keep it up, buddy!
SAI KAPHALE EH/59/00

Mr Artist,
Hope someone will find Jesus on the balls! But this is great peace of art, sublime and truly coming from the deepest subtles of an artist's imagination.
DINOS NAZZAOUR

Sam,
This is nothing but profound evidence that you are a satanic worshipper! How and why could you tear the Holy Book like that!

Wow!
This is marvellous indeed. What makes you think like these? It isn't easy to destroy your own Bible. You are a great thinker.

Keep it up.
HARRIET EH/23/00

Sam,
I always sing canticles out of your emotional work.
Mind & body rather soul & fresh converge & make a
complex super man in mind (thought).
CLEOPHAS CHIWAYA

Sam,
This is bullshit
CHRIS

Whao! Jesus! Just come down on earth and see this!
Work of an artist.
NUKA 02/08/00 1715HRS

Sam,
I don't know and can't imagine how you came up
with this idea. But I have to say it's both wonderful
and interesting. I'll tell you why in my post. The link
between art and spirituality, superstition and human
understanding. It's something though how you
attempted to make visible, is to a large extent, felt.
That's how I understand the arts in general.
(Since my limited understanding of the subject.)
Please, don't stop here!
CHARLES MATEMBA BAH/21/98

Sam,
Through Your Works Of Art, I Have Come To
Believe That Art Has Something To Do With The
Mind. You Have Brought My Body And Mind
Together. Your Creativity Has Really Aroused My

Emotions – Really Touched Me. How Did You
Come To That Especially In Bringing The Bible
In This Way?
You Are Really Special.
God Bless You.
EVANCE MWATHUNGA

Sammy,
This has been a very good experience on my journey
towards art as a professional and academic 'genre'. I
have been emotionally, physically and aesthetically
impressed with your exhibition. Despite this being
my very first time to look at an art exhibition in
my life, I have seen the true colour of what
art is. Felicitations et bravo!
You are fit to go round the world with this. Keep it
up!
MICHAEL CHILEMBA

Sam
Introduce Africanism
C. NGWALE

Sam
Congratulations!
I've never seen such an inspiring artwork before.
Bravo! At least some African who really cares for
the image.
BAH/59/00

Hi Sam,
It is new to have such a new and unexpectable
achievement. However, many people will disagree. I
think what you need to do, is to take your time

explaining to them as you have done to me.
God bless you.
AMOSI

To your beliefs it's all right, but to some denomina-
tions, you show some traits of satanism, but your
creativity and courage is admirable but wouldn't you
suggest something better than a religious matter?
KEN

Sam,
Your work is superb. The nicest and most
motivating.
ISAAC EH/69/00

I love you.

Hi Sam,
I really liked playin with your ballz. Good idea, man!
That was fun. Though at first your idea was hard
to understand.
SOPHIE

Sammy,
I didn't think somebody might think of such a
blasphemy. Bad boy.

I wish I were an artist! But if I may ask, what is
art??? Mr Kambalu, art is being crazy in mind.
Are you not?
Good coming.
KONDWANI R MSAKA EH/119/99

Dear Samson,
You made my year! Your development over the last
months has been a true exercise and exorcise in the
world of contemporary art.
Thank you so much for having the privilege to have
watched and discussed this process so closely.
Zikomo kwambiri.
MACHA ROESINK, AMSTERDAM – ZOMBA,
1999 / 2000

Sha!
I wish I were crazy upstairs like you, Sam.
RODNEY MKWEZA EH/43/99

Sam,
Indeed my soul has been exorcised. *Ayi ndanjoya.*
Izibwera bwera mipira YOYERAYI.
A JOO.

Sam,
You're crazy! And this must not be!!?!
NA MER!

Sam,
Oh what a harm to the cause of the cross. My soul
weeps for you! Repent in Jesus' name!
ISAIAH!

Sam
Kicking a ball
The centre of . . .
Kicking the Bible
The centre of . . .
Control of world

Superior systems
Sam you're out of the systems
MI STEVE PORTE

Sam,
Are you really a creation of the Almighty? Why
treating the word of God like that? I love your
creativity. You are more than a normal human being.
MOSES CHA V.

Sam,
Thanks for this marvellous creativity. You have really
shown that you are more than a human being. Such
creativity is for gods.
I appreciate your superhuman creativity. I will live to
remember such rare machangelic talent and
creativity.
Thanks.
BENSA MAPENEKA

Sam,
You have the wings,
Fly, Sam, fly!
AUSTIN MSOWOYA

Sam,
This is amazing!
S. MSOWOYA

Sam,
You are a genius. I wish Pablo Picasso was alive to
see this.
Love
TIYANYAWA MACHILA

Sam,
The world should learn about this. That we have art
in Malawian minds.
ZAITHWA LILLIAN MUWALO NQUMAYO 1-8-00

Sam,
You mean out of all material you only found the
Bible. I am not impressed. That is the word of God.
You can't abuse it as you have done. You're entitled
to your rights but some rights are a sin before God.
And this is one. Repent.
VITUMBIKO GANOKO ESQ. 3 EPS IV

Sam,
You are really crazy, whatever it is you were
thinking, I think you are going mad, watch it.
OLIVE

Mr Kambalu,
Go to church this Sunday. You need serious help. Ask
the Holy Spirit.
CONCERNED

Wonder and puzzles always succeed with free wine.
Each man could create his/her own world outlook.
And when one does, it remains to be criticised and
praised. So I did so in my own mind.
STEVE

Blasphemy.

EUROPE

We possess art lest we perish of the truth.
Friedrich Nietzsche

1

In 2000, I was awarded a four-month artist residency with the Thami Mnyele Foundation in a spacious studio on Bellamystraat in Amsterdam. I brought two suitcases with me: one filled with my clothes and the other filled with Malawian rag footballs, which I had been collecting from around the neighbourhood while lecturing at Chancellor College. The custom officials at Schiphol Airport had never heard of a country called Malawi let alone seen a passport that looked like that before. They had to look the country up on Google or something after which they detained me at the airport, not believing that those round raggedy things in my suitcase were actually footballs. They thought they were drugs, presumably Malawi Gold, but they could not find anything when they cut the balls open. It was only when they finally managed to get in touch with the Director of the Thami Mnyele Foundation that they released me into Holland.

By the time I got to the studio, I had conceived my first

work of art since moving to Europe, inspired by my ordeal at the airport: an open suitcase full of Malawian rag footballs to be installed on the floor against the wall in a gallery space. The airport tags are still on the handle of the suitcase. On the inside of the open lid is a picture of a Malawian boy, rag football in hand, standing before a makeshift goalpost. The net is too crude to stop the ball, but somehow it had to be there. The work is called *Goalkeeper*. It was eventually shown at the Liverpool Biennale as part of Bloomberg New Contemporaries 2004.

2

It was the flea (and a dead dog) that led to my fiery relationship with Susan and it was also the flea that made me ask her to marry me sooner than I had intended. Susan, who had, in the meantime, moved back to Scotland, visited me to see how I was getting on with my residency. She loved the clogs and the tulips, but the tricky bit was where to lay down those lovely brown curls. I really wished we could book a hotel, but I was broke after extensive research in the red-light district. To make matters worse there were fleas in my bed and only the romanticism of the starving artist kept me from sleeping on the floor. I couldn't report the matter to the Foundation because I was afraid of embarrassing them – the heroic artist Thamsanga Mnyele (1948–85), martyred for his seminal antiapartheid work and all he got for a memorial was a fleainfested artist residency in the backstreets of Amsterdam. Plus I couldn't really complain because I thought I was lucky to be there at all, getting free Indian-ink drawing lessons from the great Marlene Dumas – considering the nasty things Malawi had done to the ANC. Anyway, I didn't expect to find bed fleas in Europe but I suppose it's a small world.

Before Susan arrived, I sprayed every corner of the room with Doom, but the fleas kept biting us in the night. I had planned to ask her to marry me the following day over the canal, but I woke her up in the middle of the night, scratching myself all over like the bum on Kinkerstraat, and asked her to marry me right away. I figured if I waited until the morning she would have thought twice about marrying a flea-ridden artist.

3

Susan and I got married on 28 July 2001, in Perth, at Kinnoull Church. She carried pink rosebuds and I carried the Holy Ball.

We brought Mum over for the wedding and she was thoroughly impressed by Scottish industry. She wondered what was wrong with Africa and I told her that it was a long story.

Our honeymoon was a three-day trip to Loch Ness, up in the Highlands. We went looking for the monster and, of course, we found it. The secret is to take pictures of the loch with your fingers placed over the lens.

Meanwhile, my parents-in-law took my mother to the real Blantyre, to see the birthplace of David Livingstone, the man who had started all this trouble.

As I watched Mum ascending the escalator to the departure lounge at Heathrow, at the end of her three-week stay in the UK, I knew it was the last time I would see her. But I didn't think it would come so soon.

For a travelling health tip, I had told Mum not to drink directly from the tap the first few weeks after returning home, but I should have also mentioned to her not to eat the vegetables and unpeeled fruit from the local market either, because they would not be clean enough for several weeks once you've been to Europe.

As soon as Mum returned to Malawi, she got diarrhoea from her new British fresh-fruit-salad recipe. Her immune system, which had held up impressively for the seven years since her husband had died, crashed and never recovered. She lost her appetite, lived on Lucozade for a couple of months, withered into a skeleton, and that was it. She died on 18 October 2002, from Aids-related meningitis like her husband. She was the sixth in her family to die of Aids, but the eighth in all. Granny had died of throat cancer (but at least she was seventy-six), while my uncles Maurice, Mclasius and Humphrey, and aunts Maggie and Anna all died of Aids. Grandad had died of a broken heart a few weeks after Granny. His kraal was still empty.

When I got the phone call about Mum's passing, Susan and I were living in Nottingham where I was studying for an MA in Fine Art at Nottingham Trent University. When I put down the receiver, I made myself a cup of tea (for Mum had always appreciated one like me), switched off the TV and sat on the sofa to let everything sink in. On the wall behind the TV a transcription of my favourite work of art by the French conceptual artist Marcel Duchamp slowly came into focus through the tears; an epitaph he made for himself that now lies on his tombstone in Rouen:

'D'ailleurs c'est toujours les autres qui meurent.'

ACKNOWLEDGEMENTS

Big thank you:
To the Arts Council for the award that saw me through the writing of this book – thanks to Manick Govinda at the Artsadmin.

To Acme Studios, London, for the generous residency.

To Klaus Fiedler and all the authors on his project. The Kachere Series is a goldmine on Malawian history and culture – I have sampled a thing or two from J.M.W. Van Bruegel's *Chewa Traditional Religion*.

I am also grateful for materials and books employed either in direct quotation, reference or sample which include Friedrich Nietzsche's *Gay Science* and *Thus Spoke Zarathustra* translated by R.J. Hollingdale and Walter Kaufmann respectively, *Encyclopedia Britannica*, *Manson's Tropical Diseases*, The British Medical Association's *Illustrated Medical Dictionary*, Simon Goldhill's *Love, Sex and Tragedy*, busycooks.about.com's *How to Make Bread*, Nigel Cawthorne's *The Curious Cures of Old England*, John Reader's *Africa: A Biography of a Continent*, Lorenzo Loronzi's *Devils in Art*, *X-treme Latin* by Henry Beard, D.D. Phiri's *History of Malawi From the Earliest Times to 1915* and a quotation from theromantic.com on *How to French Kiss*.

To Macha Roesink who gave me a place to stand and opened up a whole new world for me.

To Josh Carney for winding me up so much with his red pen – I had to finish the book right away. Jonathan Willet for ironing out the philosophy. Dr Michael Chappell, for all the reading, discussions, booze and the football. Ted Jenner in New Zealand. Asad Farooq.

To my agent Laetitia Rutherford at Toby Eady Associates for seeing the vision and finding me the best stage possible. With her Jamie Coleman and Samar Hammam. Jennifer Joel at ICM and Amber Qureshi at Simon and Schuster.

To my editor Ellah Allfrey for her critical eye, encouragement and all the improvements in the manuscript.

To my family in Malawi and Scotland for sharing the sacrifices needed to write and think – Emily, Lucy, Joyce, Elson, Chikondi, Linda and Bond. Pam, Tom and Helen.

And finally to my shiny beautiful wife Susan for her love, company and support in red biro and cups of tea.

Samson Kambalu
London
2007